Additional praise for *The Coming Generational Storm*

"Kotlikoff has been one of the pioneers of the new economics of generational accounting. If anyone foresaw the deterioration of the U.S. government's fiscal health, he did. Now, with journalist Scott Burns, he has written a book that spells out, in crystal-clear laymen's terms, the disturbing truth about the rising tide of red ink."

—Niall Ferguson, Stern School of Business, New York University, and author of *Empire* and *The Cash Nexus*

"*The Coming Generational Storm* is one of the most important (and refreshingly irreverent) policy analyses of recent years. Laurence Kotlikoff and Scott Burns ask what will happen to our economy and way of life when the baby boom meets the current Medicare and Social Security systems. Their answers, using the innovative techniques of 'generational accounting' developed by Kotlikoff and others, demonstrate how close we are to a genuine fiscal precipice and the hard landing that awaits us. For our current presidential aspirants, the authors also provide some provocative ideas for how to ameliorate the damage this storm will certainly leave in its wake."

—Robert J. Shapiro, Senior Fellow of the Brookings Institution and the Progressive Policy Institute, and former Under Secretary of Commerce for Economic Affairs

"*The Coming Generational Storm* documents in frightening detail America's reckless fiscal trajectory as it barrels toward bankruptcy. The need to revamp Medicare and Social Security is urgent. This book is a must-read for anyone who cares about our nation's future."

—Janet Yellen, University of California, Berkeley, Member, Federal Reserve Board (1994–1997), and Chair, Council of Economic Advisers (1997–1999)

"As someone who has written extensively on global aging and its profound implications, I was delighted to read *The Coming Generational Storm*. It is an extremely important and original contribution."

—Peter G. Peterson, Chairman, The Blackstone Group, and author of *Gray Dawn: How the Coming Age Wave Will Transform America—and The World*

"*The Coming Generational Storm* is a well-written summary of an impressive and important body of carefully documented research. The book demonstrates clearly the folly of existing tax and transfer policies in the face of the impending retirement of the baby boom generation. Anyone interested in the future economic viability of American society and the economic problems we are bequeathing to our children should read this study."

—James J. Heckman, The University of Chicago, Nobel Laureate in Economic Sciences (2000)

"Kotlikoff and Burns document and analyze the most serious issue facing the American government today: the looming intergenerational conflict created by its gross failure to develop a consistent plan to fund and manage entitlements for the elderly, the cost of which will explode when the baby boom generation retires. This book is essential reading for those concerned about their own future and their childrens'."

—Daniel McFadden, Cox Professor of Economics, University of California, Berkeley, Nobel Laureate in Economic Sciences (2000)

"If Stephen King wrote about economics it would look like this. Kotlikoff and Burns have gazed into our future and seen a nightmare. The authors describe that nightmare vividly and identify why our elected officials on both sides of the political aisle are too cowardly to save us. Every U.S. citizen should read and digest this book before it is too late."

—Kevin A. Hassett, Director of Economic Policy Studies, American Enterprise Institute, and coauthor of *Dow 36,000*

The Coming Generational Storm

The Coming Generational Storm

What You Need to Know about America's Economic Future

Laurence J. Kotlikoff and Scott Burns

The MIT Press
Cambridge, Massachusetts
London, England

This book was set in Sabon by SNP Best-set Typesetter Ltd., Hong Kong.

Printed and bound in the United States of America.

Library of Congress Cataloging-in-Publication Data

Kotlikoff, Laurence J.
The coming generational storm : what you need to know about America's economic future / Laurence J. Kotlikoff and Scott Burns.
    p. cm.
Includes bibliographical references and index.
ISBN 0-262-11286-8
1. United States—Population—Economic aspects. 2. Age distribution (Demography)—Economic aspects—United States. 3. Baby boom generation—United States. 4. Aging—Economic aspects—United States. 5. Aged—Government policy—United States. 6. Retirement income—United States—Planning. 7. Population forecasting—United States. 8. Economic forecasting—United States. I. Title: America's economic future. II. Burns, Scott. III. Title.

HB3505.K68   2004
332.024'00973—dc22   2003069121

10 9 8 7 6 5 4 3

To our children and grandchildren: Stephen, Suzanne, Oliver, Alex, David, Shelby, John Taylor, Dylan, Nathan, and Aubrey

Contents

Acknowledgments

No book about a $51 trillion debt gets written without its own obligations. Elizabeth Murry at The MIT Press persuaded us to write this book, provided brilliant suggestions along the way, and ably guided its production. Her MIT Press colleagues were equally impressive editorial and production partners.

Alan Auerbach, Jagadeesh Gokhale, and Kent Smetters played a key role over the years in codeveloping the generational accounting, fiscal gap, and other analyses discussed in this book.

We're also grateful to Boston University, the National Bureau of Economic Research, the National Science Foundation, and the National Institute of Aging for supporting Kotlikoff's research over the years. Finally, we thank the *Dallas Morning News* and Universal Press Syndicate for providing Burns a special forum to research and write about the many issues covered in the book.

Our biggest debt is to our wives, Dayle Ballentine and Carolyn Burns, for supporting and encouraging us through the various stages of completing this work.

Prologue

The foundation of our Empire was not laid in the gloomy age of Ignorance and Superstition, but at an Epocha when the rights of mankind were better understood and more clearly defined, than at any former period. . . . At this auspicious period, the United States came into existence as a Nation, and if their Citizens should not be completely free and happy, the fault will be intirely their own.
—George Washington, "Circular to State Governments," June 8, 1783

2030—A Different Odyssey

Find a comfortable couch, lie back, and close your eyes. Take slow, deep breaths. Go deeply into the peaceful calm that separates your inner soul from the world around you.

Let your mind wander toward the future. Move, slowly, to the year 2030.

Now open your eyes.

What do you see?

You see a country whose collective population is older than that in Florida today. You see a country where walkers outnumber strollers. You see a country with twice as many retirees but only 18 percent more workers to support them. You see a country with large numbers of impoverished elderly citizens languishing in understaffed, overcrowded, substandard nursing homes.

You see a government in desperate trouble. It's raising taxes sky high, drastically cutting retirement and health benefits, slashing defense, education, and other critical spending, and borrowing far beyond its capacity to repay. It's also printing tons of money to "meet" its bills.

You see major tax evasion, high and rising rates of inflation, a growing underground economy, a rapidly depreciating currency, and more people exiting than entering the country. They're leaving because they're sure things will get still worse.

You see political instability, unemployment, labor strikes, high and rising crime rates, record-high interest rates. You see financial markets in ruin. In short, you see America plunging headlong toward third world status.

"No way," you'll say, as we snap our fingers and bring you back to earth. "Things can't get that bad."

Lots of people, particularly those running for reelection, would agree. Their tranquilizing view runs like this:

"Yes, the nation will be older, but our fiscal affairs and the economy will be just fine. The country's deficits are modest relative to the size of the economy and will decline through time. Sure, Social Security has some problems, but the system is close to seventy-five-year actuarial balance. The same holds for Medicare. The government can always cut fat. Technological change will bail us out. And we can always bring in more immigrants to pay our bills.

"Aging also brings economic benefits. First, we won't have so many unproductive kids to support. Second, people will be healthier and work longer. Third, old people own most of the economy's machines, factories, and other productive capital. Thus, having more oldsters around means there will be more capital available for workers to use in producing goods and services. So, yes, we'll be short on workers, but each will be more productive."

These and other purported ways of resolving the nation's aging dilemma are comforting—but they suffer from two problems: They are either wrong, or they are small potatoes when set against the fiscal imperatives of 77 million baby boomers' outstretched hands. In truth, there is no economic or demographic magic wand we can wave to make everything right. Bad things do happen to good countries, and we are heading into one God-awful fiscal storm, the full dimensions of which are hard to fathom.

To make matters worse, our captain has lost his bearings; he's got us pointed right at the storm and is gunning the motor. We've got one chance left to turn the ship around, batten down the hatches, and escape the worst, but we need to act decisively, and we need to act now.

The first step is understanding the true size of the problem. Most people realize the country is getting older and that paying for the elderly will be expensive. What they don't realize is just how old and just how expensive the elderly are going to be. Ignorance here is anything but bliss. Nor is it innocent. The public doesn't fully know what's going on for two reasons. First, the government's compass really is broken. It's using the amount of official federal debt to measure our fiscal position, when the true liabilities facing the nation are twelve times larger. Second, the government has been working overtime to either fudge or outright conceal this fact.

This book delivers a demographic and fiscal reality check, and in ways you've probably never seen before. This isn't a Stephen King novel, but what you'll read in the first two-thirds of the book will scare you, make you angry, and send you running for cover. But keep reading. Help arrives in the last part of the book in the form of new government policy proposals and personal financial moves that can save our nation and protect you from the worst-case scenario.

We're going to scare you, but we aren't trying to. We're not doomsayers. We don't sell gold coins, supplies of dehydrated food, or equipment for recharging your .357 shells. We don't have a newsletter that tells you where to make your fortune or how to keep your money safe. We're an economics professor and a financial journalist who have been watching this problem get worse year after year. We feel an intellectual and moral obligation to discuss it and offer some public policy as well as personal solutions. Our deepest motivation is very simple: we're fathers. We love our children and worry for their sake and for the sake of all of America's children about the future.

But we didn't write this book simply to assuage our consciences. We feel we have some unique insights into the demographic and economic problems facing our country based on our own research and that of other economists and financial analysts. Our goal is to leave you with a real sense of what's coming, why it's coming, when it's coming, and where national and personal economic salvation does and does not lie.

Although we take lots of shots at those politicians who put us in our current mess and are doing their best to make matters worse, we don't mean to sound partisan. Every postwar administration has passed the generational buck when it comes to paying for what it spends, so there's plenty of blame for both parties to share. But passing the buck needs to stop here, with our generation.

In the end, this book is not about politics, and it's not about which politician did exactly what exactly when. It's fundamentally about ourselves and our children. It's about how we adults, whether Republican, Democrat, Libertarian, Green, or independent, let our leaders systematically ignore, conceal, and minimize the huge dangers that lie ahead. But it's also about our desperate need to earn our titles—to act like adults by taking charge, at long last, of a very dangerous situation and beginning the serious task of protecting our beloved progeny.

Here's a guide to what lies ahead.

From Strollers to Walkers

We start by describing the tidal wave of baby boomers that is moving inexorably from changing diapers to wearing them. In particular, we discuss the boomers' numbers, their dilatory mating patterns, their meager rate of procreation, their romance with divorce, their plans to be retired *for as long as most people lived only a few centuries ago*, their prospects for an isolated, childless old age, and the protracted delay in their departure to the next world.

When it comes to aging, we also point out that the United States is not alone. The entire developed world and large parts of the developing world, including China, are in the process of getting much, much older. This won't be a one-time event. The United States and its very best buddies will not only be getting old; they will be staying old. The population shares of the old (those over age 65) and the very old (those over age 85) will grow year after year throughout the entire twenty-first century.

These remarkable demographic changes are unique in human history. They are also unstoppable. They will transform our world at the personal, national, and international levels. In particular, they will exact a fiscal toll that will shake our economy and those of Japan and Western Europe to their very foundations.

Truth Is Worse Than Fiction

Conventional politics is an unending argument about Haves and Have-Nots. Are the Haves getting more? Is it too much? Why isn't there more sharing with the Have-Nots? The Have/Have-Nots argument works to completely obscure another discussion: the Nows and the Laters. We're the Nows; our children and grandchildren are the Laters. Decade after decade, the Nows have taken from the Laters. Unfortunately, this fiscal child abuse, like the psychological kind, is hard to spot. But measure it we can, and measure it we will using a relatively new method, called *generational accounting.* Doing so leads to the following bottom line: *Unless we adults make very large sacrifices very quickly, our kids will face lifetime net tax rates that are twice those we face!*

Yes, you read that right. On each dollar earned, our kids will be faced with taxes, net of the benefits they receive, that are nearly twice what we currently pay. If you think Uncle Sam is ripping you off, imagine how your children will feel.

Another way to characterize the findings is to calculate the immediate and permanent federal personal and corporate income tax hike needed to achieve *generational balance*—the equalization of lifetime tax rates facing current and future generations. Brace yourself. *The requisite tax hike is a whopping 69 percent!*

It would be nice if we could tell you that we've calculated these numbers. Then you could say, "These guys are nuts," and discard the book. But our very own government has calculated these figures. The fact that you haven't seen these findings, which were prepared through the fall of 2002 by top economists, statisticians, actuaries, and fiscal analysts at the Department of Treasury, the Office of Management and Budget, and the Federal Reserve, is no accident. They were yanked from publication in the President's FY 2004 Budget within a couple of weeks of the budget's release for fear they would undermine President Bush's proposed third major tax cut.

Driving in LA with a Map of New York

Unfortunately, throwing out generational accounting is choosing to fly blind. The alternative guidance system—the size of the government's official debt—is worse than useless when it comes to understanding the fiscal burden we are leaving our kids. Indeed, from a scientific perspective, government debt is entirely content free. It tells us nothing about a country's fiscal policy. On the contrary, the size of a nation's official debt is purely a function of how the government labels its receipts and payments—what words it uses to describe the monies it takes in and pays out. With one set of words, the country will report one size deficit. With another, it will report a different size deficit. Indeed, with the proper choice of words, governments can make their deficits as large—or as small—as they'd like.

This message, delivered in chapter 3, is pretty radical. After all, every country in the world uses the government deficit to assess its fiscal performance. International lending institutions like the International Monetary Fund and the World Bank also use it routinely to determine whether a country qualifies for loans and other assistance. Indeed, fiscal policy discussions virtually anywhere in the world treat the deficit as the central measure of fiscal performance.

Deficit delusion has given our government (and other governments) tremendous license to expropriate future generations by taxing them to cover its unpaid bills. Most of this expropriation has occurred under the cover of "budget balance" through pay-as-you-go Social Security systems. But as chapter 3 shows, countries can report massive surpluses while simultaneously shifting huge future liabilities onto the next generation that never show up in the "official" government debt, figures that fail to show the huge cost of future commitments like Social Security and Medicare.

Popular Tonics, Snake Oils, and Other Easy Fixes

By the time you reach chapter 4, you'll be ready for a miracle cure, so we tried to find you one. We asked whether the boomers could expect to get bailed out by technological progress, the sale of government assets, a growing economy, foreigners investing in the United States, their parents, their employers, a delay in their retirement, immigration, or the elimination of wasteful government spending.

Unfortunately, the answers are no, no, no, no, no, no, no, no, and no. Technological progress will raise government expenditures by more than government receipts; selling government assets would be a wash; the economy will suffer a capital shortage; foreigners will be pulling their assets out of our country; the boomers can't expect particularly large inheritances; employers are cutting back on their retirement plans; a delay in retirement age large enough to matter is not in the cards; immigration costs almost as much as it saves; and wasteful government spending is just a drop in the bucket.

Going Critical

History is replete with examples of what happens when countries can't pay their bills. They raise taxes to exorbitant levels, default on their explicit and implicit obligations, and begin printing money like mad. This triggers inflation, drives interest rates through the roof, and sends exchange rates down the tubes. Businesses go belly up, and banks shut their doors. The result is financial and economic meltdown.

Argentina is the latest country to go critical. Brazil appears to be next on the list. Precisely when the United States will take its turn at fiscal suicide is hard to say for reasons discussed in chapter 5. But the date is close at hand unless the country miraculously changes course—not by swallowing sugar pills, but by undergoing radical surgery.

The real danger in going critical is that the country will get stuck in what economists call a bad *steady state*—one featuring ongoing and economically suffocating liabilities, sky-high tax rates, recurrent bouts of high inflation, widespread tax avoidance, capital flight, and a brain drain as the nation's most talented workers seek their fortunes on distant shores. If this happens, our kids won't be crying just about taxes as they pack their bags. They'll primarily be crying about the awful state of the economy.

Changing Course

Chapter 6 charts a new policy course for our nation by proposing bold, meaningful, new reforms of Social Security and Medicare, the two big entitlement programs that are driving us broke. Since each of these programs is serving a vital function, no reform will be accepted if it throws the baby out with the bath water. Our proposals for reforming these programs are simple, straightforward, and geared to attract support from both political parties.

Grab Your Life Jacket

Unfortunately, if history is any guide, the reforms we suggest won't be enacted for the simple reason that they require immediate and major sacrifice. Baby boomers can thus look forward to a retirement marked by extremely high taxes, substantially reduced retirement and health care benefits, very high rates of inflation, and an ailing economy. We provide examples of how this is happening—already.

Securing Your Future

Staying above water in the ensuing environment means rethinking now how much to save, where to save it, and how much to pay the professional retirement-investment complex for help. The fact is that we all need to start saving like crazy. But how we invest our savings will make a big difference. We don't want to be withdrawing lots of money from our 401(k) plans precisely at the moment the government starts raising taxes on those withdrawals. Nor do we want to be clipping fixed dollar coupons on long-term bonds when the purchasing power of that income is being eroded by inflation. This chapter shows you how to reorganize your conventional portfolio, why home ownership is likely your best investment, and why holding unconventional assets is the trick to coping with future inflation.

Epilogue

We close by recapping the size, speed, and direction of the coming generational storm, stressing the need for immediate and dramatic policy change, repeating the precise changes needed, assessing the likelihood of such change, and reviewing the steps you should take to limit your own downside risk.

A Safety Warning

Before you read on, we recommend you get into a comfortable chair, loosen your collar, and take your antidepressants.

1

From Strollers to Walkers

Old age isn't so bad when you consider the alternative.
—Maurice Chevalier

The Demographic Tidal Wave

Like it or not, ready or not, everyone reading this book will experience the greatest demographic change in human history. In less than a century, the United States will move from being "forever young" to being "forever old." The largest part of the change will happen in the next thirty years as the baby boomers retire. The most dramatic changes will be experienced outside the United States, throughout the entire industrialized world.

You can get a visceral idea of what we are facing by considering an extreme: the rising population of people at least 100 years old. By mid-century the U.S. centenarian population will exceed 600,000.[1] That's ten times the number of centenarians around today.

Housing them will require a city slightly larger than the current population of Washington, D.C. (567,000), slightly smaller than the current population of San Francisco (735,000), nearly four times the current size of Anaheim, California (165,000), and nearly equal to the combined populations of Abilene, Texas (110,000), Akron, Ohio (222,000), Albany, New York (105,000), Allentown Pennsylvania (113,000), and Amarillo, Texas (105,000). Indeed, if you check the long list of cities in America with populations of at least 100,000, only 18 are large enough to accommodate the advancing legion of centenarians.[2]

Why is this happening?

We can only remind you of the old proverb: "Be careful what you wish for. You may get it."

Imagine that you were alive in 1900. Life expectancy at birth was 47 years. The median age of all Americans (half younger, half older) was only 22.9 years. Only 4.1 percent of the population was 65 or older. Life was a constant battle. It was a struggle to be born. It was a struggle to survive infancy, let alone survive childhood. It was still another struggle to survive adulthood. It was common for a father and mother to survive one or more of their children. A husband could lose both his wife and a newborn child during childbirth. The only certainty was that survival and longevity exacted a major toll in grief.

Presented with the magical Monkey's Paw—the one with the power to grant three irreversible wishes—your first wish would have been obvious: *Let life be longer.*

And your wish would have come true.

Today, life expectancy at birth is about 76 years, a gain of 29 years. Life expectancy at 65 is now 17 years, up from 12 years in 1900. Better still, gains in life expectancy at 65 seem to be accelerating.

As a consequence, the population age 65 and over had reached 12.4 percent by 2000, nearly double the 6.8 percent of population under 5 years of age. In the course of 100 years, children had gone from outnumbering the elderly by three to one, to being rarely seen or heard (table 1.1).

By the 1950s and 1960s, the number of kids under age 5 still exceeded the number of oldsters. Kids were about 11 percent of the population in those years, while oldsters were less than 9 percent.[3] Fertility rates, however, were hitting their baby boom peaks—levels not seen since the 1920s. With the fertility rate surging toward four children per woman, a rate that would double the population in a generation, some started to worry about too much of a good thing.[4] From 76 million in 1900, our population had doubled to 151 million in 1950. Our population looked poised to double again by the millennium. In fact, it came close: 286 million. It would have exceeded 300 million without the baby bust that started in the 1970s. Today, Social Security's actuaries project we'll hit 300 million in 2006.[5]

Long lives are a great gift, but they can make a very crowded world. They can also make a very hungry world. While there was little worry

Table 1.1
Trading places: Youngsters decline, while oldsters rise

Decade	Population under age 5	Population age 65 and over (%)
1900	12.1%	4.1%
2000	6.8	12.4

Source: www/infoplease.com/ipa/a0110384.html.

that America would starve, there had already been warnings that unlimited population growth could mean hunger and starvation in China, India, and Africa.

So you made a second wish on the Monkey's Paw: *Let us all have smaller families.*

And you got your wish.

From birthrates well over 2.1 children per couple, the long-term replacement rate for population, birthrates plummeted. In some countries, birthrates fell so far that many nations in Europe will experience population declines early in this century. In the United States, the decline in births was significant, but we're still hovering near the replacement rate.

Taken by itself, the change in birthrates isn't cataclysmic. Basically, it works to accentuate the effects of the first wish, for longevity. Until the population reaches a steady state, a transition that will be measured in generations, there will be an increase in the number of old people relative to the number of young people.

But this calculation doesn't consider the baby boomers. The proverbial "pig in the python" generation that has dominated American concerns since birth, they came of age as your wish for smaller families was coming true. They had smaller families than their parents. Soon they will be starting to retire. The bumper crop of boomers born in 1946 will be reaching the age at which most people start taking Social Security, 62, in 2008. That's just four years and one presidential election away.

Unfortunately, the number of children coming of age and joining the workforce won't be nearly as large. Basically, all the forces that can enlarge the retired elderly population are in overdrive. The forces that would expand the younger (and working) population paying Social

Security and Medicare taxes are in reverse. The result is a kind of perfect demographic storm.

As we said earlier, we'll see the bulk of this change over the next thirty years, but it will continue quite a bit longer. The best way to understand the magnitude of the change is to visualize it in the form of graphs that divide the population in five-year bands from those under 5 years of age all the way to 80 and over (figure 1.1).

In 1900 the age distribution of our population was similar to what characterized all past human history. It was a pyramid—widest at the bottom and narrowing with each successive five-year interval. Only 4 percent of the population was 65 or older. There were no five-year bands beyond "65 or older." Centenarians were rare. Retirement was short. There were plenty of adult children to sustain the elderly.

By 2000 the age distribution was a very different shape. The pyramid is gone. Today the profile looks more like a house with a very tall roof. The Census Bureau has no bands beyond "80 and older." But if it did, the very top would have a narrow lightning rod—the "100 and over" population—reaching for the heavens. Instead of being the largest group at the base of the pyramid, children under 5 are about the same in number as the other groups all the way up to those in their mid-30s. The 65 and older population is now 12.4 percent of the total.

By 2030 the age distribution has a different shape again. This time it is more like a barrel. It goes almost straight up, with only minor shrinkage to the 60–64 age group. The steady shrinkage from death that defined the traditional pyramid now appears to *begin* at age 65. The population age 65 and over will have grown to 19.4 percent of the population, a huge increase in thirty years. This figure, by the way, is the *intermediate projection* used by Social Security. Other projections, including some by Social Security, have higher figures. Basically, the portion of the population age 65 and over will nearly double over the next 30 years.

If the percentage of people age 65 and over nearly doubles in the next thirty years, another part of the population will have to shrink proportionately. And that's the rub: the shrinkage will be in the working-age population, the people who pay employment taxes. Back in 1950 (when we were still worried about runaway population growth), the number of

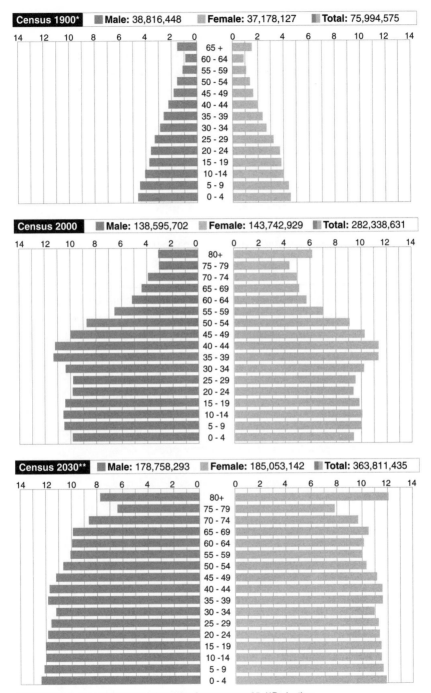

*1900 Census does not provide information for ages over 65. **Projection.

Figure 1.1
Population profiles: U.S. population by age and sex, in millions. *Source:* U.S. Census Bureau

workers per Social Security beneficiary was 16.5. By 2000 the ratio had fallen to 3.4. In the process, most workers started paying more in employment taxes than they pay in income taxes. The employment tax rose fivefold.[6] The wages subject to the Social Security tax rose as well, rising from $3,000 in 1950 to $87,000 in 2003.

Between now and 2030 we'll have the last big surge: the retirement of the boomers. At the end, we'll be close to having only two covered workers per beneficiary. Instead of having sixteen workers chip in to support one senior citizen, we'll have only two. That's a gigantic promise-killing change for Social Security. In only eighty years, the intrinsic cost of supporting retirees will have increased eightfold. In the thirty years to 2030, the intrinsic cost of supporting retirees will rise 70 percent.

Many have seen the coming wave. It is not news. It has been the subject of books, articles, and academic studies for decades. One of the most popular books on the subject, Ken Dychtwald's *Age Wave: The Challenges and Opportunities of an Aging America,* was published in 1989.

Unfortunately, when it comes to action, we're paralyzed. It's as though, having seen the perverse results of the first two wishes on the Monkey's Paw, we're afraid to make the third wish. In fact, the problems we face won't go away. Inaction will make the problem worse, not better. This is a permanent problem, not a temporary one.

Getting Old and Staying Old

The aging of America isn't a temporary event. We won't be getting older this year or this decade, and then turning back and getting younger. We are well into a change that is permanent, irreversible, and very long term.

Where we had 35.5 million people age 65 and older in 2000, we'll have 69.4 million in 2030. During those thirty years, the *dependency ratio*—the ratio of those 65 and older to those 20 to 64—will rise from 21.1 percent to 35.5 percent. That's a major increase.

Don't look around for evidence. You won't see it. We're in a quiet period. While the number of senior citizens rises each year, growth in the number of possible workers has been keeping pace since 1985. It will continue to keep up until the boomers start to retire in 2008, just one presidential election in the future.

The dependency ratio, which has hovered around 20 percent since 1985, ranging from a low of 20.6 percent projected for 2005 to a high of 21.6 percent in 1995, will start a major rise around 2015 when it hits 23.8 percent (table 1.2). By 2030 it will hit 35.5 percent.

And it won't stop there.

The intermediate population projections from the Social Security Administration show the elderly population continuing to grow through 2080, rising from 69.4 million in 2030 to 96.5 million in 2080. During the same period the aged dependency ratio will continue to climb, reaching 43.2 percent by 2080.

The most dramatic way to see how rapidly the nation is aging is to compare the number of seniors—those age 65 and over—to the number of young people. In 2000 there were 82 million people under the age of 20 in the United States. Their numbers dwarfed the 35.5 million seniors.

By 2030, however, there will be 88.6 million young people and 69.4 million seniors, approaching parity. In 2080, only fifty years later, the

Table 1.2
The dependency ratio takes off . . . and keeps going

Year	Ratio
1985	20.1%
1995	21.6
2005	20.6
2010	21.2
2015	23.8
2020	27.5
2025	31.9
2030	35.5
2040	36.8
2060	39.2
2080	43.2

Source: www.ssa.gov/OACT/TR/TR02/V_demographic.html.

number of seniors, 96.5 million, will finally exceed the number of young people, 95.8 million.

These are, of course, only projections. They could be wrong. A deadly variant on the SARS virus could create a shortage of grandparents, restore the traditional population pyramid, and "solve" the entire problem. Hardly a year passes without a population collapse movie.

The likely future is less dramatic. That's one reason the Social Security Administration regularly creates three sets of projections. There is a low-cost projection based on less positive (but not catastrophic) assumptions about future mortality rates. There is also a high-cost projection based on more positive (but well short of eternal life) assumptions about future mortality rates. The Social Security Administration characterizes the intermediate assumptions as their best bet on what will actually happen.

In fact, the Social Security Administration intermediate figures have historically tended to be on the low side, consistently underestimating advances in longevity (table 1.3). They have also been behind the curve on the decline in birthrates. If their high-cost (longer life expectancy) projections turn out to be the correct ones, the dependency ratio will almost double in thirty years and nearly triple in eighty years.

We're not bringing this up to be rude or depressing. We're just aware that few subjects attract more interest and energy than living a long and healthy life. Some may question motherhood, others may doubt apple pie, but everyone wants to live a long time.

One of the ongoing arguments·in the scientific community is whether there is a natural limit to life expectancy. Some assert there is and cal-

Table 1.3
The long-term difference assumptions make

Year	Intermediate elderly population	Intermediate dependency rate	High elderly population	High dependency rate
2000	35,516,000	21.1%	35,516,000	21.1%
2030	69,408,000	35.5	72,746,000	38.3
2080	96,545,000	43.2	106,636,000	59.7

Source: www.ssa.gov/OACT/TR/TR02/V_demographic.html.

culate the natural limit. In 1928, for instance, Louis Dublin calculated that the ultimate life expectancy was just less than 65 years, seven years higher than actual life expectancy at that time. His calculation quickly proved wrong, as have similar calculations since then.

Based on actual rates of improvement, for instance, a recent article in *Science* calculates that female life expectancy in the United States might actually range from 92.5 to 101.5 by 2070.[7] That's quite a bit higher than the 85 years that are part of the intermediate figures from the Social Security Administration.

A secondary method used by the Social Security actuaries is called *cohort life expectancies*. While the commonly used expectancy calculations assume there is no improvement in health or medicine from birth, the cohort life expectancies attempt to incorporate year-to-year improvements. Using this method, the intermediate life expectancy of a woman is 89.4 years in 2070, and the high-cost series estimate is 96.7 years.

Which will it be?

No one knows. We can only be certain of one thing. The age wave coming toward us is probably much bigger than the conventionally used figures tell us.

The Old and the Ancient

Not long ago you were considered "old" at 65. The last age category in most surveys was "65 and over." It was sufficient to hold all of the elderly, a small portion of the population. As labels go, it was perfectly adequate.

No more.

Today the taxonomy of aging is growing as fast as life expectancy. First, gerontologist Bernice Neugarten suggested that the old were really two groups: the "young-old" and the "old-old." She defined the young-old as people between 65 and 74 because they tended to be healthy, active, and functional. The old-old were closer to the elderly we imagined: frail, subject to infirmities, and likely to be suffering from physical or cognitive limitations.

The extension of life expectancy has been so great that we now have yet another category, the oldest-old. Although the definition varies a bit, the Census Bureau considers the oldest-old to be people who are 80 and older. Today the Census Bureau divides the elderly population into three categories: ages 65 to 74, 75 to 84, and 85 and over. When they project our population in the future, they estimate the number in each of those categories.

Would you like to guess which group is growing fastest?

That's right, the 85-plus crew.

Between 2000 and 2050 the 85-plus population is expected to grow from 4.3 million to 18.2 million, a 323 percent increase. During the same period, the 75 to 84 year olds will grow in number from 12.3 million to 25.9 million, a mere doubling. Those 65 to 74 will grow in number from 18.1 million to 34.7 million, somewhat less than doubling.

Before you get too impressed with the 85-plus crew, remember that this is progressive. The older the group measured, the faster the growth rate. As we pointed out in chapter 1, the centenarian population, once a virtual trace element, is projected to rise tenfold, to 600,000, over the same period. Indeed, centenarians may be the only population group growing as fast as the number of Elvis imitators.

The growth of centenarians is a worldwide phenomenon. Japan, which now holds the record for female life expectancy, has seen enormous changes in the postwar period. In 1950 a 65-year-old Japanese woman could expect to live another thirteen years. Today she can expect to live another twenty-two years. In 1950 her chances of living to 100 were only one in a thousand. Today the odds are one in twenty, a 5 percent chance.

We are looking at a major population boom. The difference is the unit of measure. While past population booms were measured in babies, this one is measured in septuagenarians, octogenarians, and nonagenarians. While their numbers are growing (in total) from 34.7 million to 78.9 million, the number of 5-and-under children in our society will rise only from 18.9 million to 27.1 million. The figures are shown in table 1.4.

Like the projections made by the actuaries at the Social Security Administration, these Census Bureau estimates are intermediate figures—the actual numbers could be higher or lower. Using different assump-

Table 1.4
Plenty of seniors, not many kids

Year	Age 5 and under	Age 65–74	Ages 75–84	Ages 85 and over	Total old	Senior-to-kid ratio
2000	18,987	18,136	12,315	4,259	34,710	1.8
2010	20,012	21,057	12,680	5,671	39,408	2.0
2020	21,967	31,385	15,375	6,460	53,220	2.4
2030	23,066	37,406	23,517	8,455	69,378	3.0
2040	24,980	33,014	28,668	13,552	75,234	3.0
2050	27,106	34,731	25,905	18,223	78,859	2.9

Source: Bureau of the Census, *Current Population Reports*, P25–1130.
Note: Population figures in thousands.

tions, two independent researchers have come up with dramatically different figures. While the Census Bureau intermediate figures project 13.5 million seniors age 85 and over, one independent researcher uses lower mortality rate figures and projects 16.8 million. Another researcher projects 23.5 million.[8]

The rising population of the old-old and oldest-old is usually credited to a dramatic and continuing decline in the expected death rates for people of that age. Between 1985 and 1995, for instance, death rates for those ages 70 to 74 in the United States fell 6 percent. Death rates for those 80 to 84 fell by 8 percent.

Barring a major resurgence of disease, we think the official figures are on the low side. Each older person, regardless of age, represents a call on Social Security and Medicare. And the longer people live, the more likely they are to outlive their assets. This means rising calls on Medicaid, which helps the poor, regardless of age, get medical care.

"More likely" isn't the same as "inevitable." While virtually everyone can tell an old-age horror story, a growing body of work suggests that there is a near "second wind" for many seniors. If they don't succumb to heart disease and cancer in their 60s and 70s, evidence suggests that those in their 80s and 90s may experience lower death rates and greater health.[9] The picture of old age that emerges from the MacArthur Foundation Study of Successful Aging is far brighter than the one presented by a long-term-care insurance sales rep.

Unfortunately, whether an older person is healthy and functional or unhealthy and nonfunctional only changes the *level* of expense they present to our economy. That expense, even at the lowest levels (Social Security retirement benefits and Medicare), is far higher than our spending on children. One indicator is the amount the federal government spends on a child compared to the amount it spends on an elderly person. In 1995 federal spending per child under age 18 was $1,693, about one-tenth of the $15,636 the federal government spent on each person age 65 and over.

Why are we bringing this up?

Simple. One of the tranquilizing arguments used to reduce concern about the coming age wave is the broad dependency ratio. Defined as the total number of children under age 20 *and* seniors 65 and over divided by the working-age population (20 to 64), the broad dependency ratio will be about the same in 2030 as it was in 1960.

No one was worried about being overwhelmed by the cost of supporting dependents in 1960. No one was talking about a "dependency crisis."

The difference, of course, is that adults—whether 65, 75, or 105 years old—cost a lot more to support than young children. In 1960, most of the dependents were children. In the future, most of the dependents will be adults.

To Die Like the Japanese!

Although women have always won the Longevity Olympics, the nationality of the winners has changed. In 1840 it was Sweden that held the female life expectancy record, clocking in at 45 years. They quickly lost it to Norwegian women, who held the title until late in the nineteenth century, having raised the record to about 52 years.

The non-Maori women of New Zealand then took the record and held it until 1940, moving the record up to about 67 years. Then it went back to Norwegian women, who traded it back and forth with Icelandic women until sometime in the 1980s, when the record hit 80 years.

That's when the women of Japan took the lead. They came out of nowhere. A Japanese woman born in 1947 could expect to live only 54 years. American women at that time had a life expectancy of 68.4 years. Japanese women surpassed them in 1970, at 75.7 years.

American women were passed as if they were standing still. Japanese women have added another ten years to their life expectancies since 1980, clocking in for 2000 at 84.6 years.

And it hasn't stopped. In August 2002, when the Japanese Health and Welfare Ministry released figures for 2001, the expectancy of Japanese women rose again, to 84.93 years. They kept the longevity record and, significantly, left America in the dust. A newborn Japanese female can expect to outlive her American counterpart by over 5 years. With an expectancy of 78 years, a newborn Japanese male can expect to outlive his American counterpart by 4.2 years.

In fact, while the women of France, Canada, and Hong Kong are pushing the women of Japan for the life expectancy record, the United States isn't even on the list of the top ten competitors. Ditto the secondary contest for male life expectancy: the Japanese are regularly challenged by Iceland, Sweden, Canada, and Hong Kong—but the United States isn't on that top ten list either.

In a book of global statistics, the *Economist* magazine ranked every nation in the world for life expectancy by averaging each country's figures for the period from 1995 through 2000.[10] Japan was first at 80 years, followed closely by Iceland (79.3 years) and Canada (78.9). France (78.8) and Hong Kong (78.8) tied for fourth place.

Where was the United States?

We tied Germany for twenty-fifth place, clocking in at 76.7 years. If you think that isn't a big difference—80 versus 76.7—you're probably less than 76 years old. Among the unlikely nations that beat us are Greece (78.1), Israel (77.7), Martinique (77.1), and Costa Rica (76.8). Indeed, we barely beat Puerto Rico (76.5), Barbados (76.4), and Cuba (76.0).

Life expectancy at birth figures are powerfully influenced by infant mortality and public health issues such as availability of clean water, so we might also examine life expectancies at age 65. There we find the same story, if somewhat less dramatic. Japanese men and women at

65 both had shorter expectancies than their American counterparts in 1970. Japanese men could expect 12.5 years of life, while American men could expect 13.1 years. Japanese women could expect 15.3 years, while American women could expect 17 years. Only ten years later Japanese men had pulled ahead. They led American men 14.6 to 14.1 years. Japanese women still trailed American women 17.7 years to 18.3. By 1998 Japanese men and women were well ahead of Americans, with men leading 17.1 years to 16 years and women leading 22 years to 19.2 years.

Now let's ask a perverse question: How long do the actuaries at the Social Security Administration think it will take for American life expectancies to catch up with Japanese life expectancies? How much of a lead do they think the Japanese have?

According to their intermediate series figures, life expectancy for American women at birth will reach 85 in 2070, giving Japanese women a 69-year lead. American men will catch up with Japanese men in 2040, giving Japanese men a lead of "only" 39 years. The life expectancy of American women at 65 will catch up with their Japanese counterparts in 2055. The life expectancy of American men at 65 will catch up with current Japanese men around 2020.

The catch-up date, of course, assumes that nothing will happen in Japan for nearly seventy years, which isn't very likely. If the established trend simply continues, the longest life expectancies in the world will continue to advance about 2.5 years per decade, a rate they have maintained for 150 years. That would bring the leading life expectancy (for women) to 92 by 2030 and 100 by around 2060.

If expectancies for women in the United States trail by their current five years, they will rise to 87 years by 2030 and 95 years by 2060. That's *five years* over the 82-year expectancy estimated by the actuaries at the Social Security Administration by 2030 and *eleven years* over the 84-year expectancy estimated for 2060.

No one can "prove" the future. But we think the evidence strongly suggests that we're being institutionally low-balled. The future U.S. population of people 65 and over is likely to be much closer to the Social Security high-cost estimates than the intermediate estimates. The age wave coming our way is larger than anyone wants to admit.

Where Have All the Children Gone?

As years go, 1957 was notable, if primitive.

Remote control for television sets had yet to be invented. This meant the 47.2 million sets in 39.5 million American households had their channels changed *by hand*, if you can imagine that. The sets were also relatively small and offered pictures only in black and white.

Elvis Presley dominated popular music with songs like "Love Me," "Too Much," "All Shook Up," and "Let Me Be Your Teddy Bear." Jack Kerouac's *On the Road* was published, introducing us to drugs and karma at the same time. Velcro was patented, General Foods introduced Tang, Ford introduced the Edsel, and a domestic first-class postage stamp cost only 3 cents.

The Soviet Union, flexing its technological muscles, successfully tested its first intercontinental ballistic missile, which grabbed our attention. Then they put the first satellite in space, *Sputnik,* which *really* grabbed our attention.

Oliver Hardy of Laurel and Hardy fame died, but Lyle Lovett was born. Lyle's birth was not much noticed at the time because 1957 was the year we produced the most babies ever born in America in a single year. We did it at the rate of one baby every seven seconds, closing the year with 4.3 million newborns, from a total population of only 172 million.

You can get an idea of what a staggering feat that was by doing a modern comparison. In spite of having 100 million more Americans today, we produced fewer than 4 million newborns a year through the late 1990s.

The difference is the birthrate. Often measured by total fertility rate—the number of expected lifetime births per woman—this figure also tells us if we can expect a growing or shrinking population in the future. If the total fertility rate is 2.1, population will stabilize after a number of decades. This is the birthrate sought by ZPG (Zero Population Growth) and other organizations interested in population control.

In 1957 our total fertility rate hit a record, 3.68, a figure that approaches the fertility rates of underdeveloped nations. The rate (not to mention the 4.3 million babies) frightened those concerned with population growth and set in motion Malthusian fears of global starvation. In fact, neither the number of babies born nor the total fertility rate has been that high since.

After 1957 the total fertility rate declined. It hit 2.48 in 1970 and dropped to 2.27 in 1971. And it was well below replacement rate through most of the 1970s and early 1980s. It bottomed at 1.74 in 1976. The baby bust of the seventies and the Birth Dearth of the eighties replaced the baby boom of the fifties (see figure 1.2).

If longer life expectancies and lower birthrates can radically reshape the age distribution of a population, causing major changes in the number of retirees depending on younger workers, the juxtaposition of a baby boom with a period of baby bust works to accentuate the change still further.

Today, we teeter around the replacement rate, surrounded by ominous portents of lower birthrates in the future. As we'll show shortly, a combination of higher education, later marriages, and delays in the birth of the first child may reduce future total fertility rates below the 2.1 replacement rate. If that happens, our future will have the stresses currently being faced in Europe, Japan, and China.

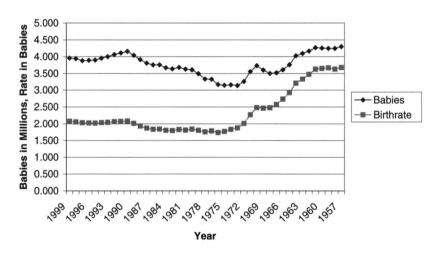

Figure 1.2
From boom to near bust. *Source:* Population Reference Bureau
a-FERT_USFerti/1.x/s

However, the operative word here is *may*. Whatever problems we face due to the rising number of elderly people, the only certainty is that we can't expect much sympathy from the rest of the world. Elsewhere, the problems are far worse. If we don't adapt and cope, there will be no one to bail us out.

You can understand this if you divide the nations of the world in two dimensions: life expectancy and birthrate. Let's make life expectancy the vertical axis and birthrate the horizontal axis, creating four quadrants (figure 1.3). Setting the cross-hairs at a life expectancy of 60 and a birthrate of 2.1 we find two quadrants of disaster, one of major upheaval, and one of possible Panglossian balance. In the United States, we're on the tattered edge of Panglossian balance—and still face a future with gigantic generational imbalances.

High life expectancy

The Decrepit Quarter High life expectancy (76.9), low birthrate (1.5) Most of Europe, Japan, China	**Panglossian Balance** High life expectancy (73.4), low birthrate (2.1) United States
Postmodern Malthusian Hell Low life expectancy (58.0), low birthrate (1.4) Russia, most states of former Soviet Union	**Traditional Malthusian Hell** Low life expectancy (52.3), high birthrate (4.9) Most of Africa, other undeveloped nations

Low birthrate (left)   *High birthrate* (right)

Low life expectancy

Figure 1.3
The four quadrants of demography

Like Sisyphus, most of the world plugs on in a traditional Malthusian Hell. Life expectancies are low because public health efforts are limited, incomes are low, and starvation is a daily possibility. Birthrates are high to cope with the losses.

The starkest picture of the future comes from Postmodern Malthusian Hell, dominated by the states of the former Soviet Union. There, *both* life expectancies and birthrates have plummeted. The total fertility rate has fallen to 1.3, and life expectancies for men dropped to 57 years. As a consequence, the population of Russia could fall from its current 148 million to only 58 million by 2040—less than forty years off. This is a decline of 60 percent. That's what happened during the plague years of fourteenth-century Europe. The only difference is that Russia, with forty years, will have time to bury its dead. Cities hit by the plague lost so many people in such a short time that burying the dead became impossible.[11]

Waiting for Mr./Ms. Perfect

The funniest and most demographically telling section in David Brooks's *BoBos in Paradise: The New Upper Class and How They Got There* is his comparison of current and past wedding announcements in the *New York Times*. Thirty years ago the wedding announcements were as much about the bride and groom's parents as the bride and groom. Today, Brooks observes, the wedding announcements read more like résumés:

When America had a pedigreed elite, the page emphasized noble birth and breeding. But in America today it is genius and geniality that enable you to join the elect. And when you look at the *Times* weddings page, you can almost feel the force of the mingling SAT scores. It's Dartmouth marries Berkeley, MBA weds Ph.D., Fulbright hitches with Rhodes, Lazard Freres joins CBS, and summa cum laude embraces summa cum laude (you rarely see a summa settling for a magna— the tension in such a marriage would be too great). The *Times* emphasizes four things about a person—college degrees, graduate degrees, career path, and parents' professions—for these are the markers of upscale Americans today.[12]

Thirty years ago the education of the bride was somewhat important (it gave strong signals about the quality of the match) but her employment wasn't. Today, her résumé is as important as the groom's:

"These two awesome résumés collided at a wedding ceremony in Manhattan, and given all the school chums who must have attended, the combined tuition bills in that room must have been staggering," Brooks wrote.[13]

One reason for this shift is that both the bride and groom are older— much older. Another reason is that both the bride and groom work. Both expect to work after marriage as well as before. For women, the job-as-way-station to marriage is history. The June wedding following college graduation is history. Today, marriage can be delayed for graduate school, first job, and longer. As a consequence, today's wedding bells are accompanied by the loud chiming of a biological clock.

Between 1950 and 1960, the peak years of the baby boom, the median age at first marriage for women was a tender 20.3 years. The corresponding age for men was only 22.8 years. Age at first marriage had barely advanced by 1970, the beginnings of the birth dearth. In 1970 the median age at first marriage for women was 20.8 years, only half a year greater. The median age at first marriage for men was 23.2 years. Again, it was only half a year greater.

But that was the end of young marriages.

By 1980 the median age for women was 22 years; by 1990 it was 23.9, and by 2000 it was 25.1. In only thirty years, median age at first marriage advanced 4.3 years.[14]

Grooms aged nearly as much. By 1980 the median age at first marriage for men was at 24.7 years; by 1990 it was 26.1; and by 2000 it was 26.8—a 3.6-year advance in thirty years.

To be sure, they still seem like kids to anyone who is over 40. But the rude fact is they have lost four of their best reproductive years, and the result is showing up in the total fertility rate. Another way to see the same shift is to examine how old the average American woman is at the birth of her first child. In 1970 the average age was 21.4 years, only slightly older than the median age at first marriage. (Given the indelicate difference of only 0.6 years—a tad more than seven months—we hasten to point out that one figure is an average, the other a median. In addition, as many proud grandparents will tell you, many first grandchildren are born prematurely.)

Table 1.5
Births per thousand women of all races

Year	15–19	20–24	25–29	30–34	35–39	40–44	15–44
1970	53.7	78.2	31.2	7.3	2.1	0.4	34.2
1980	41.4	57.3	38.2	12.8	2.6	0.3	29.5
1990	45.1	55.2	44.1	21.2	6.7	1.0	29.0
1999	38.9	50.9	43.1	25.6	8.5	1.6	26.6
Change	−27.6%	−34.9%	38.1%	350.7%	404.8%	400.0%	−22.2%

Source: National Center for Health Statistics www.cdc.qov/nchs/data/

Thirty years later the average age at the birth of the first child was 24.6 years, an increase of 3.2 years from 1970. While first births have increased in women 25 and older, the increase has not offset the decrease in first births in women under 25. When the rate at which first children are born declines, the overall birthrate also declines. You can see the shift in the figures in table 1.5, which represent the number of live births for every thousand women (of all races) in different age groups over the past 30 years.

First births to teenagers have declined. So have first births to women in their early twenties. Meanwhile, there has been a boom in first children born to women over 30—the increase from the 1970s is over 350 percent! The first child boom for women over 30, however, started from such a small base that it completely fails to offset the decline in first babies born to women under 25.

Another effect of later marriages and childbearing doesn't even show up in the age-at-first-birth figures. For some women, the long wait means they won't have any children *at all*. Between 1980 and 1998, for instance, the proportion of women who were 40 to 44 years old and childless virtually doubled, rising from 10 percent to 19 percent. Today, nearly one woman in five can expect to be childless. Madelyn Caens's book *The Childless Revolution* lets us know this is not an obscure event. Popular medical miracles and fanatical exercise notwithstanding, there is no "catching up" on motherhood at age 45.

This isn't a quirky statistical footnote. What we're seeing here is a change in reproduction that is without precedent: *the willing deferral of childbearing raises the odds of being childless.* Combine this with rapid advances in life expectancy, and you have the formula for the generational storm coming our way. Basically, we made a massive societal bet on the ability of our children to support the elderly. Then, like the well-known slogan emblazoned on T-shirts in the 1980s, we forgot to have children.

Why is this happening?

The subject is rich in speculation. We see three major forces at work: the increasing education of women, their growing role in the workplace, and the crucial role women play in creating the affluent two-income household.

Education, Work, and Condoms

It would be difficult to overestimate the economic contribution of women. Of the 118.9 million people employed in 2000, women accounted for 55.6 million. In the last half-century the proportion of men who are employed has declined. The proportion of women who are employed has soared. Indeed, most affluent households—perhaps even the *idea* of affluent households (think "yuppies," "DINKS")—would not exist today if women had not become major contributors to the world of paid work.

We could also argue that women are the secret heroines of Social Security. If they had not joined the labor force in droves, the financial condition of the Social Security system would be materially worse than it is today. As we show by examples in chapter 6, women pay the full burden of employment taxes but have received only a marginal increase in benefits.

The growing strength of women in the workplace has not been without cost. The most measurable human cost is quite easy to see: fewer children. Rising levels of education have increased the economic value of women in the marketplace. The same education has brought more and more women into the workplace. But it has also reduced the total fertility rate. Women who are educated and working have fewer children than women who are less educated and not working.

A 1997 study, for instance, found that education level was the single best predictor of how many children a woman would have.[15] Women educated no further than eighth grade have an average of 3.2 children, women who are high school graduates average 2.7 children, and women college graduates average 1.6 to 2.0 children, depending on their race. Among college graduates, non-Hispanic white women average 1.7, non-Hispanic black women average 1.6, and Hispanic women average 2.0.

College-educated women, in other words, don't have enough children to sustain current population levels. If all women had college educations, the birthrate in the United States would be close to the very low rates being experienced in Europe, where population is expected to shrink over the next thirty years.

Now consider the trend in education. In 1960 men earned 66 percent of all degrees beyond high school. In that year 254,000 men, but only 138,000 women, received bachelor's degrees. It was the same for master's degrees: men received 51,000 while women received 24,000. Raise the ante to the doctorate level, and the disproportion was even more extreme: 9,000 for men, 1,000 for women.

The educational gender imbalance was even more striking for recipients of professional degrees. In 1960 only 5.5 percent of M.D. degrees went to women; a bare trace element of D.D.S. or D.M.D. degrees, 0.8 percent, were conferred on women; only 2.5 percent of all new law degrees went to women. Women earned only 2.3 percent of all theological degrees.

No more.

The number of associate's degrees earned by women exceeded the number of associate's degrees earned by men before 1980; the number of bachelor's degrees earned by women exceeded the number earned by men by 1985. Ditto the number of master's degrees.

The advance has been slower (and tougher) for Ph.D. degrees and professional degrees, but the numbers are changing rapidly. By 1994 women were receiving 38 percent of all M.D. degrees, 38 percent of all dentistry degrees, 43 percent of all law degrees, and 25 percent of all theology degrees. Recent projections indicate that women should achieve near parity in Ph.D. degrees early in this decade but will have slowed their advance in professional degrees. But those are only projections. In fact, the number of women enrolled in medical school is already greater than the number of men in medical school.

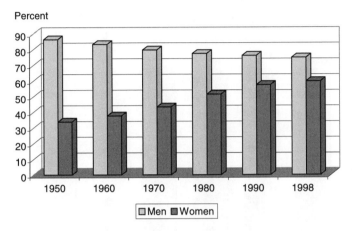

Percent

Figure 1.4
Women rising, men falling (labor force participation rates). *Source:* Adapted from Howard N. Fullerton, Jr., "Labor Force Participation: 75 Years of Change, 1950–1998 and 1998–2025," *Monthly Labor Review*, December 1999. www.bls.gov.opub/mlr/1999/12/art1full.pdf

Glass ceilings notwithstanding, the forty-year surge to educational parity (and then some) allowed women to expand their share of the job market. Between 1950 and 1999 the number of people in the labor force grew from 62.2 million to 139.4 million, an increase of 77.2 million. Of that number, women were 46.5 million or 60 percent.[16] If men and women were products, we'd have to say women were gaining market share and men were losing it.

You can see this reality most directly in the labor force participation rate figures developed by the Labor Department (figure 1.4). From 1950 to the present, the male labor force participation rate has declined steadily, from 86.4 percent to 74.9 percent. The same figures for women have shown a steady increase. While only 33.9 percent of women were labor force participants in 1950, 59.8 percent are participants today.

Most striking is that fact that male participation rates have fallen for every age group (figure 1.5). The largest declines, as many would suspect from newspaper reporting over the past twenty years, have been among men 55 and over. For them, the participation rate has fallen from 86.9 percent in 1950 to 68.1 percent in 1998. For men 65 and over,

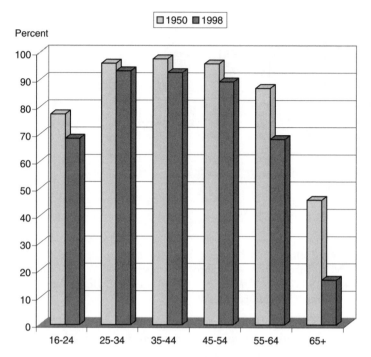

Figure 1.5
Men in the work force, 1950–1998. *Source:* Adapted from Howard N. Fullerton, Jr., "Labor Force Participation: 75 Years of Change, 1950–1998 and 1998–2025," *Monthly Labor Review*, December 1999. www.bls.gov.opub/mlr/1999/12/art1full.pdf

the decline has been even steeper: from 45.8 percent in 1950 to 16.5 percent in 1998.

Female participation rates have risen for every age group, with the single exception of those 65 and older (figure 1.6). There, the rate has fallen from 9.7 percent to only 8.7 percent.

At first glance it would seem that the choice being made is simple and direct: Women can seek an opportunity for education and the employment that follows, or they can seek an opportunity for motherhood. But a closer look at the figures tells us that women are trying very hard to do both. In 1975 the labor force participation rate for women with children under 3 years of age was 32.7 percent. For women with children under age 1, the rate was only 30.8 percent.

Percent

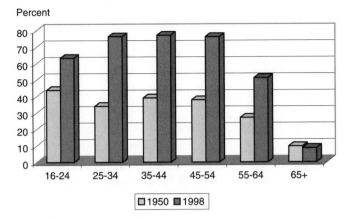

Figure 1.6
Women in the work force, 1950–1998. *Source:* Adapted from Howard N. Fullerton, Jr., "Labor Force Participation: 75 Years of Change, 1950–1998 and 1998–2025," *Monthly Labor Review*, December 1999. www.bls.gov.opub/mlr/1999/12/art1full.pdf

By 1998 there were 3.7 million women with infants under the age of 1. An amazing 59 percent were in the labor force with 36 percent employed full time, 17 percent part time, and 6 percent seeking employment. The same research found that an incredible 73 percent of the 31.3 million mothers without infants were in the workforce, with 52 percent working full time, 17 percent working part time, and 4 percent seeking employment.[17]

Small wonder that we see articles on "Having It All" and great concern with the availability and quality of child care. What it all comes down to, regardless of effort, is that the third child is never conceived, and some women have fewer than two children.

As a society, we've been remarkably inattentive to these extraordinary changes. We've been even less attentive to how women are doing it— dancing backward and on high heels, like Ginger Rogers. The idea that "having it all" may not be such a good deal for women has been stewing for a long time; witness Sylvia Ann Hewitts's 2002 book, *Creating a Life: Professional Women and the Quest for Children*.[18] We experience the price in one of the most painful experiences a person can endure: divorce.

Divorce American Style

Modern weddings can be disorienting. At one wedding not many years ago, a reporter watched the bride and groom exchange vows in a Catholic and deeply death-do-us-part ceremony. Nothing in their family histories, however, offered encouragement. The mother of the bride, who had been divorced from the father for many years, was unaccompanied. The father of the bride brought his most recent girlfriend. The bride's brother arrived with his wife. Her parents had divorced many years earlier. The father of the groom, who had remarried, arrived with his second wife. The mother of the groom, who had also remarried after divorcing the groom's father, arrived with her new husband. He brought his two sons by his first marriage. The groom's sister, who had married a few months earlier, brought her husband. His parents were also divorced.

While this may sound like the basic ingredients for a play that combines *Who's Afraid of Virginia Woolf?* and *Three Weddings and a Funeral*, it is, in fact, fairly typical of conjugal gatherings in America. Small wonder that people like to quote Rita Rudner: "When I meet a man I ask myself: Is this the man I want my children to spend their weekends with?"[19]

While no one ever said marriage was easy, it seems to be particularly difficult in the United States, a reality with long-term consequences as we become an older country. Many Americans now live in familial isolation, an isolation that will worsen as they age.

Is our situation extreme?

Very. In the divorce Olympics, we win the bronze medal. With 4.34 divorces per thousand inhabitants per year, we trail only Maldives (10.97) and Belarus (4.63). While it is unlikely we'll ever capture the gold (given the Maldives record), we're positioned to move up to silver and unlikely to be challenged by any of the also-rans. Cuba, which placed fourth at 3.72 divorces per 1,000 inhabitants per year, is well behind us. So are Estonia (3.65), Panama (3.61), and Puerto Rico (3.61).[20]

Compared to other industrialized nations, we're the Demolition Derby; they're the Grand Prix of Monaco. The divorce rate in Sweden, once reported to be the home of free love, is 2.4 per thousand inhabitants. That's only a tad lower than the 2.6 rate for Great Britain.

Germany scores a modest 2.3, France 2.0, and Italy a mere 0.6. In Japan the rate is 2.3. Barring some major change, marriage will continue to be nearly twice as difficult in the United States as in the rest of the industrialized world.[21]

Indeed, examining the statistics of marriage, we could easily conclude that marriage in America is much like Thomas Hobbes's description of preindustrial life—"nasty, brutish, and short."

Knowledge of the difficulty of marriage doesn't keep us from trying. At one time or another in our lives, usually sooner than later, about 95 percent of us try matrimony. Some keep trying with a second and third marriage. Only 1 percent of us, however, are game for four or more marriages.

The most recent complete examination of our mating habits was published in 2002 based on data collected from several very large surveys in 1995. Romantically titled *Cohabitation, Marriage, Divorce, and Remarriage in the United States*, it tells us how everything from race to generalized anxiety disorder affects the odds a marriage will survive. On first marriages, it notes they are "less likely to break up, and more likely to succeed, if the wife grew up in a two-parent home, is Asian, was 20 years of age or over at marriage, did not have any children when she got married, is college-educated, has more income, or has any religious affiliation."[22]

As you can see in figure 1.7, for women between 15 and 44 years of age in 1995, half of all first marriages were likely to fail by the twenty-second year.

The same study also shows the flux of marital status as women age and the enduring drive to live as couples (table 1.6). At age 20 to 24, for instance, 11.2 percent of women are cohabitating, 56.1 percent have never been married, 5.5 percent are "formerly married," and 27.2 percent are married. Twenty years later, by age 40 to 44, cohabitation has declined to 4.1 percent, only 8.8 percent have never been married, 18.1 percent are formerly married, and 68.6 percent are married. The positive story here is that if marriage is a major social goal, more than two-thirds of all women eventually succeed. The other figures simply show that it isn't easy. (Sadly, the study offers no information at all on women over age 44.)

Percent

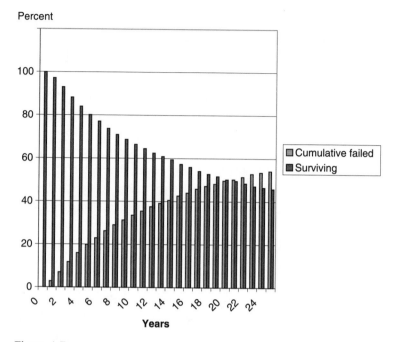

Figure 1.7
First marriage life table. *Source:* Adapted from Rose M. Kreider and Jason M. Fields, "Number, Timing, and Duration of Marriages and Divorces: 1996," *Current Population Reports,* February 2002.

Table 1.6
The long drive to marriage—more than two-thirds of women succeed

Age at interview	Currently cohabitating	Not cohabitating		
		Never married	Formerly married	Currently married
15–19	4.1	91.5	0.6	3.8
20–24	11.2	56.1	5.5	27.2
25–29	9.8	28.9	8.8	52.5
30–34	7.5	16.2	11.6	64.7
35–39	5.3	11.9	15.0	67.9
40–44	4.4	8.8	18.1	68.6

Source: Matthew D. Bramlett and William D. Mosher, "Cohabitation, Marriage, Divorce, and Remarriage in the United States," *CDC Vital and Health Statistics,* July 2002.

While it is commonly observed that it is the destiny of most women to live alone late in their lives, these figures make it clear that a substantial minority of women live without a significant other most of their lives: nearly 27 percent of women 40 to 44 had either never married or were formerly married (table 1.6). This means a substantial minority of women doesn't have the economic or health benefits of marriage. They are likely to enter their old age in a more vulnerable position than those who are married.

Unfortunately, these figures don't show the decline in marital success for women who came of age more recently. Another study, which analyzes marriages by year in which the marriage occurred, shows that women who first married in 1945 to 1949 had a 95 percent chance of reaching their fifth anniversary and a 90 percent chance of reaching their tenth anniversary.[23] The marital longevity figures decline year by year. Women who first married in 1980 to 1984, for instance, had only an 86 percent of reaching their fifth anniversary and a 73 percent chance of reaching their tenth anniversary.

The study also examines the marital status of women over the entire life cycle, revealing that widowhood supplants divorce after age 60. Examined by age group, we learn that women are most likely to be in a marriage from the age of 30 through 59. In that period roughly two-thirds are married. Before age 30 women are looking for mates (sometimes a second or third mate). At 60 and older, raw mortality struts on stage. The higher mortality rate of men begins to expose an increasing number of women to living alone. At 60 and older, 54.5 percent of women are currently widowed, and 58.3 percent have been widowed at one time.

The corresponding figures for men are dramatically lower: only 18.6 percent are currently widowed at 70 and older and only 25.1 percent have ever been widowed. If we look from the other side, 73.9 percent of men 70 and older have married only once, 55.5 percent are still married to the same woman, and 71.3 percent are currently married, though some have married three times to get there.

Will these figures hold? We doubt it. Divorce is more accepted, more common, and much easier today than it was in 1950, 1960, or 1970.

Dividing all women into different age groups tells us how each age group is doing now (table 1.7). It tells us much less about how they will be doing in the future. We can't, for instance, blithely assume that women now ages 30 to 34 will age forty years and simply replace the current group of 70-and-older women. There are several reasons for this, but we'll name just the big ones. The first is a pure numbers game: higher divorce rates for everyone and lower death rates for women. Like a morbid game of musical chairs from which male "chairs" are removed in increasing numbers, some women will simply lose their "place." Raw mortality will make replacement impossible. There is a reason women outnumber men in nursing homes: men don't live long enough to get there.

The second reason has to do with choice. Fifty years ago, marriage was a social and material necessity for women. Today, glass ceilings notwithstanding, an increasing proportion of all women earn more than their husbands. With more women earning undergraduate degrees than men, that proportion is likely to increase. Indeed, men of all colors could become the "super masculine menials" that Eldridge Cleaver described long ago.

For women today, marriage is a social choice and a material convenience. In the poker game of life, it no longer takes "a pair or better" to open.

What does this mean for the elderly of the future? Their only non-institutional source of help and support in their old age, whether it is physical or financial, may be their children—if they have any. As we've already seen, the supply of children—and the working adults they become—is shrinking.

Empty Nests

Robert Schroeder died an enviable death.

Widowed at 82, he spent the last two years of his life in active contact with his children, grandchildren, and great grandchildren. All lived in the same city, less than an hour from him, and all loved his company. He worked part time, drove his car, enjoyed the security of living independently in a continuing care community, and embraced every day as a new opportunity.

Table 1.7
Women and marriage through life, by age group

Marital status	15–19	20–24	25–29	30–34	35–39	40–49	50–59	60–69	70 and over
Never married	96.6	67.0	35.3	18.7	14.1	8.6	5.0	3.7	4.2
Married once, still married	3.0	27.4	48.9	57.0	53.3	49.2	50.3	48.4	28.1
Married twice, still married	×	1.1	4.6	9.6	12.0	15.5	13.2	10.5	6.0
Married three times or more, still married	×	×	0.3	1.1	2.3	3.4	3.9	2.4	0.9
Currently divorced	×	2.1	7.1	9.5	12.8	17.2	16.6	11.5	5.6
Currently widowed	×	0.2	0.2	0.3	1.0	2.6	8.2	21.6	54.5
Total married	3.0	28.5	53.8	67.7	67.6	68.1	67.4	61.3	35.0
Total unattached	96.6	69.3	42.6	28.5	27.9	28.4	29.8	36.8	64.3

Source: Rose M. Kreider and Jason M. Fields "Number, Timing, and Duration of Marriages and Divorces: 1996," *Current Population Reports*, February 2002.

On the morning of a party to celebrate his eighty-fourth birthday, he had a mild stroke and inhaled some material into his lungs, starting an infection. Within four days the infection was overwhelming his body. No amount of antibiotic could stop it. Three days after that, conscious to the very last, he looked silently at each of the eleven family members gathered around him. Each was touching him. And then he was gone.

George Blasius followed him only a few months later. After George married his third wife, they moved to Sarasota. When she had a stroke and had to stay in a nursing home, he visited every day, rolling the oxygen tank he needed to cope with his emphysema. Finally, he fell in the night and was hospitalized for exhaustion. With a son from his first marriage, a stepson and three sons from his second marriage, and a near-son from his third marriage, he was not without support or help. "The boys" (who ranged in age from 38 to 62) were spread around the country—Maine, New Jersey, Texas, Colorado, and California.

They flew in, one after another. The ones with air miles contributed tickets, and they rotated their visits. In the final months they pooled enough money so that one of the brothers could stay in Florida. On Father's Day three boys went to lunch with him. The next day two boys and a grandson helped him in a physical therapy session. He died that night.

Several months later, to escape the conflict over where he should be buried, the boys gathered again. This time they took a yacht volunteered by a family friend into the Gulf of Mexico. They shared straight shots of George's beloved Canadian Club and anointed the water. Then, one by one, they shared the task of dropping his ashes into the glassy swells of the gulf.

These are two of our stories. If you don't have a story about the death of a parent, you are either very young or very lucky. Like it or not, these stories are destiny: each of us will have a story about how our mother and father died.

The hard part is that the stories are changing. As marriages shorten, as mothers have fewer children, and as we become geographically dispersed around the country, the care and support elderly people could hope for—no, expect—from their children is shrinking. Sometimes it simply isn't there. They are old and alone.

Table 1.8
Women alone

Marital status	50–59	60–69	70 and over
Never married	5.0	3.7	4.2
Currently divorced	16.6	11.5	5.6
Currently widowed	8.2	21.6	54.5
Total unattached	29.8	36.8	64.3
Total married	67.4	61.3	35.0

Source: Rose M. Kreider and Jason M. Fields, "Number, Timing, and Duration of Marriages and Divorces: 1996," *Current Population Reports*, February 2002.

We've worried about social connection for a long time. David Reisman did it in *The Lonely Crowd* in 1950; Philip Slater did it in *The Pursuit of Loneliness* in 1970. Most recently, Robert Putnam did it in *Bowling Alone* (2000). These concerns were rooted in observation of broad social change. They could always be dismissed as dour speculation or the inevitable social nagging of the intellectual community.

Today our worry has hard demographic roots. Table 1.8 examines the marital status of women in later life. While two-thirds of women in their 50s are married, the odds drop precipitously when they are 70 and older. Then, only one woman in three is still married. With higher divorce rates among younger women, the proportion is likely to grow in the future.

Most men escape this fate. But they do it the hard way, by dying.

After spouses, the next measure of connection is children. In traditional societies, adults had children to care and provide for them in their old age. Today, we have fewer children, they are geographically mobile, and their sense of obligation may have been reduced by divorce.

You can get some idea about the odds against family care by considering the findings of a study. In "How Much Care Do the Aged Receive from Their Children?" the lives of 5,000 elderly people were examined.[24] In addition to considering whether they were single or married, the study examined the number of children, the number of daughters, how many lived less than an hour away, and the amount of time their children spent with them on a weekly basis. The researchers learned:

- That 22.4 percent of the elderly have no children
- That another 19.8 percent had only one child
- That 40.5 percent have no daughters
- That most of the single elderly live by themselves
- That 10 percent of those with children had no children within an hour's distance
- That over 40 percent of the "vulnerable" elderly lived by themselves
- That less than 20 percent of the elderly live with their children
- That institutionalized elderly have less contact with children, not more
- That transfers of money from child to parent (or vice versa) were rare, regardless of income

It's not a pretty picture—and that's the way things were over ten years ago. As Phyllis Diller once joked, "Always be nice to your children because they are the ones who will choose your rest home."[25]

What will familial care and support look like in 2030? That's a matter of speculation. One optimistic speculation is that the relatively high number of siblings that baby boomers have may offset their smaller number of children. Others have speculated that definitions of "family" or "kin" might include the stepchildren as well as natural children. The counter-argument is that siblings, however willing, may not be capable of providing care and support because they will be relatively old themselves. How many newspaper stories have you read about a 60- or 70-year-old daughter being exhausted by caring for her 90-year-old mother? Similarly, while the number of people we are connected to may expand through two or more marriages, multiple marriages also work to expand the number of aging people children and stepchildren may be called on to help. Call it a wash.

Kenneth W. Wachter, a researcher at the University of California at Berkeley, examined the issue using computer simulations of family patterns.[26] The results offered some hope: the increasing number of stepchildren and step-grandchildren will offset most of the anticipated decline of close biological kin. Numbers, however, aren't the same as actual support. Unless the kinship ties with stepchildren become stronger in the future, they won't be a substitute for biological kin.

What we are heading toward is a nation in which familial and institutional caring will be strained and reduced at the same time. The natural caring of family is strained and reduced by the same demographic change that will put the nonfamily substitutes—Social Security and Medicare—under extreme financial pressure.

Big, Blue, and Wrinkled All Over

America is getting older. But it isn't alone.

The entire planet is aging, much of it faster than we are. Most of the developed world is aging faster for two reasons. First, Americans aren't contenders in the Life Expectancy Olympics, so we're not increasing our elderly population as fast as other countries. Second, our birthrate, while flagging, isn't so low that our population will shrink over the next fifty years.

In most of Europe, it will. The problems we face are mild compared to those of many other nations.

You won't see much about this on TV. There, the cardinal rule is, "If it bleeds, it leads." You won't read much about this in most newspapers either. Stories about population, life expectancy, and birthrates tend to get put in the Sunday "think piece" bin.

In fact, virtually nothing in the daily news will change how we live and what we do more than the global population shift now under way. No story is more newsworthy. We are heading toward a planet that is big, blue, and wrinkled all over.

How old? How wrinkled?

Very. At the Second World Assembly on Ageing in Madrid in 2002, those attending heard astounding figures. By 2050 the number of older persons *in the world* would exceed the number of young people *for the first time in history*. The number of children is expected to grow by only 140 million, but the number of people in their 60s is expected to grow by 600 million. The number of people in their 70s will grow by 448 million. The number of people in their 80s will grow by 253 million. And the number of people at least age 90 will grow by 56 million. While children worldwide outnumber older people by three to one today, the ratio will be one to one by 2050. This is a gigantic change.

Another way to see the shift is to examine the changes in median age between 2000 and 2050. As you can see from table 1.9, we're going from

Table 1.9
The advancing median age in years

Country or area	2000	2025	2050	Change 2000/2050
World	26.5	32.0	36.2	9.7
United States	35.5	39.3	40.7	5.2
China	30.0	39.0	43.8	13.8
More developed regions	37.4	44.1	46.4	9.0
Europe	37.7	45.4	49.5	11.8
Japan	41.2	50.0	53.1	11.9

Source: United Nations, *World Population Ageing: 1950–2050* (New York: United Nations, 2002).

a world in its 20s to a world in its 30s—and that includes the entire less developed world. The developed world will age much more. By 2050 the median age in Japan will be 53. The entire developed world will be in its 40s.

The world of 2050 is how the developed nations of the world could be described in 1998. Over the next fifty years, nations like Mexico, Peru, Brazil, and India will catch up. Currently, Mexico has nearly eight children (those under 15) for every elderly person (those 65 and over). In India, the ratio is seven; in Brazil, six; and in Peru, eight. After centuries where few people were old and nurturing children was the primary social concern, children will become a small minority around the globe. The primary social concern will be caring for the elderly.

Meanwhile, the developed nations will continue to age. In Europe, there will be 2.1 old people *per child* by 2025, increasing to 2.6 by 2050. Europe will definitely be "the old country."

This will not be a phase. We will be older forever.

Two powerful forces, rising life expectancy and declining birthrates, drive the aging of the planet.

While the population of the United States will still be rising in 2050, the population of the *entire developed world* will be slightly lower than it is today (table 1.10). Some areas and countries will experience sharp declines. The population of Europe (as defined in the U.N. report), for instance, will shrink by 124 million, an amount greater than the current population of France and Italy combined.[27] The only way both countries

Table 1.10
The aging world and coming population decline

Country or area	2000	2025	2050	%60+ in 2050
United States	283.2	346.8	397.1	26.9
More developed regions	1,191.4	**1,218.8**	1,181.1	33.5
Europe	727.3	683.5	603.3	36.6
France	59.2	62.7	61.8	32.7
Germany	82	78.9	70.8	38.1
Italy	57.5	52.4	43	42.3
Russia	145.5	125.7	104.3	37.2
Japan	127.1	123.8	109.2	42.3
China	1,275.1	**1,470.8**	1,462.1	29.9

Source: United Nations, *World Population Ageing: 1950–2050* (New York: United Nations, 2002).
Notes: The peak period is in bold type; population figures are in millions.

will avoid an increasingly quaint (and abandoned) countryside is to sell their homes and towns to wealthy foreigners seeking a second or third home.

The population of Russia will fall by 41.2 million, or 28 percent—and some consider that estimate wildly optimistic. Lacking a Tuscany or Provence, Russia could develop whole areas like the "Buffalo Commons" that some American environmentalists dream of for the mountain states.[28] They would like to see large areas of New Mexico, Colorado, Wyoming, and Montana return to vast, unfenced grazing areas unpopulated by humans. The difference is that Russia will be an ecological disaster area.

Japan will likely be the oldest nation in the world, with 42 percent of its population 60 or older. Fifteen percent will be 80 and over. The centenarian population will be approaching 1 million—even though Japan's population will be down to 109 million. In a single century Japan will have gone from a nation with 4.6 children for every old person to a nation with 3.4 old people per child.

One of the most dramatic changes will be in the most populous nation in the world, China. While its population will continue to grow in the early part of this century, it will be declining by 2050. It will also be getting older fast, with the median age rising from 30 in 2000 to 39.0 in 2025 and 43.8 in 2050. By 2025 China will have 287.6 million people who are at least 60 years old, a number that exceeds the entire current population of the United States. By 2050 China will have 437 million people who are at least 60 years old. Ranked as a subnation, Old China will be larger than the total population of any nation in the world, except India.

In addition, China's population will be profoundly unbalanced because males will continue to outnumber females at all ages through the early 60s. Referred to as the "missing girls problem," the imbalance has its roots in a long-standing cultural preference for male children, a preference that was exacerbated by a government edict limiting the number of children a woman could have. Today, males age 15 to 59 outnumber females in the same age range by 25.4 million. By 2025 the mismatch will reach 30.7 million, 31.3 million by 2050.

Examining the gender gap closely, one demographer noted that "by 2020, for example, the surplus of China's males in their 20s will likely exceed the entire female population of the island of Taiwan!" The demographer calculates that about one in six Chinese men will either have to find a bride outside China or remain unmarried.

Will we see population growth anywhere?

Perhaps. While most of us read or hear the news of HIV prevalence in Africa and envision a complete population collapse, the United Nations researchers have projected that the current devastation will recede and that high birthrates will lead to major population growth there. A United Nations report from 2000 says, "Even in Botswana, where HIV prevalence is 36 percent or in Swaziland and Zimbabwe, where it is above 25 percent, the population is projected to increase significantly between 2000 and 2050: by 37 percent in Botswana, 148 percent in Swaziland and 86 percent in Zimbabwe."[29]

Similarly, less developed nations not burdened with major HIV incidence are likely to continue their high birthrates. Basically, while the less developed world will continue to be a Malthusian nightmare of high birthrates, the developed world will be plunging into a new demography: inescapable old age.

Is it the end of the world?

No. History and life are full of surprises. But the raw numbers tell us two important things. The first is that human demography, driven by simple changes in life expectancy and childbearing, is about to trump the power of economic growth. The second is that the shift in the United States may be major, but it's minor compared to what the rest of the developed world will experience.

If we get into trouble, there will be no rescue. We're on our own.

2

Truth Is Worse Than Fiction

The second vice is lying, the first is running in debt. . . . Lying rides upon debt's back.

—Benjamin Franklin, *The Way to Wealth*

The Incredible Shrinking Government

As we saw in chapter 1, when it comes to demographics, we're not in Kansas. Instead, we're living in one very big and rapidly expanding retirement community. And life in this community is getting damn expensive.

Of course, you wouldn't know this from listening to our elected leaders. To the contrary, they've spent so much time ignoring the future that they might just as well have outlawed it. In so doing, they've left us with a fiscal problem so big that it's hard to comprehend. Once you see it, your reaction will be: Why the hell didn't anyone tell us?

The answer was delivered by Jack Nicholson, the embittered, overbearing colonel in *A Few Good Men* when he screams at an upstart lieutenant Tom Cruise, "YOU CAN'T HANDLE THE TRUTH!"

That's right. None of us can stand the truth, and for good reason. Avoiding reality is a natural instinct and one of life's greatest pleasures. We all fantasize about getting rich. We all play the lottery. We all watch the millionaire dating game. And we all put off the trip to the dentist, doing our taxes, and making financial plans. The last thing we want is Uncle Sam telling us to save now to pay for a tidal wave of obligations coming when the baby boomers retire. So we make sure that doesn't happen. We hire politicians who tell us what we want to hear. They also dig us a deeper hole from which to emerge.

Down in Washington, the production of official disinformation about our future obligations has developed into an art form requiring skill, dedication, and a finely honed sense of what's politically feasible. Every government forecaster, economist, and actuary knows to get a "sign-off" on any written or oral statements she or he makes about the future performance of the economy, the federal government's finances, or the financial status of particular programs, like Social Security and Medicare. If the signer-offers—the political appointees in the White House, the Department of Treasury, the Office of Management and Budget, the Congressional Budget Office, the Social Security Administration, the Centers for Medicare and Medicaid Services, and others—aren't on board, the statement doesn't get made—unless, of course, the appointee is willing to risk her job.

I (Kotlikoff) remember a meeting I attended while working as a senior economist at the President's Council of Economic Advisors (CEA) during the first Reagan administration. The meeting's goal was to come up with a rosy economic forecast to help the administration defend its huge tax cut, which budget director David Stockman referred to as "pigs feeding at the trough."

Neither the CEA chairman, Murray Weidenbaum, nor any of the other economists around the table was happy with what we were being forced to do. At one point, after a painful discussion of what parameters could be tweaked, twisted, and squeezed to reach the "proper" conclusion, Murray turned to me and asked, "And in what course do they teach this in graduate school?" My answer was quick: "Creative writing."

Murray and his successor, Martin Feldstein, it must be said, both risked their jobs at various points during their terms as CEA chairmen to provide honest assessments of where the country was headed economically and fiscally. Indeed, Feldstein's reward for questioning—*in public*—deficit forecasts that he felt were outlandish was being called "Dr. Doom" on national television by Treasury Secretary Donald Regan. The fact that this was Feldstein's finest and Regan's worst hour was lost on subsequent CEA chairs, who, with rare exceptions, followed the party line when publicly discussing the economy's future.[1]

Speaking of parties, is one political party more honest than the other when it comes to disclosing the mess we are handing our kids? No. Each party has its constituents, all of whom share the convenient property of being alive and being able to vote. Future kids don't have that luxury, and current kids are kept far away from the polling booths. So the goal becomes to make the grown-ups happy. The Democratic grown-ups are happy when the government spends more money (on them). The Republican grown-ups are happy when the government raises less taxes (from them). The ideal solution, then, is to spend more and tax less.

In achieving this solution, it helps having compliant directors of the Congressional Budget Office (CBO) ready and able to invent the future. The CBO is charged with providing Congress and, by extension, the nation with projections of the government's finances. There's no requirement, however, that these projections be accurate or, indeed, bear any resemblance to economic reality.[2]

Take the CBO's ten-year budget forecasts. During the Clinton administration, the CBO routinely projected that regardless of inflation or economic growth, the federal government would spend precisely the same number of dollars year in and year out on everything apart from Social Security, Medicare, and other entitlements. At the same time, the CBO assumed federal taxes would grow at roughly 6 percent per year. The result was the incredibly shrinking government spewing forth budget surpluses as big as Kansas.

In the run-up to the 2000 presidential election, these phantom surpluses totaled close to $7 trillion over the ten-year projection window! The prospect of so much black ink was just what both parties wanted since it provided each with play money to bribe us for our votes. In the case of Democratic candidate Al Gore, the bribe was in the form of promised future spending. In the case of George W. Bush, the Republican nominee, the bribe was in the form of major tax cuts.

Once the election was over, the CBO decided that failing to adjust projected discretionary spending for inflation was no longer "useful or viable." This adjustment reduced the CBO's projected 2002–2011 surplus from $6.8 trillion to $5.6 trillion. Today, after a recession, September 11th, the Afghan war, the ongoing Iraq war, three tax cuts, and passage of the new Medicare drug benefit, the projected ten-year "surplus" has disappeared. Indeed, according to the CBO, if discretionary spending grows with the economy, if expiring tax cuts are extended and the alternative minimum tax is reformed—both of which are highly likely—the 2002–2011 deficit will total $4.6 trillion. As we write, the CBO forecasts almost a half-trillion-dollar deficit for 2004 alone!

To paraphrase former Senator Everett McKinley Dirksen, a trillion here, a trillion there, and suddenly you're talking real money. The difference between running a surplus over this decade of $6.8 trillion and a deficit of $4.6 trillion is $11.4 trillion more debt for the decade than the CBO forecast prior to the election! This is almost three times the current outstanding stock of federal debt!

Unfortunately, as bad as they really are, the short-term official debt projections don't begin to approximate the mess we're in.

Measuring the Big Whammy

All of us know we have to pay our bills—maybe not immediately but sometime in the future. If we don't, we face the modern-day version of debtor's prison: bankruptcy, loss of credit cards, the inability to get a mortgage, the surrendering of liquid assets, and at least some degree of social ignominy. This lesson—that we must pay for what we spend—somehow gets lost when it comes to discussions of government finance. The reason is that we can get someone else, namely our kids, to cover the spending we do through the government.

The method is simple: Have the government hold the bill and hand it over to the kids to pay when they hit the workforce.

Think of it. If we were all able to go to the mall and charge our purchases to Bill Gates, the mall would be awfully crowded. Or would it? We'd realize that even if it were legal, stealing from Bill Gates isn't exactly sanctified by the Ten Commandments or whatever moral creed we endorse. Now suppose that it wasn't Bill Gates who'd be sent the bill, but rather that the bill would be sent to someone like us, but someone we didn't know. Then we'd really have second thoughts. Given the frustration that crashing Windows operating systems have caused us over the years, stealing at least one copy of XP may seem justified, but ripping off people we don't know, even if the government says it's OK, wouldn't feel right.

Does it feel better if those unknown victims of our rapacity are someone else's children and the children of those children and the children of those children of those children? It shouldn't. Sure, the next generation may have it better off than we do, but isn't that the point? We have it better than our parents did, and they wouldn't have had it the other way around. Bill Gates has it better than all of us, but we still don't feel right taking more than one copy of XP. (Well, OK, but no more than two.)

Our moral concern would turn to outrage if we were told that people we don't know had government permission to shop with our own kids' credit cards. Such a policy wouldn't last a day. But it has lasted a day. Indeed, it has lasted for decades. We just haven't fully recognized it because (a) we've let the government do the shopping for us and (b) we've conveniently arranged not to total up our kid's bills.

Generational accounting fixes this situation. It directly measures the fiscal burden we are leaving our kids, whether their bills will come from paying for our Social Security, Medicare, and Medicaid benefits, or for Stealth bombers and the president's cigars, or for things that directly benefit children, like education.

Generational accounting may sound new, but it's been around for about fifteen years and has been applied in roughly thirty countries. The International Monetary Fund, the World Bank, the Bank of England and Her Majesty's Treasury, the German Bundesbank, the European Union, the Treasury of New Zealand, the Bank of Japan, and the Finance Ministry of Norway are some of the official institutions that have sponsored generational accounting studies. Geographically speaking, generational accounting has spread to countries as far-flung as Argentina, Finland, Iceland, Thailand, Korea, and Israel. And it has been done repeatedly in the United States, even though the authorities have quashed it from time to time.

For now, let's get to the task at hand: understanding how generational accounting measures the big whammy—the burden we're placing on future generations. The best place to start is with our own household *lifetime budget constraints*.

$E = S + M.$

On the left-hand side of this pretty friendly looking equation is E, which stands for all the money you earn after paying taxes and receiving transfer payments, such as Social Security benefits. According to the equation, this amount E must cover all the spending, S, that you are going to do plus M, which stands for your current mortgage and other debts net of any assets you own.

"But wait just a second. I don't have to pay off my mortgage right now, so why should my current earnings have to cover my entire mortgage?" you might ask. Good question. The answer is that E doesn't stand for just your current net labor earnings. It stands for your *future* net earnings as well. Indeed, E is the value in the present of all your current and future earnings. And S is also a *present value*. It measures the value today (the value in the present) of all future spending. M is already measured as a present value. That's what your mortgage balance is—the present value of your future mortgage payments. If you have assets, M is measured net of the present values of those assets, also referred to as their market values.

So what's a present value? Here's an example. Suppose the interest rate is 10 percent and you're thinking of spending $50,000 a year from now on the most beautiful car ever made—a 1952 Jaguar roadster in British racing green, with red leather seats and, get this, no outside door handles. (Anyone cool enough to own this car would have the top down and be able to swing his or her legs over the door.)

Anyway, you've been working on your spouse for years to let you buy it, and you think maybe you'll have enough money in a year if you continue to bank what you've saved so far. So how much do you need now to end up with $50,000 in a year? The answer is found by dividing $50,000 by 1.10 (one plus the interest rate). The resulting number is $45,454.54. Why is this the right amount? Because if you put that sum in the bank, a year from now the principal plus interest will equal $45,454.54 multiplied by 1.10, which is exactly $50,000. Hence, to get to $50,000 a year from now, you need $45,454.54 today. Stated differently, having $45,454.54 in the present has the same value as having $50,000 a year from now. That's why we say that $45,454.54 is the present value (the value today) of the future $50,000.

The number 1.10 that we divide $50,000 by to get its present value is called the *discount factor*. It's called that because we are discounting, in the sense of *making less of*, money that is coming in the future. Telling your 12 year old you'll give him his allowance in a year isn't the same to him as having the ten bucks in his sweaty little palms right now. As you'd expect, the discount factor is bigger the further in the future is the amount we are trying to value in the present. Intuitively, getting $50,000 in twenty years isn't worth as much as getting it in a year.[3]

Any future dollar amount that you will earn or expect to pay can be measured as a present value in just the same way we expressed the cost today of your future purchase of the Jag, which, incidentally, can be viewed at http://www.motorcities.com/contents/03FMG394833214.html.

So, what does $E = S + M$ tell us? If you hate equations and want to think about it in words, it reads like this:

The present		The present		Debts
value of	*equals*	value of	*plus*	net of
earnings		spending		assets.

It says that that *E*—the value, measured in the present, of everything you will earn, on net, through the rest of your life—must cover your net debts, including your mortgage, plus *S*—the value, again measured in the present, of everything you'll spend. If *S* (spending) plus *M* (debt) exceeds *E* (earnings), you have one option: cut back *S* (spending) or work harder to raise *E* (earnings). If *M* (debt) by itself exceeds *E* (earnings), call a lawyer quick and file for bankruptcy.

The government has an *intertemporal* (an across-time) *budget constraint* that is very similar to the one you face. The only real difference is that current and future generations—not a single household—must collectively pay for what the government spends as well as the official net debt.

Here's the equation, and, we promise, it's the last one in the book:

$A + B = C + D$.

This absolutely terrifying mathematical expression can be grasped even by sixth graders and should be lesson 1 in their civics courses. The *C* stands for the value, measured in the present, of all government purchases, from $500 toilet seats, to Boston's $14 billion and growing Big Dig, to the Texas beef ribs smothered with hickory sauce savored by Bush the Second.

"Hold on, hold on. Aren't you mixing in federal spending with state spending including, for example, Boston's Big Dig?" Yes, good catch. Generational accounting is comprehensive. It includes all of government, at the local, state, and federal levels.

"So, what do A, B, and D stand for?" Well D stands for government official debt, net of assets. Assets here include financial assets, tangible assets, like the roughly $50 billion in gold bars the federal government holds in Fort Knox, and the market values of state-owned enterprises, like NASA's commercial satellite launching service that uses the Space Shuttle.

The B stands for the present value (the value in the present) of the net taxes to be paid by everyone alive when the analysis is made. *Net tax* refers to all the future taxes paid net minus all future transfer payments received. The A is the big whammy: the amount, again measured in present value, that future generations will have to pay.

Here's what the whole thing looks like in words:

The present value of net taxes of future generations		The present value of net taxes of current generations		The present value of government purchases		Official debt net of official assets.
	plus		*equals*		*plus*	

So, how come the present value of net taxes of future and current generations has to add up to the present value of government purchases plus its net debt? The answer is fundamental. *There is no free lunch.* Just as we have to cover the present value of our own spending and debts with the present value of our own lifetime earnings, current and future generations must jointly pay with their net taxes, measured in present value, for the government's bills, also measured in present value.

If we want to express the burden on the future generations by itself, we can do so by rearranging the equation to this:

$A = C + D - B.$

In words, it reads like this:

The present value of net taxes of future generations	*equals*	The present value of government purchases equals	*plus*	Official debt minus official assets	*minus*	The present value of net taxes of current generations.

(No, we didn't lie. This doesn't represent a new equation, just a rewrite of the previous one.) Expressed this way, the big whammy—the amount being left for future Americans to pay—equals the amount of government bills less the contributions of current generations to paying these bills. Stated differently, *given the size of the government's bills, the less that current generations pay of them, the greater is the burden that will be left for those coming in the future.*

Before revealing the size of A, the burden on our children, we're going to raise your blood pressure slowly by pointing out that the main reason A is so big is that B is so small. B is so small because it represents taxes to be paid *net* of transfer payments to be received by everyone now alive. This includes the 77 million baby boomers.

Miles to Go and Promises to Keep

We promised you no more equations. Well, sorry, we lied. But it's for your own good. Anyway, in this third version of the basic generational accounting equation, we've broken B, the net payment of currently living generations, into T, the present value of their projected future taxes, less V, the present value of their promised future transfer payments. Replacing B by T-V in A = C + D − B gives:

$$A = C + D + V - T$$

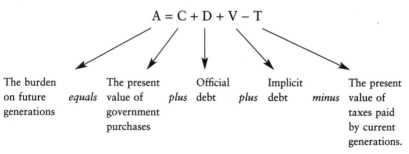

The burden on future generations	*equals*	The present value of government purchases	*plus*	Official debt	*plus*	Implicit debt	*minus*	The present value of taxes paid by current generations.

Writing the equation this way lets you see that the burden on future generations depends on *implicit debt, V,* in exactly the same way it depends on explicit debt, *D.* Implicit debt refers to the present value of Social Security, Medicare, food stamps, welfare payments, Medicaid, and all the other transfer payments promised to boomers and others now alive. If "implicit debt" doesn't seem very real to you, talk to a senior citizen who depends on Social Security and Medicare. Many retirees know these programs are their major assets.

The equation says a deal's a deal. Whether the government promises your Aunt Tilly to pay interest plus principal on her U.S. Savings Bonds or whether it promises to pay her Social Security benefits, the implications for future generations, in terms of having to pay the bills we don't cover with our taxes, are the same.

Stated differently, *from a generational accounting perspective, the composition of the government's promises as separated between official and unofficial obligations makes no difference to the burden to be born by future generations.* We put this statement in italics for a reason. It's going to provide the basis for our questioning the definition of official debt later in the book—an analysis that will blow your mind. But for the moment, we'll accept the government's definition of official debt and, for that matter, implicit debt and compare the magnitude of the two measures.

Gross U.S. official federal debt is now $4.4 trillion, or 40 percent of gross domestic product (GDP). That's a BIG number. It's about $31,000 per American worker. Paying off this debt immediately would require each and every working American to work for almost three-fifths of a year and hand every penny earned over to the government. Only then would the Feds have enough money to pay back all the money they've borrowed on our behalf.

Having a debt-to-GDP ratio of 40 percent is not pretty except in comparison to some other well-known countries whose ratios are much higher. Take Japan, which has the second largest economy in the world. Its debt is 164 percent of its GDP! Italy's gross debt is 118 percent of its GDP. Belgium places third with a debt-to-GDP ratio of 98 percent. Altogether, a third of the twenty-four other members of the Organization for Economic Cooperation and Development (OECD), an economic club whose members are developed countries, have ratios of debt to GDP that equal or exceed that of the United States.[4]

Because the ratio of debt to GDP in the United States is not way out of line internationally or historically most politicians have a hard time getting exercised over the fiscal plight of the next generation. "Yes," they'll admit, "our debt would be very tough to pay off overnight, but there's no need to do so. Pay it off gradually, and it's no big deal for either us or our kids."

Unfortunately, using the official debt by itself to assess the sum of official plus implicit debt is like mistaking Iceland for Greenland. One's smaller than Kentucky; the other's three times the size of Texas.

In fact, the amount of implicit debt (V in the equation) that Americans need to pay is simply enormous. The Social Security component of this present value is, by itself, $22 trillion. Add in Medicare's and Medicaid's gross benefit obligations/liabilities, and you're up to $72 trillion. To pay off this liability, today's workers would have to work for nothing not for three-fifths of a year but for ten years.

If your palms are getting sweaty and your breathing is becoming rapid, good. Or you may be cool, calm, and collected because you figure we can just blow away these unofficial promises any time we want. Sure thing. Just let us be there when you tell your Aunt Tilly, who's living solely off Social Security and Medicare, that she can get by with four fewer monthly checks each year and needs to pick up a lot more of her medical expenses.

In fact, a large share of the elderly are in Aunt Tilly's or similar-sized shoes. That fact and the fact that the elderly vote with great regularity means it's probably easier to default on official debt than on unofficial promises, particularly those indexed to inflation.

The most common way to renege on official debt is to create inflation. For a quick tutorial in how to do it, just drop by heaven, purgatory, or an even deeper location that may be housing former president Nixon. Ask him to tell you how he reneged on official debt to pay for the Vietnam War. He'll tell you that he sold bonds to the public to get the money to pay the military. Then he got his buddy Arthur Burns at the Federal Reserve to print money to buy back the bonds.

Sure enough, inflation took off. Nominal interest rates, which are used to discount the interest and principal, shot up, and the real value of federal debt declined dramatically.[5] This helps explain why the ratio of debt to GDP hit a postwar nadir in 1974, the year our nation gave Tricky Dick the boot.

President Clinton (otherwise known as "Slick Willy") also managed to have the economy outgrow its official liabilities, but he did so without using inflation. When President Clinton took office in 1992, federal debt was 48 percent of GDP. By 1996, despite a tax hike, debt was an even larger share of output. Having made a big deal of being fiscally conservative, this wasn't building the presidential legacy.

But the "Comeback Kid" came through in the end. According to Clinton adviser Paul Begala and Clinton's other disciples, the president grew the economy with his bare hands in his second term to the point that debt was only 35 percent of GDP by the time his moving van pulled up to the White House and started pilfering the place.[6] Mind you, economists tend to credit the production of goods and services not to a single person, no matter how talented, but to the roughly 143 million workers and trillions of dollars of capital actually used to produce them. And they ascribe the boom in the late 1990s as having a lot to do with a plethora of high-tech investment, not to mention the invention by Albert Gore of the Internet, in the previous decade.

In any case, lowering the debt-to-GDP ratio while comforting Monica, testifying to grand juries, fighting impeachment, and pardoning Mark Rich wasn't President Clinton's only fiscal accomplishment in his second term or even his finest. Figures 2.1 and 2.2 show that during his term, federal purchases and federal taxes, both measured relative to GDP, declined and rose to their lowest and highest postwar values, respectively.

Given that the burden (A) on future kids is smaller if official debt (D) is smaller, the present value of future government purchases (C) is smaller, and the present value of future taxes paid by current generations (T) is larger, one would think the Clinton policy was really effective in reducing A measured relative to the size of the economy. Well, think again. A also depends on the present value of transfer payments, V. And

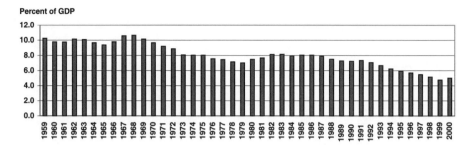

Figure 2.1
Federal government purchases as a share of GDP. *Source:* Congressional Budget Office

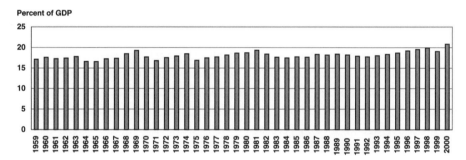

Figure 2.2
Federal taxes as a share of GDP. *Source:* Congressional Budget Office

Bill wasn't able to lower transfers as a share of output—not during his eight glorious years in office and certainly not for the long term. As figure 2.3 indicates, transfer payments, measured as a share of GDP, were higher when President Clinton left than when he took office. The president no doubt had just too many things in his lap to come up with long-term solutions for Social Security, Medicare, or Medicaid.

As figure 2.3 shows, Clinton's failure, like that of his immediate predecessors, to meaningfully reform the big three transfer programs has left us with projections of transfer payments as a share of GDP that rise insanely over the next seven decades. The figure focuses on Social Security, Medicare, and Medicaid, showing total outlays on these programs relative to GDP from 1950 through 2075.

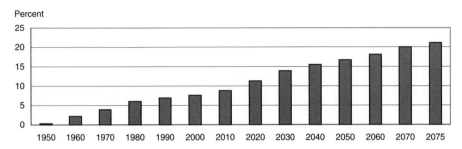

Figure 2.3
Social Security, Medicare, and Medicaid transfers as a percent of GDP. *Source:* "The Economic Costs of Long-Term Federal Obligations," testimony before the Committee on the Budget, U.S. House of Representatives, by Douglas Holtz-Eakin, Director, Congressional Budget Office, July 24, 2003. http://www.cbo.gov/showdoc.cfm?index=4439&sequence=0.

The source of this chart is the very latest long-term projections by the Congressional Budget Office. They show the share of output spent on these programs rising from 7.6 percent in 2000 to 13.9 percent in 2030 and 21.1 percent in 2075! To put these figures in perspective, payroll taxes average about 6.5 percent of GDP, so paying for these transfers would require doubling the payroll tax rate in the short run and tripling it in the long run!

Clearly, we have a problem. This is true notwithstanding all the short-term fiscal miracles that President Clinton performed and which President Bush is working overtime to reverse. Since taking office, George the Second has presided over three tax cuts—two major and one minor— and increased federal discretionary spending at more than twice the rate of growth of the economy. Now that's really putting your supply-side economics where your kids' mouths are.

The moral to this story is simple: *It's the Future, Stupid!* Yes, short-term fiscal discipline helps, but the terms in the generational accounting program are present values that take into account future as well as current taxes, transfers, and government purchases. While Clinton raised taxes in the short run, he also allowed long-term transfers to rise, which made the policy a net loser when it comes to our progeny. All the diddling that Clinton and Bush did and are doing in raising and then cutting and probably soon raising again the income tax isn't going to prevent 77 million baby boomers from starting to collect their old age benefits in just five years. Nor is it going to prevent medical costs in the future from growing much more rapidly than the economy as they have in essentially every year since 1963. Nor will it prevent Americans from starting to die like the Japanese—at a very ripe and medically very expensive old age. President Clinton, to his credit, did some short-term fiscal good, but like his predecessors, he left fully intact the slowly growing fiscal tumor that seeks to devour the next generation.

Playing Against Our Kids

The *A*, *B*, *C*s of generational accounting make one thing clear: Paying for what the government spends is a zero-sum game, and it's one we're playing against our own flesh and blood. Either we pay the government's bills, or we leave them for our kids to pay. It's that simple.

Or is it? The Republicans, who have yet to meet a tax they like, claim that cutting the taxes of current generations, particularly those of its richest members, will so stimulate entrepreneurship and the economy that these tax cuts will pay for themselves in terms of higher tax revenues. Their *voodoo economics*, as it was labeled by none other than George the First, says we can have our cake and eat it too. We can cut our own tax rates and not only help ourselves, but also help future generations.

When this argument evokes laughter, the Republicans fall back on their primary rationale for cutting taxes. They claim that making current generations pay more (making T larger in $A = C + D + V - T$) won't lower the burden on future generations (won't reduce A), because the Democrats will just spend the additional revenue on education and other government purchases (thereby raising C) or on transfer payments (thereby raising V). According to the Republicans, "Any dollar left in the government's hand will be wasted. Taxing more is just feeding the beast. The thing to do is to tax less and cut off the beast's food supply."

As we've seen, some facts support this view. When the father of voodoo economics, Ronald Reagan, dramatically cut taxes in the early 1980s, federal discretionary spending began to fall as a share of GDP.

Whether it was the pressure of the tax cuts or the collapse of the Soviet Union that kept the lid on discretionary spending is hard to say. But discretionary spending kept falling relative to the economy until George the Second took office. On the other hand, over the same two decades, Social Security, Medicare, and Medicaid expenditures continued to grow faster than the economy. By 2000, spending on these programs took up 25 percent more of GDP than it did in 1980.

So what happened to overall federal expenditures during the 1980s and 1990s? On balance, they grew more slowly than GDP. That's the good news.

The bad news for our kids and for believers in Republican witchcraft is that the ratio of federal debt to GDP rose by a third. Even worse was the dramatic increase in future projected spending associated with the rapid growth in entitlement benefits. The bottom line is that the so-called Reagan revolution was just a continuation of a decades-long policy of passing the buck to the next generation.

Remember that old saying, "If you don't learn from history, you're condemned to repeat it." Well, apparently, one failed supply-side experiment wasn't enough. When George the Second took office, he found an old trunk in the White House attic full of Reagan's voodoo donkey dolls. After sticking them with assorted pins, needles, and General Patton's sword, Bush the Second decided that massive tax cuts could not only pay for a new, fabulously expensive Medicare drug benefit, but they could also pay for a huge military buildup, wars in Afghanistan and Iraq, homeland security, and additional discretionary spending. So the president set to work over the next three years to grow discretionary spending three times faster and entitlement spending two times faster than the economy.

His black magic didn't work. This time, instead of revenues growing more rapidly than the economy, they fell dramatically. Indeed, real federal tax revenues are now 11 percent lower than when this president took office.

The Democrats, who feel everyone else's pain as long as they're available to vote, have their own excuses for engaging in fiscal malfeasance. "Cutting spending," the Democrats will tell you, "is regressive. Big business knows how to take care of itself. So spending cuts will just hurt the poor. Furthermore, spending cuts won't be saved. They'll just lead the Republicans to cut taxes." In terms of our algebra, the Democrats claim that any reduction in government purchases, C, or transfer payments, V, will lead to an equal-sized reduction in taxes, T, leaving the burden, A, on future generations unchanged.

Setting up the debate this way gives both sides what they want: an excuse to tax too little and spend too much.

But isn't this overstating the case? After all, George the First raised taxes after telling God and country at the 1988 Republican convention: "Read my lips. No new taxes." And Clinton cut welfare spending to the eternal antipathy of some of his closest supporters.

To be honest, these two instances were just sideshows to appease deficit hawks in both parties and convince the rest of us that we actually managed to elect a grown-up. The reality is that each postwar administration, starting with Eisenhower, picked the pockets of children and those coming in the future to benefit current taxpayers. Moreover, even when taxes were raised to pay for spending, the young generally got to pay the taxes and the elderly generally got to enjoy the spending.

In sticking up for the next generation, we're not arguing that current and future kids should get off scot-free (that A should be zero) when it comes to paying for the government's bills. After all, our kids, we hope, will earn a good living. Indeed, if economic growth continues, they should earn a lot more, on average, than we earn. Since 1970, labor productivity has grown at close to 2 percent per year. Assuming productivity growth continues at this pace, we can expect lifetime earnings to roughly double from generation to generation.

The real question is, *How much* do we want our children, grandchildren, and other descendants to pay? The answer is not solely a matter of generational ethics. There is a limit to the fiscal burden we can impose on any generation. You can't get blood from a stone, and you can't tax a generation more than it earns. Indeed, at some point short of a 100 percent tax rate, confiscating a higher share of a generation's income will lower revenues because the generation will either stop working or stop paying taxes. If this sounds like supply-side economics, we plead guilty. The real difference between non–supply siders and supply siders is not that this happens, but rather the level of tax rates at which it happens.

In any case, the fact that there is a limit to the tax rates we can impose on future generations means there is a limit to *intergenerational fiscal progressivity*—how much we can hit up potentially richer future generations to benefit those now alive. If, for example, we want each generation to face tax rates that are 10 percent higher than the previous generations faced, these tax rates will grow very rapidly from one generation to the next and quickly run into the upper limit. Indeed, any fixed rate of growth of generation-specific tax rates will eventually run up against the upper limit. Basic economics tells us that, at some point, we need to stabilize the tax rates levied on successive generations. The alternative is confiscatory taxation that will drive not only tax revenues, but also the economy, down the tubes.

The tax rate we have in mind here is a comprehensive one. It's the *lifetime net tax rate*—the share of lifetime labor earnings that a generation pays to federal, state, and local governments in taxes of all kinds, net of the benefits of all kinds received from those governments.

To calculate a generation's lifetime net tax rate, we first discount back to the generation's year of birth all the taxes it pays net of all the benefits it receives in each year of its life. The resulting present value *lifetime net tax payment* can then be divided by the present value of lifetime earnings (the discounted value of all the money the generation earns over its lifetime) to form a *lifetime net tax rate*.

For generations now alive, the lifetime net tax rate is roughly 20 percent. This means that current generations are, on average, handing over twenty cents of every dollar earned to either the federal government or a state or local government in taxes net of transfer payments received.

A 20 percent tax rate may sound low, but bear in mind that it's a *net* tax rate. Benefits received are netted out against taxes paid. It's also an average tax rate rather than a *marginal* tax rate. What's the difference? Suppose you earn $50,000 and pay no tax on the first $40,000 you earn, but pay a 50 percent tax on every dollar you earn above $40,000. This makes your total tax payment $5,000. Your average tax rate is calculated by dividing your tax payments—the $5,000—by your total earn-

Table 2.1
Net marginal work tax rates

Multiple of the minimum wage	Hourly wage	Initial household income	Tax rate
1	$5.15	21.4	66.5%
1.5	7.73	32.1	80.6
2	10.30	42.8	72.2
3	15.45	64.3	63.0
4	20.60	85.7	59.1
5	25.75	107.1	57.5
6	30.90	128.5	57.5
7	36.05	150.0	57.0
8	41.20	171.4	56.6
9	46.35	192.8	56.1
10	55.00	214.2	55.7
15	77.25	321.4	55.2
20	110.00	428.5	54.7
30	154.50	642.7	54.2
40	206.00	857.0	54.0

Source: Jagadeesh Gokhale and Laurence J. Kotlikoff, *Does It Pay to Work?* (Washington, D.C. American Enterprise Institute, forthcoming).

ings—the $50,000. Your average tax rate is 10 percent, but your *marginal* rate is 50 percent because, at the margin, each additional dollar you earn is taxed at a 50 percent rate.

When it comes to figuring out how much to work and whether to report one's taxes honestly, it's the marginal tax rate that matters. As table 2.1 shows, the marginal tax rates facing Americans—poor, middle class, and rich alike—are already extremely high. The tax rates presented are actually *marginal net tax rates*. They consider not just the additional lifetime taxes Americans pay for working each year throughout their working lives. They also include the change in any lifetime benefits associated with those additional earnings.[7]

If you're poor in America today, making more money can mean losing some or all of your welfare benefits, food stamps, Medicaid benefits, earned income tax allowance, housing assistance, and so forth. But whether you're poor or rich, making more money can raise your future Social Security benefits. The marginal net tax rates in table 2.1 include the impact of additional earnings on the receipt of every major transfer benefit provided by federal and state governments.[8] The table considers the marginal net tax on representative married couples in deciding whether to work full time over their working lives.[9] The results are presented for couples earning different multiples of the minimum wage.

The findings indicate that *we all face marginal net tax rates of at least 50 percent if we decide to work full time over our working lives*. This means that for every extra dollar we earn, the government confiscates at least fifty cents above and beyond any additional benefits we receive from having higher earnings. For the poorest among us, the marginal net tax rate can exceed 80 percent because they lose lots of welfare benefits when they earn more money. Table 2.1 shows at a glance why nobody feels like paying more taxes. At the margin, the taxes everyone in the country faces from working are already extremely high.

These marginal tax rates should also give pause to anyone who believes we can tax future generations at still higher rates. That would push marginal net tax rates so high that Sweden would start looking like a tax haven.

But couldn't we get a lot more revenue with lower marginal tax rates if we replaced the federal income tax with a flat tax under which all earnings above a threshold are taxed at the same rate? No. There are six reasons why.

First, to keep the poor from bearing a much higher tax burden, the threshold would have to be very high. Second, because the threshold would be high, the flat tax rate would have to be quite high—about 30 percent. Third, although 30 percent is a lower marginal federal income tax for the rich, it's a higher marginal federal income tax for the middle class. So switching to a flat tax would lower the marginal rates of the rich but raise those of the middle class. Fourth, the very poor don't pay income taxes anyway. Their very high marginal tax rates reflect their *loss* of benefits and tax credits, not the taxes they pay. And fifth, the middle class would strongly object to paying more in order to lower the tax burden on the rich. Finally, the flat tax has been proposed and rejected repeatedly by the political process over the past two decades. Two Republicans—*Forbes* magazine publisher Steven Forbes and Indiana senator Richard Lugar—ran for the Republican presidential nomination with flat tax platforms and lost. And various members of Congress have introduced flat tax bills as well as consumption and value-added tax proposals that were flat taxes in sheep's clothing. None of these reforms saw the light of day.

The Size of the Big Whammy

Now for the really bad news you've been so patiently awaiting—the size of the big whammy, *A*. Recall that *A* is the collective fiscal burden facing future generations *assuming* we (1) don't raise the net taxes of current generations, (2) don't cut government purchases, and (3) don't renege on official debt. The absolute value of *A*, which is in the tens of trillions of dollars, doesn't mean much by itself. But when we divide it by the labor income that future generations are projected to earn (also measured in present value), we find that future generations face a lifetime net tax rate that is twice the rate we're paying!

If you think your taxes are too high, imagine how the next generation will feel paying twice as much in net taxes on every dollar earned. And bear in mind that the calculation assumes this sky-high net tax rate is imposed over the lifetimes of all Americans born in the future starting with babies born next year. Giving Americans born in the near term a pass on this higher tax rate means hitting subsequent generations even harder.

"Impossible!" you say.

You're absolutely right. There is just no way we can double the tax rates of future Americans. They'll stop working, stop reporting their income, or leave the country. So either this calculation is bogus, or we need to make some immediate and very painful sacrifices to protect our descendants and save our nation.

Rest assured, the calculation isn't bogus.[10] It was made by our own government, specifically by Dr. Jagadeesh Gokhale, a highly respected government economist who serves as senior economic adviser to the Federal Reserve Bank of Cleveland. Moreover, all the projections Gokhale used to make the calculation were generated by U.S.

government agencies. For example, he used the Social Security trustees' intermediate demographic projections. He also used, with one exception, the Congressional Budget Office's (CBO) long-term forecast of government receipts and payments.[11] The exception is that he assumed that federal discretionary spending would stay even with the economy.

The calculation certainly passes the initial sniff test. But is it predicated on overly pessimistic assumptions? No. In fact, if anything, it's based on overly optimistic assumptions. Consider, for example, the Social Security trustees' projected increase in Americans' longevity, which plays a big role in calculating the burden on future generations. Recall that the trustees assume it's going to take over a half-century for Americans to start living as long as the Japanese now live. That seems to us a long time to wait. It also seems that way to the nation's top demographers. Professor Ronald Lee, director of the Center on the Economics and Demographics of Aging at the University of California at Berkeley and a member of the National Academy of Sciences, is one of them.

In 1999 Lee joined other leading demographers and economists to serve on the Social Security Administration's Technical Advisory Panel. This panel was asked by the trustees to review the economic and demographic assumptions underlying the Social Security Trustees' Report— the annual statement of Social Security's long-term finances. Lee and his colleagues voted unanimously to recommend that the trustees raise their long-run life expectancy assumption by four years. Four years of additional longevity is a big difference in the world of demography. It also makes a big difference to the projected solvency of the Social Security system, which is precisely the reason the trustees told their own technical panel to get lost.

Shocked? You shouldn't be. Don't forget, the trustees in 1999 were all Democratic political appointees. Declaring that Social Security, the party's most sacred of sacred cows, would have to pay future retirees benefits, on average, for four more years and was in far worse trouble than anyone thought would not have gone down well with the party faithful. Nor would it have helped the prospects of Albert Gore, who was campaigning on a platform of READ MY LIPS—NO SOCIAL SECURITY REFORM.

Another reason that Gokhale's measure of the big whammy is likely to be an understatement is that the CBO's revenue forecast assumes real wages (wages adjusted for inflation), which help determine the tax base, will grow at 2.2 percent per year. This is rather high by historical standards. Since 1959 real wages have grown at 1.7 percent per year, and since 1975 they've grown at only 1.2 percent per year.

The third and most important downward bias in the measured size of the whammy arises from highly optimistic assumptions about future growth in Medicare expenditures. Gokhale uses the CBO's Medicare expenditure projections, and the CBO gets these projections from the Medicare trustees. The current trustees—all Republican appointees—are much more optimistic about long-term Medicare outlays than were their predecessors.

In 1997 the Medicare trustees projected that Medicare spending in 2030, when baby boomers are in the middle of their old age, would equal 7.1 percent of GDP. In 2003 they projected 2030 spending would total only 4.7 percent of GDP. The 2.4 percent of GDP discrepancy between these numbers is enormous when you consider that Medicare expenditures are currently about 2.6 percent of GDP. Hence, compared with the 1997 trustees, the 2003 trustees assumed away an amount of 2030 spending on Medicare, which, when scaled relative to the economy, equals roughly the size of the current program.

What happened to make the Medicare trustees so much more upbeat about the program's future costs? The answer is that growth in Medicare spending per beneficiary slowed considerably between 1998 and 2000. This gave the 1998 trustees, Democrats to a man (and one woman), the green light to engage in lots of wishful thinking. When the Republican trustees replaced them in 2001, they too realized that honesty isn't necessarily the best policy if it undermines your patron's agenda.

Unfortunately, in 2001, Medicare spending per beneficiary started picking up again. By 2003 it was 11 percent higher after inflation than it was two years earlier. To appreciate what providing an 11 percent Medicare bonus represents, let's multiply .11 times $21,363 trillion, which is the present value of Medicare benefits owed to current adults. The resulting number, $2.3 trillion, is the additional bill (the addition to A) that future generations will have to pick up, assuming that current generations don't pay for this largesse and the government doesn't cut back on other spending to fund this expected future outlay. Note that this figure dwarfs the formal budget deficits that receive so much attention.

The fact that the Medicare trustees' long-run projections are so different today than they were only a few years ago means three things. First, the trustees are anchoring much of what they expect Medicare to cost in future years to a couple of outlier years with respect to Medicare spending growth. Second, they are paying little attention to the fact that the most recent growth rates in real Medicare spending per beneficiary are among the highest they've ever been. Third, there is no guarantee that the much higher future costs projected in 1997 won't be projected again in a few years.

To summarize, the big whammy—the birth bill we're leaving our kids—is huge, and if more realistic assumptions were made, it would be even larger. Because doubling the lifetime net tax rates facing our kids, grandkids, and on down the line isn't feasible, we need to consider the alternatives, which brings us to the *menu of pain*.

The Menu of Pain

In the fall of 2002, the U.S. treasury secretary, Paul O'Neill, asked Dr. Kent Smetters to prepare a study, for inclusion in the President's FY 2004 Budget, of the federal government's long-term liabilities. Smetters, an economics professor at the University of Pennsylvania, was spending two years serving in the Treasury as deputy assistant secretary for economic policy. He agreed and immediately asked Dr. Gokhale to spend the fall at the Treasury to help with the project.

The two decided to measure the *fiscal gap*—the difference, in present value, between the government's future receipts and future expenditures assuming future generations faced the same net tax rates as current generations. This variant on generational accounting has the attractive feature that it treats current and future generations symmetrically in terms of the tax rates we can expect them to face. The fiscal gap also provides a single, comprehensive dollar measure of the government's red ink.[12]

Gokhale and Smetters consulted extensively with the Office of Management and Budget, the Social Security Administration, and the Centers for Medicare and Medicaid Services to obtain and produce the most accurate and up-to-date projections of future receipts and payments, including debt service. They and their assistants worked long days and weekends meticulously preparing the study. They checked and double-checked the figures. They developed new, more accurate projection methodologies, and they formed their present values using the prevailing long-term interest rate on inflation-indexed government bonds.

The fiscal gap they calculated is $45 trillion—big bucks by anyone's standard. It's eleven times larger than the current official debt and roughly four times the size of the country's annual output.

During the period they were making this measurement, the net worth of the American people, as measured by the Federal Reserve Consumer Balance Sheet figures, was less than $40 trillion.[13] We are thus technically bankrupt.

Another way to come to grips with $45 trillion of red ink is to ask what it would take to pay it off. Gokhale and Smetters also posed this question in their study. Their answer is given in the menu of pain in table 2.2, which details alternative immediate and permanent policies that would generate, in present value, either $45 trillion in additional revenues or $45 trillion in reduced expenditures.

The menu lists the following entreés. We could, starting today, raise federal income taxes (individual and corporate) by 69 percent. Or we could, starting today, raise payroll taxes by 95 percent. Or we could

Table 2.2
Menu of pain

Policy	Percentage change
Increase federal income taxes	69
Increase payroll taxes	95
Cut federal purchases	106
Cut Social Security and Medicare	45

immediately and permanently cut federal discretionary spending by 106 percent, which, of course, is infeasible. Or we could immediately and permanently cut Social Security and Medicare benefits by 45 percent.

Another option is to go for a combination of smaller portions of each of these varieties of castor oil. For example, we could simultaneously raise income taxes by 17 percent, raise payroll taxes by 24 percent, cut federal purchases by 26 percent, and cut Social Security and Medicare benefits by 11 percent.

Taking any one or any combination of these medicines will be brutal. But continuing to ignore the problem will simply let more generations, particularly older ones, off the hook, and dump an even bigger problem in our kids' laps. Gokhale and Smetters point this out. Their *menu of delayed pain* (table 2.3) indicates the alternative immediate and permanent fiscal adjustments that would be needed starting in 2008 if nothing were done before then.

Delay has a significant cost. Waiting five years, for example, to raise federal income taxes means having to raise them by 74 percent rather than 69 percent. The reason delay matters is that the $45 trillion of red ink, like our credit card bills and any other liability we fail to pay, accumulates at the rate of interest. The real interest rate Gokhale and Smetters used in their study was 3.6 percent.

If you owe a dollar and have to pay 3.6 percent interest, how much will you owe after five years if you pay nothing back in between? The answer is $1.19. After ten years it's $1.42, and after fifteen years it's

Table 2.3
Menu of delayed pain

Policy	Percentage change if policy enacted in 2003	Percentage change if policy enacted in 2008
Increase federal income taxes	69	74
Increase payroll taxes	95	103
Cut federal purchases	106	115
Cut Social Security and Medicare	45	47

$1.70. Compound interest takes no prisoners. Waiting fifteen years, after half the boomers have reached retirement age, to start dealing with today's $45 trillion problem transforms it into a $76 trillion problem. Worse yet, half of the baby boomers will no longer be in a position to be taxed on their earnings because they will have already retired. And the other half will have fifteen fewer years of earnings that can be taxed. Those earnings that could and should have been taxed will either have been consumed or saved. To the extent they have been saved, they may have been invested in housing and other assets that aren't subject to capital income taxes.

If depression is setting in, we can help you switch moods by promoting an alternative emotion: anger. Just take the following steps. Go to http://www.whitehouse.gov/omb/budget/fy2004/ and print out all 13 megabytes worth of the president's 2004 budget, including its appendix. Next proceed to read the roughly 3,000 pages. See if you can find the Gokhale-Smetters study with its menus of pain.

Trust us. You won't. The study was yanked from the FY 2004 budget a few days after Secretary O'Neill was unceremoniously fired for being far too comfortable with the truth. Unfortunately, this occurred several weeks before the budget was to be published. When the new treasury secretary, John Snow, came on board, some anxious staffers showed him the report, and that was the end of it. Apparently, it was too politically dangerous even to be hidden in the budget's enormous appendix.

Snow's sensitivity is understandable. Reporters might well have found the study. They might have asked the Treasury embarassing questions, like, "How much of the pain in the menu of pain is due to the president's first two tax cuts?"

The answer: about 15 percent. This would hardly have helped in the selling of Bush the Second's third major tax cut. Nor would it have helped the president sell his Medicare drug benefit. In November 2003 Congress passed a drug benefit that is roughly twice as expensive as President Bush proposed. *According to Gokhale and Smetters, it raises the $45 trillion fiscal gap by $6 trillion to $51 trillion!*

To be clear, limiting our need to know the true size of our long-term fiscal obligations is not just a Republican responsibility. The last time generational accounting was almost published in the president's budget was 1994, when President Clinton's staffer, Gene Sperling, pulled the same trick. In this case, the analysis ran only about five pages and was slated to be buried very deep in the appendix. Its preparation and publication had been approved by Dr. Alice Rivlin, then deputy director of the Office of Management and Budget. But Sperling, who at that point was masquerading as an economist in his position as deputy director of the National Economic Council, trumped Rivlin. Ironically, Sperling now champions Social Security reform, but when it counted, he put politics ahead of his own and everyone else's children.

In its second term, the Clinton administration had another opportunity to quash generational accounting, of which it took full advantage. The director of the Fiscal Affairs Division of the OECD asked Treasury undersecretary Lawrence Summers to endorse their annual production of generational accounts for all member countries, which happen to comprise every developed country in the world. Summers punted the ball to his junior assistant, Ted Truman, who spent roughly three seconds deciding the United States had no interest in such analysis.

Fortunately, we live in a free country. And the John Snows, Ted Trumans, and Gene Sperlings of the world notwithstanding, truth has a way of surfacing. The fiscal gap study, which we've dubbed *The Treasury Papers*, has now been released by Gokhale and Smetters in the form of a report of the American Enterprise Institute. It's posted at http://www.aei.org/docLib/20030723_SmettersFinalCC.pdf

But the condition for its publication was that it contain no visible trace to the Treasury.[14]

It doesn't.

Payback

Secretary O'Neill was able to land a good right hook before he got completely decked. The secretary of the treasury serves as the managing trustee of Social Security's Board of Trustees, whose main job is to produce the annual Trustees Report that assesses the long-run financial solvency of the Social Security system. The report includes its own entreé of pain. It shows the immediate and permanent increase in the payroll tax rate needed to achieve present value budget balance over the next seventy-five years.

Smetters convinced O'Neill that the trustees' long-term financial reporting was not to be trusted precisely because it ignored years beyond the seventy-five-year window. While seventy-five years may seem like a long enough horizon, projected Social Security deficits in seventy-six years and beyond are extremely large—on the order of three-quarters of a trillion dollars, measured in today's dollars. Ignoring the major deficits in years 76 and thereafter guarantees that each successive seventy-five-year projection will look worse because they will replace, in the prevailing seventy-five-year window, surplus or low-deficit years with very high-deficit years. As a result, the seventy-five-year projection that we make, say, in the year 2015 will show a really huge seventy-five-year funding shortfall, and we will essentially repeat today's debates about how and when to reform the system.

You know Viagra salesman Bob Dole? The U.S. senator, and an important one at that, who ran for president? Indeed, during the 1996 presidential campaign, he debated Bill Clinton and claimed to have "saved Social Security."

Come again?

Here's the story. In 1983 Dole served on the Greenspan Commission, which was headed by (now) Federal Reserve Board chairman Alan Greenspan. The commission was charged with putting Social Security on a firm long-term financial footing. Greenspan, Dole, and the other commissioners did what, at the time, seemed a reasonable job in adjusting the system's finances for the next seventy-five years. But in ignoring the years beyond seventy-five, they knew—or should have known—they were leaving a big problem that would come back to haunt the country.

So here we are, in 2004, twenty-one years after Social Security was "saved" and the current seventy-five-year entrée of pain is a 2 percentage point hike in the payroll tax rate. This may seem like small potatoes, but we have only 100 pennies out of each dollar we earn to give to local, state, and federal governments, and all of us are already handing over lots of pennies to these governments at the margin.

The fact that we're now in 2004 means that part of the reason we're facing a seventy-five-year Social Security shortfall is that the *current* seventy-five-year projection window includes twenty-one years that the commission ignored. It turns out that about three-fifths of today's seventy-five-year funding shortfall could have been anticipated in 1983. The other two-fifths reflects the commission's use of overly optimistic assumptions and technical mistakes made in projecting future Social Security receipts and payments. Ironically, the combination of commission omissions, wishful thinking, and mistakes has left us today with a larger seventy-five-year problem than the commission faced back in 1983.

Bob Dole, as we know all too well, is a *very* active guy. But he's not getting much sleep from the sounds of it, and he's getting on in age. So when he tells us he saved Social Security, we wonder if he means he saved it for himself.

For his part, Secretary O'Neill realized that the real goal is not saving the Social Security system but saving our kids *from* the system. So he instructed the Social Security actuaries to include in the Trustees Report a measure of the entreé of pain that did not assume the world ends after seventy-five years.

This analysis survived O'Neill's exodus and was included in the 2003 Trustees Report. Mind you, the analysis is tucked far away in the back of the report in a section entitled "Actuarial Estimates" and with an obscure title that only an economist could decipher. But if you surf over to http://www.ssa.gov/OACT/TR/TR03/IV_LRest.html#wp253771 and check out Table IV.B7, you'll see the numbers $3.5 trillion and $10.5 trillion. The $3.5 trillion stands for the present value of the Social Security's fiscal gap looking out seventy-five years. The $10.5 trillion figure is the fiscal gap if we look out seventy-five years as well as beyond seventy-five years.

Rather than being hidden, this table should have been the first thing to appear in the Trustees Report because it shows that Social Security's long-run finances are precisely *three times* worse than the public has been led to believe. Stated differently, we don't need an immediate and permanent 2 percentage point hike in payroll taxes to cover future Social Security benefit obligations. We need a roughly 4.5 percentage point hike. Since the combined employer-employee Social Security payroll tax rate is 12.4 percent, we're talking here about raising Social Security payroll tax rates by close to 30 percent.[15] Because the menu of pain says that eliminating the nation's overall fiscal gap would require a 95 percent immediate and permanent increase in payroll taxes, it's clear that Social Security is a large part of the overall problem.

And Medicare plays an even larger role in the nation's massive fiscal gap which, to repeat, now equals $51 trillion thanks to the new Medicare drug benefit. The Bush II administration made sure to keep the true cost of this drug benefit under wraps until it was passed by Congress. Indeed, Richard Foster, Medicare's chief actuary, was told he'd be fired if he gave Congress the true cost estimates. Foster, to his great credit, risked his job and went public with the truth.

3

Driving in LA with a Map of New York

"When I use a word," Humpty Dumpty said in rather a scornful tone, "it means just what I choose it to mean—neither more nor less."
—Lewis Carroll, *Alice in Wonderland*

Figures Lie and Liars Figure

John Mitchell, who headed the Department of Justice under President Nixon, had a pet expression he used whenever confronted with numbers that undercut the administration's views: "Figures lie, and liars figure." Mitchell knew what he was taking about. He served time in a federal penitentiary for lying to Congress about the Watergate scandal.

Indeed, we've already documented the second half of Mitchell's dictum. To recap, the CBO assumes the government will miraculously shrink, the Clinton administration censored generational accounting, the Bush II administration has yanked publication of the fiscal gap, the Treasury blocked generational accounting by the OECD, the Social Security trustees have ignored their own technical experts in forecasting longevity, the CBO is ignoring its board of advisers' generational accounting recommendations, the Social Security trustees have understated the system's financial problem by a factor of three and buried the truth deep inside their annual report, and the Centers for Medicare and Medicaid Services have low-balled future growth in Medicare expenditures by a factor of two.

To describe this as a conspiracy to hide the truth would be close to the mark except for that fact that it's not centrally directed. It doesn't have to be. Each political appointee, whether she's running the CBO, the

Treasury, Social Security, Centers for Medicare and Medicaid Services, the National Economic Council, Office of Management and Budget, or something else, knows that the truth will set her free—free, that is, from her job. Just ask Rick Foster.

Given this, let's turn to the first part of Mitchell's message: "Figures lie." As we'll now show you, the figures that are lying are those relating to official government debt. The issue here is not the dishonest nature of the deficit projections; rather the issue is whether government deficits, even were they honestly forecast, actually tell us anything. Do they, in and of themselves, reveal our true or, indeed, any aspect of our true fiscal condition? The answer, according to economic science, is no.

This negative answer matters because at the same time the government is either refusing to do proper long-term budgeting or censoring its findings, it is using the reported level of federal debt as its measure of fiscal solvency. In so doing, it's in bad company. Every country around the world uses official debt as *the* key indicator of fiscal policy. So do international lending agencies, like the International Monetary Fund and the World Bank, in deciding whether to lend money to poor countries or to use their leverage to force countries to change their policies. A county's ratio of official debt to GDP is also foremost in the minds of equity, bond, and currency traders in considering whether to buy or sell that country's securities.

If, as we contend, government debt is a measure in search of a concept, using it to guide fiscal policy is like driving in New York with a map of Los Angeles. Indeed, countries with the highest debt-to-GDP ratios can be in much better fiscal shape than those with the lowest.

If all this sounds like Alice in Fiscal Land, keep reading.

Alice in Fiscal Land

One day a girl named Alice fell down a very deep hole near a tree in the park. After lots of adventures and bumping into strange-looking accountants, actuaries, and tax attorneys, Alice finds herself face to face with Tweedledum and Tweedledee, two citizens of different countries in Fiscal Land. The two are having a heated debate about which country has the better fiscal policy:

Table 3.1
Deficit delusion in fiscal land

Transaction	Tweedledum's country	Tweedledee's country
Net payment when young	$1,000	$1,000
Net receipt when old	$1,000	$1,000
Description of net payment when young	A $1,000 tax payment	Purchase of a $1,000 government bond
Description of net receipt when old	A transfer payment	Payment of $1,100 in principal and interest less a $100 tax

Tweedledum: We tax the young $1,000 each to help the old. But we're debt free.

Tweedledee: Well, we also help the old, but we do it by borrowing $1,000 each from the young. And we tax the old $100 each to pay the interest on the debt.

Tweedledum: Well, you have debt. That's bad.

Tweedledee: Well, you tax young people. That's worse.

Tweedledum: Debt erodes one's moral fiber.

Tweedledee: Taxing the young to support the old is exploitive.

Back and forth, back and forth, the two argue, hour after hour, until Alice, who has a Ph.D. in linguistics, screams, "Your countries have the exact same fiscal policy!" "No way," they both reply. "His has debt, and mine doesn't," says Tweedledum. "And his taxes the young and mine taxes the old," yells Tweedledee.

"Of course you're right, but actually you're wrong." Alice says as she shows them table 3.1. "Look," Alice says, "in both countries, the young hand over $1,000 each to the government, and the old receive, on balance, $1,000 from the government. In one country, the government takes $1,000 from the young and calls it a tax. In the other, it calls it borrowing. In one country, the government hands $1,000 to the old and calls it a transfer payment. In the other, the government hands $1,000 to the old and calls it a return of principal plus interest (P&I) of $1,100 less a tax of $100. So you have the *same* policies; you're just calling them different things."

The two Tweedles stare dumbfounded at Alice and then exclaim: "Oh, we get it. You're an economist. That's why we don't understand a word you're saying."

"Trust me," Alice says. "I'm nothing of the kind. This is just a matter of logic. In your country, Tweedledum, young people get back in old age what they pay in taxes when young, but they don't earn any interest. And in your country, Tweedledee, young people get back in old age with interest what they paid in principal when young, but then the interest is taken away from them."

"You really are an economist," shout the Tweedles. "You interrupt a critically important policy debate with some cockamamie theory that has no connection to reality. How about getting lost?"

At this, Alice breaks down in tears and runs headlong into the Queen of Hearts, who promptly arrests her for promoting tax evasion.

Fiscal Relativity

As far as we know, poor Alice is still sitting in a dungeon explaining to the Queen's guards that in and of itself, the level of government debt and its change over time tell us nothing whatsoever about a country's fiscal policy. For people, particularly economists, who have spent their entire adult lives discussing fiscal policy in terms of the size of the government's deficit and comparing countries' debt-to-GDP ratios, this proposition, if true, should be highly disturbing.

It's true.

A country's current or future time path of official debt bears no intrinsic relationship to its actual fiscal policy. Stated differently, a country can run whatever fiscal policy it wishes, including whatever generational policy, while reporting absolutely any time path of deficits or surpluses.[1] The reason is simple: the government is completely free to choose how it wants to label its receipts and payments. There is nothing in economic theory that tells a country whether to discuss its fiscal policy in French, German, Chinese, or English, and there is nothing that tells it how to label the monies it collects and distributes.

Two more examples will help drive home this point. Suppose in Dum's country, where fiscal prudence is a source of national pride, the govern-

Table 3.2
"Running" more conservative and liberal fiscal policies: Fiscal language after "policy changes" are enacted

Transaction	Tweedledum's prudent country	Tweedledee's stimulated country
Net payment when young	$1,000	$1,000
Net receipt when old	$1,000	$1,000
Description of net payment when young	A $6,000 tax payment less the extension of a $5,000 government loan	Purchase of a $5,000 government bond less a $4,000 transfer payment
Description of net receipt when old	A transfer payment of $6,500, less repayment of $5,500 in P&I	Payment of $5,500 in P&I less a $4,500 tax

ment decides to "run" a $5,000 surplus per young person. And suppose in Dee's country, where deficit finance is believed crucial to stimulate the economy, the government decides to "run" a $5,000 deficit per young person. Table 3.2 shows that each country can change its reported debt by simply modifying its language, *while making no changes whatsoever to its underlying real fiscal policy.*

Under the "new" policies, each government still takes $1,000 from each young person. In Dum's country, the government calls it a $6,000 tax on the young, less the extension of a $5,000 loan to the young. In Dee's country, the government calls it the purchase by the young person of a $5,000 bond, less a $4,000 transfer payment to him or her. And each government still hands $1,000 to each old person. In Dum's country, the government calls it a $6,500 transfer payment, less a $5,500 payback of P&I on the loan extended to the person when young. In Dee's country, the government calls it return of $5,500 in P&I on the bond purchased when young, less a $4,500 tax.

Once the countries complete their policy "reforms" (change their fiscal labels), they'll have permanently different official surpluses and debts.[2] Dum's country will report a $5,000 surplus per young person because at any point in time, the government will have this amount of money lent out to the current elderly. And in Dee's country, the government will report a $5,000 debt per young person because at any point in time, the government will owe this amount to the current elderly.

There is nothing special about these "policies." The government of Tweedledum could equally well "run" a $5 trillion surplus per young person and that of Tweedledee a $5 trillion debt per young person. In addition, either country is free to change its labels any time it wants, so that it can, for example, have a "balanced budget this period," a $5 trillion surplus next period, and a $5 trillion debt the following period.

The fact that the government debt has no real meaning in these examples doesn't mean there's no real policy being run. On the contrary, *in both countries, the government is taking $1,000 from the young and giving it to the old.* Whenever the countries started this practice, they made the initial elderly better off, and they hurt the contemporaneous young and all future young, since all of these generations receive in old age no interest on the $1,000 they surrender when young. Stated differently, the policy represents a lifetime net tax on the initial and all subsequent generations of young equal to the present value of $100, which, given the 10 percent interest rate assumed, equals $90.90.

Einstein's theory of relativity tells us that measurements of time and distance are not absolute. Instead, they depend on the observer's perspective. The proposition being advanced here—that the level of a country's debt is in the eye (actually mouth) of the beholder—might well be dubbed *fiscal relativity*. Fiscal relativity can be very quickly understood by thinking about the method of economic science.

Economic science proceeds using the development of mathematical models in which three principal actors—households, business firms, and the government—interact to achieve particular economic or social ends. Each of the actors (as well as the economic institutions they construct) is assumed to be rational. Rationality doesn't mean that the actors know everything about everything or that they never make mistakes. Nor does it mean that the world is certain or that markets work perfectly. What it does mean is that the actors aren't systematically fooled and that they can distinguish real policy changes from a relabeling of existing ones.

When economists formulate their mathematical models, including those built to determine the economic impacts of alternative fiscal policies, they use symbols, typically Greek letters, to refer to the variables or terms in their equations. One term might stand for how much the government consumes. Another might stand for how much the household earns. A third might stand for business profits. Regardless of what symbols are used, the implications of the model, once it's constructed, can be discussed in whatever language one chooses—Celtic, Swahili, English, you name it. And whatever the model has to teach us about the economy doesn't change based on the language used to discuss it.

If you agree with the last sentence, you should see immediately why fiscal labeling is arbitrary. Each choice of fiscal labels simply represents a different language we might use to discuss an economic model, that is, a different set of words that we associate with the mathematical terms in the model. In discussing Tweedledum's and Tweedledee's economies, we used different sets of labels (different words) to describe the $1,000, which we might denote by θ in a formal model, flowing from the young to the government and the $1,000, that we might denote by ϕ, flowing from the government to the old.

Fiscal relativity has four important implications:

1. Deficit accounting has no intrinsic economic meaning.

2. It's not simply deficits that are not well defined. Measures of annual taxes and transfer payments are also meaningless, as are related concepts like personal saving and disposable income.

3. Any particular fiscal policy or component of a fiscal policy can be relabeled, which invalidates separate accounting for particular policies, such as Social Security.

4. Most important, fundamental aspects of a country's fiscal policy, such as the fiscal burden, A, that could land in the laps of future generations, are well defined and can be measured with any set of labels because the resulting measure will be the same.

To see this last point, consider the four different ways we've labeled the lifetime net taxes facing the young in the countries of Tweedledum and Tweedledee. Regardless of which of the four alternative sets of labels we use, the discounted present value of lifetime net taxes imposed on the young in each country is always $90.90.[3]

To clarify this last point, let's go back to our A, B, Cs.

Some Things Change and Some Things Stay the Same

Recall the formula for the net taxes of future generations (otherwise known as the big whammy), A: namely $A = C + D - B$. Each term is a present value. C stands for government purchases, D for net official debt, and B for net taxes paid by current generations.

Given *any* set of labels, we can find values of C, D, and B and therefore determine the value of A. So what happens if we now choose a different set of labels? The answer is that we'll change the values of D and B by the same amount, leaving their difference unchanged and therefore leaving A unchanged.

To make this point concrete, suppose the U.S. government chose to label this year's roughly $800 billion in payroll tax contributions as "loans" from workers to the government instead of "taxes." Also suppose that instead of calling the future Social Security and Medicare benefits it promises to pay current workers in exchange for these contributions "transfer payments," it instead calls them "return of principal plus interest" on these loans less an "old age tax" (levied at the time contributors receive their benefits).

This alternative set of words would leave the U.S. government reporting an $800 billion larger deficit this year, putting the overall budget in deficit to the tune of more than $1.3 trillion! A year from now, the government's debt D would be $800 billion larger, but B, the net future taxes of currently living generations, would also be larger by $800 billion since their future "old age tax" would now be part of the calculation of B. So the difference, $D - B$, remains the same, as does A.

Can We Trust Our Trust Funds?

A corollary of the fact that B (the present value of net taxes of current generations) by itself is not well defined is that components of B are not well defined. This means that labeling some government transfers and taxes as part of "Social Security" and some of them as part of "Medicare" has no economic justification. While the government may call a payment it receives from a worker a "payroll tax to pay for Social Security benefits," the worker herself might call it a "payroll tax to pay for antiballistic missiles." Since money is fungible (can be freely exchanged for any number of items), there is no way to say who is right. But if we use the government's words, the Social Security system's finances will be deemed to be in better shape than if we use the worker's.

The ongoing confusion in our national discussion of Social Security's finances, particularly whether the Social Security Trust Fund is real or just a mirage, is simply this point writ large. The government could label enough of its taxes to be "Social Security taxes" and thereby fully fund the system. Other parts of the government's finances, however, would then have to be described as being more unfunded. *The overall degree of unfundedness of the entire fiscal enterprise, which is measured by A, would not change.*

Alternatively, the Treasury could hand the Social Security Trust Fund an IOU and claim that it has "funded" the system and improved its long-term finances. This would create an asset for the Social Security system but a liability for the rest of the government. The additional asset and additional liability would net out, leaving D unchanged. Hence, the woman on the street is free to say that the Social Security Trust Fund is simply internal bookkeeping—that this asset is offset by an additional liability of the Treasury and that there is, in fact, no real existing asset or improvement in the system's finances.[4]

We live in a free country where everyone can choose her or his own language. If the government wants to say that Social Security is in great shape and the rest of the government's finances are in terrible shape and someone else wants to say that Social Security is in terrible shape but that the rest of the government is in great shape, who can stop them? This argument cannot be won because it's about linguistics, not economics.

The only meaningful analysis to assess our fiscal condition looks at all the government's programs comprehensively based on what economists call the *government's intertemporal budget constraint*. This constraint requires the government to cover the present value of all its expenditures (including debt service) with the present value of all its receipts. This is a fundamental relationship. It says there is no free lunch, even in government.

This is the equation we've been using to measure A—the collective burden on future generations if the government spends no less and current generations pay no more. It's also the equation we've been using to measure the fiscal gap—the present value difference between future government expenditures and receipts assuming future generations are taxed over their lifetimes at the same net rates as current ones. Finally, the government's intertemporal budget constraint also lets us keep track of different forms of fiscal child abuse, a subject to which we now turn.

Fiscal Child Abuse—Now You See It, Now You Don't

There's nothing sacrosanct about the government's choice of fiscal labels. Each of us is free to substitute our own words for those of the government and claim the government is running a larger or smaller deficit that it says it's running. This point is particularly troubling for the small army of academic, government, and business economists who routinely try to explain interest rates, currency valuations, and other economic variables by relating those variables to the government's reported deficit. Whatever relationship these analyses suggest exists between "the" deficit and economic variables can be overturned in a nanosecond by offering an alternative, but equally valid, deficit series that's high when the old series is low and low when the old series is high.

In addition to not knowing what to make of the government's past deficits, it's impossible to know what to make of changes in its deficit through time. If the government tells us it's going to help future generations by immediately raising taxes and running a smaller deficit, should we view this as a real policy change or simply a change in labels?

Unfortunately, we can't know how A will change unless the government articulates fully how the policy will affect B, C, and D. It could be, for example, that the government is modestly raising taxes now but will dramatically lower taxes in the future. In present value, this will lower B and thereby raise A. *Understanding the government's policy requires it to spell out not only what it's doing now but what it intends to do in the future.* This is one of the virtues of generational accounting. It forces governments to discuss the future time path of policy. To be specific, it forces the government to disclose how its policies will change each generation's remaining lifetime net taxes as well as the time path of government discretionary spending.

The fact that governments can redistribute income from future to current generations (by reducing B and raising A) under the cover of a surplus or a balanced budget doesn't mean our government has actually done so. Could it be that our own government has arranged its language to coincide with its policy by announcing higher levels of debt whenever it raises A?

The answer is decidedly no.

For over half a century, ardent discussions of budget balance have been used as a cover for what is really happening: a massive redistribution from young and future Americans to currently living adults. Our de facto generational policy has been to indulge the present at the expense of children living and unborn. This gives new meaning to "no taxation without representation."

The expansion of Social Security benefits is a case in point. Apart from recent Social Security "surpluses," Social Security benefits have risen in line with Social Security payroll taxes; that is, the program has had (given the government's labeling) a balanced budget. But whenever payroll taxes and benefit levels were simultaneously increased, young people got to pay the higher taxes and old people received the higher benefits.

The young, of course, figured out how to play this game. They understood that winning Pass the Generational Buck (lowering B and raising A) requires making sure that benefits are increased when you hit old age. This explains the dramatic increase over time in the rate of Social Security payroll taxation.

The formation of the American Association of Retired Persons (AARP) in 1958 was instrumental in this regard. Membership in the AARP, which now totals 35 million, grew like wildfire, and the organization was soon at the forefront of campaigns to raise benefits for the elderly. Much of the AARP's lobbying campaign was centered on the need to help poor elderly. But when the benefit hikes occurred, the big winners were the rank-and-file members of AARP—middle class and rich retirees as well as middle class and rich prospective retirees.

Today the AARP is no longer called the American Association of Retired Persons. It's just the AARP. The lobby group has dropped the word *retired* to attract members in their 50s who aren't yet retired but have the same interest as current retirees: ripping off the next generation. This strategy has worked. Fully a third of current AARP members are under age 60, but above age 50, the minimum age permitted for membership. The choice of age 50 is no accident. It's roughly the age at which one switches from being among the expropriated to being among the expropriators when it comes to balanced budget expansions of Social Security.

The history of Social Security's balanced budget benefits and tax hikes provides the opportunity to reassess which of our past presidents was a fiscal conservative and which was not. When the system began collecting taxes in 1937, the combined employer-employee tax rate was 2 percent, and the ceiling on taxable earnings was $3,000. Today's rate is 12.4 percent, and the ceiling is close to $90,000. Although the payroll tax rate rose every couple of years between 1950 and 1990, the biggest increases occurred under Republican presidents. Eisenhower increased the tax rate by 3 percentage points, Nixon by 2.7 percentage points, and Reagan by 1.4 percentage points. Together, these three presidents account for more than half of the system's historic expansion as measured by its current tax rate.

Does this mean that Dwight Eisenhower, who is generally viewed as the most fiscally conservative president of the postwar era, was actually more profligate than is commonly believed, if profligacy is measured in terms of bills left for future generations? It does indeed.

Rockefeller Republicans—traditional Republicans who think the government should pay for what it spends—will no doubt find this view of Eisenhower hard to swallow. But conventional economic notions are turned upside down when considered from the perspective of generational accounting. Take structural tax reform, such as replacing the income tax with a consumption tax that generates the same revenue. Most observers would think such a policy has no particular generational consequences. Nothing could be further from the truth. Switching from income to consumption taxation is one of the most fiscally conservative policies the government could undertake because it places a much larger fiscal burden on current older generations and a much smaller burden on future generations (it significantly raises B and lowers A).

The reason is easy to see. Under an income tax, the elderly, who are retired, pay taxes only on the income they earn on their assets, but they finance their consumption not just from the income on their assets but also by spending down principal. Hence, taxing consumption is like taxing the elderly on their wealth holdings; every time the elderly spend their wealth on consumption, they pay a tax.

Before passing away in 1990, Malcolm Forbes, the incredibly wealthy publisher of *Forbes Magazine,* threw himself a special 70th birthday party. He flew 800 guests on a 747, a DC-8, and the Concorde, to a lavish party in Tangiers, Morocco. The party featured six hundred acrobats, jugglers, snake charmers, and belly dancers, an honor guard of three hundred Berber horsemen, and the consumption of 216 magnums of the world's finest champagne. As a display of conspicuous consumption, the party was hard to beat. According to the papers, the fete cost Malcolm millions.

How nice for Malcolm that he could send himself off in such style. But it's really too bad that the country had no federal consumption tax in place to help Malcolm relieve him of some of his money. Had we replaced the federal income tax with, say, a 30 percent federal retail sales tax (which would generate roughly the same revenue), Malcolm's soirée would have netted us taxpayers at least $3 million.

Ironically, Malcolm's son, Steve, has been trying for years to get the country to switch from taxing income to taxing consumption. Steve, who took over for his dad in publishing the magazine, has run twice for president on a *flat tax* platform. It's not clear whether Steve knows this, but his flat tax is just a consumption tax that has been labeled in such a way as to make it look like simplified income tax.

The tax base of the flat tax is income minus investment. Capital income is taxed at the business level, and wage income above a high exemption level is taxed at the personal level. Businesses are also allowed to expense (deduct) their investment from their taxable income. Since investment equals saving, the flat tax is effectively taxing income minus saving, which equals consumption.

So how would a flat tax generate a tax on wealth, most of which is owned by the elderly? Under an explicit consumption tax, retail prices rise by the amount of the tax, so that when Malcolm spends his wealth, some of it has to be spent on consumption taxes. Under a flat tax, retail prices don't change, but the market value of Malcom's wealth drops, leaving poor Malcolm in the same position.

Come again? Why does the market value of Malcolm's wealth fall? The answer is pretty subtle, but bear with us. Under a flat tax, business firms get to write off—deduct—their new investment. But this gives an advantage to new investment goods that isn't available to existing investment goods—what economists call old capital. Since Malcolm's wealth represents claims to old capital, its market price falls because it has to compete with new capital goods, which can be expensed for tax purposes.

Why are we telling you this? To point out that generational policy not only can be conducted but *is* routinely conducted, and in very subtle ways. Indeed, it is seldom discussed. When it is discussed, it is seldom characterized correctly.

To recap, we've shown that major increases in the fiscal burden on future generations (A) and reductions in the present value of net taxes of current generations (B) can occur under the heading of budget balance fiscal policy by raising benefits for the old and taxes on the young or by lowering taxes on the old and raising them on the young. We're now showing that the government can also use the stock market to redistribute across generations. Generational accounting, if done correctly, records even this especially subtle form of redistribution.

Summing Up

In this chapter, we've been harping—harping on the fact that the government has literally no idea what it's talking about when it uses conventional measures to discuss fiscal affairs. Harping isn't all that much fun for either the harper or the harpee. But understanding the implications of fiscal relativity, the need for generational accounting, and the findings of generational accounting is essential to appreciating our nation's precarious position.

If there were an easy way out of our country's jam, we'd have spared you the trip to fiscal wonderland and all the equations. But there isn't. Indeed, as the next chapter explains, all the magic bullets that people have proposed to cure our demographic and fiscal woes are blanks.

4

Popular Tonics, Snake Oils, and Other Easy Fixes

I think Social Security is off the table for the foreseeable future. We have so many other, more pressing and more immediate problems, and we ought to focus on the ones that are immediate, not the ones that are 20 years out.
—Newt Gingrich, upon becoming Speaker of the U.S. House of Representatives in 1994

Technological Progress

In the fall of 1999, an economist we know named Kotlikoff flew to Washington, D.C., to testify to the House Budget Committee on Social Security's long-term financial imbalance. As luck would have it, Kotlikoff was seated on the plane next to his congressman, Edward Markey. A senior Democrat and a very distinguished member of the House of Representatives, Markey has represented the Massachusetts Seventh District for over a quarter-century. The congressman, a real force of nature on Capitol Hill, has been at the forefront of telecommunications reform, environmental policy, energy deregulation, privacy rights, and a host of other important issues.

Kotlikoff had never met Markey, but recognized him immediately from the pictures on his campaign brochures that show up in his mailbox every two years. After introducing himself, Kotlikoff decided to tell his congressman about the scary generational accounting numbers that he was presenting to the congressman's colleagues later that day.

Congressman Markey listened politely for a minute or two. Then he interupted, "You ivory tower guys worry too much. The economy is growing like crazy. Technological progress has never been this rapid. Do you have any idea what's going on in high tech? We're going to outgrow these financial problems. It's time to get real."

Kotlikoff, realizing that Markey held the economics profession in precisely the same high regard as did Kotlikoff's wife, mumbled some words of dissent, and hid his face behind a newspaper.

That was then—back when dot-coms were king and "irrational exuberance" filled the air.

Now a half million telecom workers are unemployed, two in five software executives are looking for work, and computer engineers once earning six-figure salaries are selling shoes at the mall. As Markey was waxing eloquent about the "new" economy and scoffing at concerns about paying for the boomers' retirement, hundreds of telecommunications companies and thousands of dot-com firms were about to close their doors. And technology stocks were about to lose at least half their market values.

The lesson here is that we can't be sure about technology and future economic growth. Actually, we can't even be sure about *past* economic growth.

Come again? Well, the measurement of economic growth is far from perfect, and some of what gets recorded as increases in national output is anything but a real and permanent gain.

Take, for example, economic growth during the Clinton administration. Was it as fast and steady as Markey and other fans of Clintonomics claim? Apparently, it was not. Ever hear of *dark fiber*? This term refers to the millions of miles of long-distance fiber lines that now crisscross the globe thanks to enormous investments made by telecom companies in the late 1990s. These companies, most of which are either bankrupt or close to it, include Global Crossing, WorldCom, and Qwest Communications.[1] The term *dark* references the fact that a huge number of the fiber lines laid by these and other companies are not being used. They aren't carrying tiny particles of light—photons—representing voice or Internet transmissions (primarily penis enlargement ads) for a simple reason: they aren't needed. As the telecom industry so nicely puts it, there's a *fiber glut*. And once this glut became apparent, there was a great sucking sound heard on Wall Street—the sound of $1 trillion being sucked out of the stock values of the firms that so ably "grew" the economy.[2]

Now here's the important point. When the investments were made, they were counted as raising the nation's output and productivity. But when the investments turned sour, our national income accountants didn't go back and correct the growth record of the 1990s. Nor did they lower output, growth, and productivity in the year that the investments lost their market values. The reason is that our national income accountants use book (historic cost) rather than current market values to determine depreciation.

The 1990s was marked not only by lots of useless telecom investment, but by tens of billions of dollars of investment in Internet companies, like pets.com, that are now defunct. All that computer code, all those beautiful Web sites, all the advertisements, all the public relations campaigns, and all the fabulous business plans went down the tubes with the dot-coms that generated them. *This debacle shows up nowhere in the measure of U.S. productivity growth.* This matters because if anyone wants to hang his hat on productivity growth as the potential savior with respect to our demographic and fiscal dilemma, he undoubtedly is going to point to the "halcyon" days of the 1990s.

Suppose Congressman Markey was right—that recent economic growth was real and that we can count on it again. He'd still be wrong about growth bailing out our government's fiscal finances. As discussed in the next chapter, our social insurance benefits are structured, explicitly or implicitly, to ensure that they grow with productivity. In addition, since the costs of the goods and services purchased by the government are closely linked to real wages, higher levels of labor productivity will raise real wages *and* real government purchases.

Another thing to bear in mind is the interaction of population and productivity growth when it comes to future Social Security and Medicare benefit payments. The fact that the beneficiary population will be growing much more rapidly than the workforce means expenditures will grow more rapidly than taxes even if there is higher productivity growth.

This point comes across loud and clear in the Gokhale-Smetters study.[3] Recall that the baseline fiscal gap is $45 trillion, assuming a 1.7 percent annual rate of labor productivity growth. If productivity grows yearly at 2.2 percent, the present value of expenditures increases more than does the present value of receipts. The fiscal gap rises to $56 trillion! On the other hand, since the wage base that would be available to cover this larger imbalance is itself bigger, the requisite tax rate hike needed to deal with this larger fiscal gap isn't much different from that in the base case.

The bottom line? Unless we change the explicit and implicit linkages connecting productivity growth and federal expenditures, we can't count on growth, no matter how high it gets and how long it lasts, to bail us out of our fiscal shortfall. It's hard to know how Congressman Markey would respond to all this, but if he were smart, he'd change the subject. Indeed, he might conjure up another miracle cure, like selling off government assets.

The National Yard Sale

If you forget its liabilities, the federal government is very rich. At last count, the Feds had over $1.5 trillion in fixed assets and $600 billion in financial assets. That's 400 times richer than Bill Gates.

Fixed assets refer to machines and buildings. Two-thirds of our government's fixed assets are used in our nation's defense. They include tanks, aircraft carriers, and military bases in far-away locations. The nondefense fixed assets consist primarily of government buildings, like the U.S. Capitol and the Smithsonian.

Well, what about selling these assets? True, the sale proceeds wouldn't cover much of our $51 trillion fiscal gap, but it would make a contribution, wouldn't it?

The answer, actually, is no. To see why, suppose we sold the Capitol Building. We'd certainly rake in a bundle, but we'd also end up with no place to put our senators, representatives, and their staff. Relegating them to the ballroom of the Hilton Hotel or to even less comfortable digs has a certain appeal, but after a few weeks we'd probably want to see them back in the Capitol.

The question is how? To get them back, we'd be forced to rent the building from the same people to whom we'd just sold it. Assuming the rent we'd have to pay was set at a fair market value, the present discounted value of all the future rent payments would simply equal the proceeds from the building's sale. So each and every dollar we'd make by selling the Capitol would be needed to pay rent on the Capitol through time. In other words, this sale and lease-back transaction would net us nothing whatsoever.[4] The same point applies to the Bradley fighting vehicles, the *U.S.S. Kennedy*, the Stealth fighters, and all the other fixed assets that the government uses to do its thing.

Well, what about selling the $600 billion in financial assets, most of which consists of bars of gold sitting in Fort Knox, foreign bonds, other international reserves, and IOUs signed by students and others who have borrowed money from Uncle Sam? Cashing in these assets and using them today to pay some of the government's current bills is certainly feasible. But that would deprive us of both the income and the return of principal we'd otherwise receive over time on those assets—money that we'd use to help pay for future government bills. If the sale of our nation's financial assets were done at fair market value, the sales proceeds would exactly equal the discounted present value of the loss of the future receipts from holding onto those assets. Another wash. Like the sale of the Capitol Building or any other fixed assets, this transaction would generate no net income.

All this makes the benign assumption that government assets can be sold at fair market value. In fact, government sales, because they are large and conducted by governments, tend to drive down prices. The best recent example is the gigantic fire sale conducted by the Resolution Trust Corporation in the early 1990s. Created in 1989 as the receiver for the failed thrifts and all their assets, the Resolution Trust Corporation set about to "clean up" the savings and loan mess and help get the nation's banking system liquid and functional again.

They did this by organizing auctions of real estate assets, mortgage loans, bank loans, and other goodies to the investing public. They also spent a lot of time and money suing anything that moved or contradicted them. The process created a whole new generation of real estate and finance millionaires at the expense of the taxpayers. It also helped a good many lawyers build their dream houses. It was taxpayers who paid the bill, picking up the difference between the book value of the assets and what they brought in a quick sale, which was below their true market values.

The idea that assets yield either in-kind services or explicit income, which is sacrificed when the assets are sold, is subtle. Most countries that consider asset sales simply don't get it. Historically, government asset sales have made big headlines and bad public finance.

Argentina is a case in point. In the 1990s, Argentina engaged in an orgy of privatization, selling virtually every state-owned enterprise in sight to private companies—the national electric company, the national telephone company, the national airline, the national railroad, and the postal service. The state even sold off the country's highways to private companies. Today, it's the private companies that are collecting the highway tolls, selling stamps, train and air tickets, and phone service. Unfortunately, the Argentine government treated all the sales proceeds as free money—*as new income*. Officials used it as an excuse to raise government expenditures far above what would otherwise have occurred.

These points—that asset sales are at best a wash, and are likely to be a major fiscal loser—can be understood immediately using the *A, B, Cs* of generational accounting.

Here again is our beloved equation:

$$A = C + D + V - T - H$$

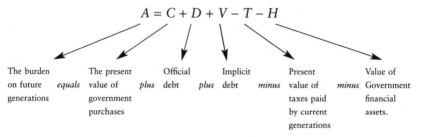

| The burden on future generations | equals | The present value of government purchases | plus | Official debt | plus | Implicit debt | minus | Present value of taxes paid by current generations | minus | Value of Government financial assets. |

In terms of this equation, simply having a national yard sale has no impact on the burden, *A*, facing future generations. To see this, first consider the sale of fixed assets. The equation doesn't explicitly include the value of fixed assets, but were we to sell the country's fixed assets, *H* would rise by the amount of money collected because the sale converts the fixed assets into financial assets. On the other hand, *C*—the present value of government purchases of goods and services—would also rise.

Indeed, it would rise by an equivalent amount because of the need to rent the fixed assets that had just been sold. The net impact on A would therefore be zero. As they say in Maine, "You can't get there from here."

Next, consider the sale of the government's financial assets. Simply selling the securities comprising H for cash has no impact per se on the size of H because cash is also a financial asset. This is just like your selling shares of stock: It reduces your holdings of stock but increases your holdings of cash, leaving your overall financial assets unchanged. Because H doesn't change, A, *the burden on future generations,* remains the same unless the asset sale triggers some other policy change.

The real issue with selling government assets, whether they are fixed or financial, is not what happens to H. It is what happens to the values of C, V (the present value of transfer payments to current generations), and T (the present value of tax payments of current generations). Otherwise, there is no impact on the other side of the equation, A, which again measures the future fiscal liabilities of future generations.

Unfortunately, neither our government nor the Argentine government nor, for that matter, any other government on earth uses the above intertemporal budgeting framework to do its bookkeeping. Instead, they treat the sale of assets as equivalent to receiving more immediate tax revenue since that will lower the government's reported deficit.[5]

In fact, the prevailing practice is rather convenient. It leads them to report smaller deficits, if they were otherwise running deficits, or larger surpluses, if they were otherwise running surpluses. Either way, they are in a position to claim that their fiscal affairs are in better shape owing to asset sales, so they can "afford" to spend more and tax less, the historically proven path to reelection. That, however, will raise C, government spending, raise V, implicit debt, or lower T, the burden on current generations, or generate some combination of those three responses. The end result is always a bigger burden on future generations—the A on the other side of the equation. In the case of the sale of fixed assets, we're talking here about C (government spending) rising by more, and potentially a lot more, than H (government financial assets) rises.

In Argentina's case, it appears that all three things happened. The government raised its spending by more than the increase in its financial assets; it raised implicit debt, and it also reduced the tax burden on current generations. In other words, Argentina didn't use the proceeds from the sale of its state enterprises to pay off bills it would otherwise have had to pay. Instead, it *spent* the sales proceeds in the sense that it used the cover of smaller short-run deficits to jack up government purchases and transfer payments and cut taxes.

At a personal level, this is the same as taking out a second mortgage on your home, but instead of using the funds to pay off your credit card bills and other nonhousing debts, using the money to go on a shopping spree.

Bottom line: When we're finally driven to a national yard sale, it will be a break-even event—or worse. And it won't solve the problem.

The Capital Deepening Cure

A valid criticism of the scary generational accounting we presented back in chapter 2 is that it ignores the response of the macroeconomy to the demographic transition. Economists refer to this feedback as *general equilibrium effects*. In principal, general equilibrium effects can be very important. Suppose the economy does much better because of these effects. Then tax bases will be much larger, and we'll get a lot more tax revenue for the same tax rates. This means our fiscal problems will be a lot smaller. By the same token, if the general equilibrium effects are very negative, our fiscal problems will be greatly exacerbated.

In the current context, the critical macroeconomic feedback to consider is the potential of population aging to generate *capital deepening*, which refers to an increase over time in the amount of capital per worker. The term *capital,* as we've previously indicated, stands for the equipment, plant, commercial structures, and other tools that workers use to produce the economy's myriad goods and services. Giving workers more and better tools makes them more productive. This leads, in a competitive labor market, to their being paid more, which in turn raises the nation's overall wage tax base. A larger wage tax base will generate more payroll tax and income tax revenue for the same set of tax rates, so capital deepening holds the promise of limiting, indeed greatly limiting, the major tax hikes that would otherwise be needed to pay the future elderly their benefits.

Surprisingly, instead of praying for capital deepening to help bail us out of our aging woes, the cognoscenti on Wall Street have been pulling out their hair over the prospect. They've decided that the 77 million baby boomers will bring so much wealth into retirement that they'll create a tremendous capital glut. (Wealth, recall, represents ownership claims to capital, so more wealth means more capital.) In Wall Street's nightmare scenario, the boomers all dump their assets on the financial market on exactly the same day in order to pay their nursing home bills. Stock, bond, and real estate markets plummet. Banks collapse. The dollar is vaporized. Brokers jump out of office buildings (old ones, whose windows open). And so on.

Wall Street can breathe easy. Even were we to experience capital deepening, there's no reason to expect a sudden crash in the market in response to an economic phenomenon that will materialize over decades, not days. The oldest boomers are 18 years older than the youngest, so they aren't all going to retire on the same day or even in the same decade.

But the real reason Wall Street can relax is that as far as economists know, capital deepening won't take place. Instead, we're likely to see a decline in capital per worker, labor productivity, and real wages (apart from any increases in the latter two variables associated with technological progress). In other words, *the nation's aging is going to hurt, not help, the economy and inflict a double whammy on our kids.* They'll face not only sky-high tax rates but also lower real wages (again, apart from growth in real wages that is driven by technological progress).

The reason for the projected capital shortage is the tax hikes projected over the next three decades. The higher taxes will suck up so much of the wages that baby boomers and the Generation Xers (those now in their late 20s and 30s) would otherwise be saving for retirement and investing in capital that the alleged capital glut will turn into a capital shortage.

How do economists reach this conclusion? They do so by constructing and simulating rather elaborate computer models of the economy that incorporate our nation's changing demographics as well as its current and likely future fiscal policies. In these *life cycle* models, households live for a realistic number of years, have a realistic number of children, and work until their early 60s. The households save for their retirement out of the income they have left over after they pay their taxes. They also leave bequests to their children.

The simulation models include all the major fiscal policy variables, including Social Security, Medicare, deficit finance, the federal personal and corporate income taxes, state income taxation, and state and federal sales and excise taxes. These fiscal policies, along with other model parameters, are calibrated to generate realistic economic, demographic, and fiscal conditions, like the nation's saving rate, age structure, and payroll tax rate.

Generations in these models are *overlapping*, meaning that there are households of all ages interacting in the economy at every point in time. Households differ not only with respect to their year of birth, but also with respect to their lifetime earnings ability. Including this feature in the modeling is important. With it, the models show not only which generations get nailed by particular policy responses to the nation's aging, but also whether it's the poor, middle class, or rich in those generations who get hammered the hardest. As we'll show in chapter 6, the current and future poor really need to watch out. Two likely courses of future policy—dramatic payroll tax hikes and major Social Security and Medicare benefit cuts—are horribly regressive.

Building and calibrating a dynamic life cycle computer simulation model is a big job that generally takes a year or more to complete. The computer code, which would fill up a small book, needs to be tested carefully to make sure all the economic actors, including the government, are living within their means. And although today's computers are incredibly fast and powerful, the models can take days to calculate because they need to converge on the economy's *general equilibrium transition path*. This refers to the path the economy will take when the model's households and firms correctly perceive where the economy is heading, as well as the fiscal policies they will face.

Finding the economy's general equilibrium transition path requires a lot of iteration because of a nasty chicken and egg problem, which economists refer to as a *simultaneity problem*. This problem arises because the economic decisions, like how much to save and how many workers to hire, that the models' households and firms take in a given period depend on what they think wages, interest rates, tax rates, and other variables will be in the future. But the future values of these variables depend on what happens in the present. For example, current saving determines the amount of future capital, which helps determine the level of future wages, which in turn affects the size of the future payroll tax base, which in turn affects the level of future payroll tax rates.

So current decisions depend on future outcomes, but future outcomes depend on current decisions. The only way to solve this problem is to solve for both current decisions and future outcomes simultaneously—hence the term *simultaneity problem*. In practice, the solution begins by simply guessing future outcomes. These guesses are then used to determine current decisions.

Next, the current decisions are used to update the guesses of future outcomes, which are then used to generate a new set of current decisions, new updates of future outcomes, and on and on until the model has *converged*. Convergence here means that the procedure has found a set of current decisions that generate the same future outcomes as had been guessed on the previous round and that were used to determine the current decisions.

To make sure their models are working correctly, economists typically try them out assuming stable demographics and simple fiscal policies that don't cause the simulated economies too much grief. Once the models have been fully tested, economists see how well they can handle realistic demographic conditions and fiscal policies.

These models aren't the exact equivalent of lab rats, but they can help us think about the amount of fiscal stress an economy can handle. And one message that comes across loud and clear from pushing these models is that simulated economies can get—and stay—very, very sick. Indeed, if the simulated government waits too long to get its fiscal house in order, the model will do the human equivalent of throwing up—it won't converge to a solution. This is the model's way of saying that running that fiscal policy isn't feasible; there is no way to satisfy the government's intertemporal budget constraint.

The most recent and realistic simulation model that economists have built to study America's demographic transition is described in "Finding a Way Out of America's Demographic Dilemma." The study was produced by one of us (Kotlikoff) together with University of

Pennsylvania economist Professor Kent Smetters and World Bank economist Dr. Jan Walliser.[6] The Kotlikoff, Smetters, and Walliser model does a very good job lining up with the Social Security Administration population projections. In 2030, the model predicts there will be 22.8 percent more Americans alive than are now living. The comparable Social Security figure is 22.6 percent. The model also does a pretty good job tracking population shares. For example, in 2075, both the model and the Social Security Administration predict that 23 percent of the population will be age 65 and older.

The study's baseline simulation assumes that payroll tax rates will simply rise through time to pay for all the baby boomers' Social Security and Medicare benefits as they come due. This simulation lets us see whether the macroeconomy improves or deteriorates over time assuming status quo policy. Unfortunately, the macroeconomy deteriorates. Over time the stock of capital falls relative to the supply of labor by one-third percent and real wages fall by 10 percent. This bad economic news will no doubt cheer Wall Street because it also portends a long-term 300 basis point rise in the real return to capital.

Why does capital become scarce, leading wages to fall and returns to capital to rise? Cherchez les taxes. According to the model, payroll tax rates double over time. Income tax rates rise as well—by 10 percent. These hefty tax hikes leave the models' baby boomers and Generation Xers with little scope for saving prior to retirement.

If we add together the model's projected tax increases and real wage decline, our kids are looking at 40 percent lower take-home pay when they hit the workforce than the amount we now receive. This abstracts from the real wage increases our kids will enjoy owing to technological change, but whatever technological progress occurs, our kids will be earning 40 percent less than would otherwise have been the case. *Stated differently, we're on our way to depriving the next generation of two-fifths of its natural economic inheritance—its ability to earn income through the sweat of its brow—because of our unwillingness to start correcting the situation now.*

Technological change is also no freebie. Yes, there are geniuses coming up with brilliant new discoveries and inventions every day, but paying for their work and transforming their ideas into practical applications cost money. And when a country saves and invests less, one of the things it invests less in is research and development. Moreover, most new technologies are delivered to us in the form of new machines. So less investment means fewer new machines, which means less embedded and embodied technological progress. Since economists believe that roughly half of technological progress is embodied in new capital goods, killing off new investment through higher taxes will also significantly limit technological progress.

Capital goes where it is treated best and has the greatest opportunities. While we like to believe that America is at a permanent pinnacle of power, that our technology will always be the best in the world, and that no nation can surpass us, the long historical view is less positive.

Today, manufacturing investment is pouring into China, which is fast becoming the world's low-cost supplier. Manufacturing jobs are disappearing not only from the United States but also from the countries to which U.S. manufacturing jobs once emigrated, like Mexico. Sure, labor is dirt cheap in Mexico, but why build your factories there when labor is even cheaper and just as reliable in China?

In his book *The Clash of Civilizations and the Remaking of World Order*, Harvard professor Samuel P. Huntington points out that China and India once dominated world manufacturing. They accounted for more than 50 percent of global manufacturing in 1750, but were heading for "deindustrialization" as productivity and technology in the West pulled ahead. Their share of world manufacturing fell from 57 percent in 1750 to a mere 5 percent in 1913. During the same period, Western nations' share of manufacturing rose from 18 to 82 percent.

"Beginning in the mid-nineteenth century," Huntington writes, "the Western share rose dramatically, peaking in 1928 at 84.2 percent of world manufacturing output. Thereafter, the West's share declined as its rate of growth remained modest and as less industrialized countries expanded their output rapidly after World War II. By 1980 the West accounted for 57.8 percent of global manufacturing output, roughly the share it had 120 years earlier in the 1860's."[7]

As Huntington sees it, Western industrial dominance is a two-hundred-year blip in history. Basically, everything we've experienced has been inside a fortuitous bubble. If that's what is happening—and note that

Western manufacturing share peaked over seventy-five years ago—there is little reason to believe Americans will experience capital deepening. The real likelihood is that China and the rest of the developing world will suck out (attract) ever larger shares of the U.S. capital stock, leaving American workers with fewer tools with which to work and with lower wages to pay their taxes.

Help from Abroad

If the United States is going to be short of capital, can it import the capital it needs from abroad? Well, we hate to be such nattering nabobs of negativism, as Spiro Agnew, President Nixon's vice president and convicted extortionist, used to call the press. But the answer is no. Incorporating international capital flows into the picture doesn't help. Actually, it significantly worsens the picture.

The U.S. economy is an open economy, meaning that it is highly open to international trade and investment. Foreigners are free to invest their savings in our country as well as to pull their assets out if they feel they can earn a higher return elsewhere. We have regular scares about the Japanese failing to show up at the weekly Treasury auctions.

We too can take our money and go, though few do. One of the most repeated mantras of financial planners is asset diversification, but most people have little or nothing invested overseas. That could change if conditions warrant.

The foreigners who matter the most when it comes to investing in the United States are those residing in Japan and the European Union. Apart from us, the Japanese and EUers are the only other fat cats on the block. Indeed, if you combine all the assets owned by Americans, Japanese, and citizens of the EU, you arrive at the vast bulk of the world's total wealth. So if foreign investment is going to prevent a U.S. capital shortage, Americans will not only need to leave their marbles at home, but the Japanese and EUers will have to invest, in spades, in the United States.

Unfortunately, Japan and the EU are aging more rapidly and more dramatically than we are. This fact, plus relatively high levels of support of the elderly, has left Japan and the EU in even worse fiscal shape than the United States. Like the United States, Japan and the EU are doing little or nothing to fix their problems. Germany's and Italy's recent pension reforms have been largely cosmetic. France can't even hold a public discussion of pension reform without incurring a general strike. And Japan is so worried about recession and deflation that any talk of fiscal restraint is considered ridiculous.

What all this spells is a more severe capital shortage in Japan and the EU than in the United States. Consequently, future capital flows won't run from Japan and the EU to the United States but in the opposite direction. Foreigners will stop investing in our country. We'll make matters worse by moving our own capital abroad—probably to Asia.

This means our impending capital shortage will be even more pronounced than predicted by the Kotlikoff-Smetters-Walliser model (which is a closed economy model with no foreign trade or international capital flows). Kotlikoff is finding exactly this in ongoing research he is conducting with Professor Hans Fehr of the University of Wurtzberg. Their work builds on the Kotlikoff-Smetters-Walliser model by including all three regions in a single model of aging and international capital mobility. Preliminary results from the new model indicate a long-run decline in after-tax U.S. wages (apart from technological change) of almost 20 percent, which is twice the decline predicted by the earlier model.

Looking to Mommy and Daddy

A few years back when the stock market was surging, brokers around the country began to fantasize about a huge $14 trillion wealth transfer to the boomers from their parents. The transfer would be so massive it would leave the boomers scrambling to hire brokers to manage their money. The $14 trillion estimate came courtesy of two economists, Robert Avery and Michael Rendall, in a study published by the American Statistical Association.[8]

A close look at the Avery-Rendall study shows it to be a hoax. The only question is whether the authors were fooling themselves as well as their readers. Their $14 trillion figure isn't the inheritance of boomers per se, but of everyone who will receive an inheritance over the next half-century. This includes Generation Xers, children of the boomers, and even parents of the boomers. Moreover, the measure simply adds up the annual flows of inheritance with no adjustment for the time value of money—the fact that a dollar received today is not worth anything like a dollar received in 2050. Finally, the study makes no attempt to scale its big number against the other big numbers in our big economy, like the baby boomers' total labor earnings.

Avery and Rendall's answer is suspect, but their question is interesting. How much *will* the boomers receive when their parents make their way to the happy hunting ground? Will boomers be able to rely more on inheritance to support them in old age than was the case for their parents? Will their inheritance be large enough to insulate them from the major Social Security and Medicare benefit cuts they're surely going to face?

To address these questions, Jagadeesh Gokhale and, yes, Kotlikoff measured the flow of inheritance as a share of the flow of labor earnings. Like Avery and Rendall, they used a Federal Reserve survey that disproportionately samples the rich and "killed off" sample members based on their probabilities of dying. They then asked how much the designated decedents would have left in assets and life insurance proceeds had they actually died. But unlike Avery and Rendall, Gokhale and Kotlikoff compared their results for the late 1990s with those for the early 1960s. Gokhale and Kotlikoff report that inheritances are roughly the same share of labor income today as was the case forty years ago. *In other words, baby boomers are not going to be able to rely on inheritances to finance their retirement to a greater extent than their parents.*

Were price-earnings ratios on the stock market closer to historical norms, inheritances would actually be a much smaller share of labor income than was the case in 1960. This is what one should expect. The boomers are very large in number. Stated differently, any given boomer typically has lots of siblings. Hence, whatever bequests the boomers' parents make will be divided among lots of outstretched hands. The magnitude of this effect can be gauged by assuming that parents are generally 25 years older than their children and taking the ratio of those in their 40s and 50s (roughly the boomers) to those aged 65 to 80 (their parents). This ratio is roughly 30 percent larger today than it was when the boomers' parents were their kids' age.

Another reason to expect a smaller level of bequests relative to labor income today than in the past is the remarkable postwar increase in the *annuitization* of the elderly. Annuities refer to income and in-kind benefits that end when you end. This includes your private pensions, your Social Security, Medicare, and Medicaid benefits, and your labor earnings. The more of your resources that are annuitized, the less you'll leave as bequests to your heirs on your way out the door.

If you went back half a century and did some checking, you'd find that over four-fifths of the resources of oldsters were in the form of fungible (tradeable) assets that would be left to their children if they died.[9] Today, thanks to annuitization, that proportion is close to *one-half*. In addition, if the current low interest rate environment persists, retirees who were just able to pay their bills on 5 percent interest will annuitize more of their personal savings. Already, research from TIAA-CREF has shown that the substitution of life income annuities for some portfolio assets increases the odds of long-term portfolio survival.[10] Since the number one fear of retirees is, "Will I run out of money?" life annuities are likely to be as popular in this decade as technology funds were in the late 1990s.

Who's responsible for this change? It's dear old Uncle Sam. When the boomers' parents were working, the government took lots of money from them in the form of payroll taxes and promised them lots of future Social Security and health benefits in exchange. Consequently, none of these earnings that were handed over in payroll taxes ended up being saved. Instead of showing up in old age with lots of bequeathable private assets, the boomers' parents showed up with huge claims on nonbequeathable government benefits.

Mind you, the boomers' parents had the option to offset this compulsory annuitization of their old age resources. All they had to do was buy more private life insurance. But they didn't. They actually reduced their life insurance holdings relative to their resources for reasons that aren't yet entirely clear.[11]

To make matters worse, the boomers' parents are spending down their assets at a much faster clip than previous generations of oldsters. Back in 1960, the typical 80 year old would spend about 9 percent of her remaining resources within a given year. Today that spending is close to

14 percent.[12] This higher *propensity to consume* may reflect the fact that with Uncle Sam sending monthly checks and covering most medical bills, the elderly are less worried about running out of money. Their higher spending rate coupled with their longer life expectancy means the boomers' parents are poised to deplete many of the assets they would otherwise have bequeathed to their children.

Finally, boomer inheritances may be diminished by a decline in the bequest ethic. Drive around Florida (and elsewhere) these days, and you're bound to see a bumper sticker that reads: "Retired—Spending My Children's Inheritance." These five words are shorthand for: "I've done my bit. My kids can take care of themselves. If my kids get into financial trouble, it's their problem. Spend 'til the end. Party time!"

It's difficult to imagine such sentiments being expressed publicly in 1950, let alone conveyed as a point of pride. But things have changed in more ways than one. Back in 1950, families were much more closely knit. According to the U.S. Census, almost all of the elderly lived with their children. Now, this figure is less than 10 percent. Indeed, today's elderly are lucky if their children live in the same state.

The dirty little secret here is that the boomers have, in many cases, given mom and dad the boot.[13] They've made it clear that short visits are okay, but prolonged stays are out of the question. How can one say this? The answer is "by comparing the living arrangements of rich parents and poor kids with those of poor parents and rich kids." The former pairing of parents and kids is more likely to live together than the latter pairing.

Note that if love conquered all, it wouldn't matter how resources were divided between the elderly and their kids. All economic decisions, from who lived with whom, to how much parents and their adult kids got to spend, to who got to go on what vacation, to how large a house one would buy, would be the same regardless of whether you or your parents had all the money. Any government that tried to get your parents to spend more on themselves by taking money from you and giving to them would end up frustrated. Your parents would realize you'd been robbed and give you the money back as either a gift or a bequest.

Economists view such behavior as evidence of *intergenerational altruism*—the theoretical proposition that parents (kids) care not only about their own welfare but also about their kids' (parents') welfare. Intergenerational altruism has been tested in the United States not only in the context of living arrangement decisions, but also with respect to annual consumption expenditures. It's been tested using cohort data, data on extended families, data on nuclear families, and data on families in which some members are actively making transfers to other members.[14] Regardless of what data set one uses and what empirical or statistical testing method one applies, intergenerational altruism is very strongly rejected.

One of the powerful pieces of evidence here is what's happened over time to the relative consumption of the young and the old. Recall that our government has spent fifty years taking ever larger sums from workers and handing these to their older parents in the form of Social Security, Medicare, and Medicaid benefits. Had the parents simply handed the money back to their kids, the relative consumption of the old and young would not have changed, but change it did. Since the early 1960s, consumption per retiree has almost doubled relative to consumption per worker. *Indeed, when you include all the in-kind health care benefits they receive, the boomers' parents now appear to be consuming more, on average, than the boomers themselves!*[15]

The fact that inheritances are not a general solution to our coming fiscal problems doesn't mean they aren't a solution for particular baby boomers. But those baby boomers are precisely the ones we are least worried about. They're the children of the rich for whom Social Security benefits are a pittance—people who would think nothing of paying out of pocket for their own bypass surgery. As the Gokhale-Kotlikoff study points out, inheritances, like the overall distribution of wealth, are incredibly unequally divided. In examining the 1998 Federal Reserve Survey of Consumer Finances, they found that the vast majority of households (92 percent) reported receiving no inheritances. Of the small minority that did report receiving an inheritance, most reported receiving less than $25,000. Only 1.6 percent of the sample reported receiving an inheritance of $100,000 or more, and this group consisted disproportionately of households with high incomes.

The other thing to bear in mind is that we've been writing here about *positive* inheritances. Inheritances can also be negative. A negative inheritance refers to children supporting their parents. Negative inheritances can be huge if the support, which is often the case, includes paying for parents' nursing home bills. For the country as a whole, the net flow of inheritances is positive, meaning that what children receive exceeds what they provide to their parents. But since inheritances are so highly skewed, this statement is also consistent with most baby boomers paying more to support their parents than they end up receiving from them.

Relying on Our Employers

Close to half of America's workers are enrolled in an employer-based retirement plan.[16] These plans are of two main types—*defined benefit plans*, or *DB plans*, which provide workers with pensions when they retire, and *defined contribution plans*, or *DC plans*, which establish saving and investment accounts for participating workers. If DB and DC plans were really generous and secure, workers wouldn't need to worry about income tax hikes and Social Security benefit cuts marring their retirements.

Alas, DB and DC plans are neither really generous nor really secure. To see why, let's first consider DB plans. Granted, receiving a pension year in and year out in retirement sounds great, but only a fifth of the workforce is so eligible. And for those lucky few, the amount they receive will likely to be far less than they expect, for four reasons.

First, the annual reports sent to participating workers make their future DB benefits look huge because there is no adjustment for inflation. Since most current pension plan participants can't make the adjustment on their own, they are led to believe their future living standards will be much higher than will in fact be the case. When we think about this form of reporting, it makes us nuts. But it's also perfectly legal.

Second, the real—inflation-adjusted—benefits provided by most pension plans are severely *backloaded*.[17] The biggest increases in benefits are in the last few years before retirement, after long periods of service. This is true notwithstanding anti-backloading provisions in ERISA—the Employee Retirement Incomes Security Act. If, like most other workers, you switch jobs frequently, your employer-provided pensions aren't likely to amount to very much. Moreover, understanding backloading requires a very good grasp of actuarial techniques. Add to this the fact that DB pension provisions can be very complicated, and you again see that workers are being promised something they have no real hope of understanding.

The third concern about most DB pension benefits is that once you start receiving them, that's it. Your benefit's your benefit, regardless of whether inflation is 2 percent or 20 percent per year. Consequently, inflation will erode the real (inflation-adjusted) value of what you receive.

It doesn't take much inflation to do a real (sorry for the pun) number on your pension benefit. At a 3 percent annual inflation rate, the real value of an unindexed pension that you start receiving at age 60 will be cut in half by the time you reach age 85. At a 10 percent annual inflation rate, your real benefit will be cut in half by the time your reach age 70! And, as discussed in the next chapter, very high rates of future inflation are almost guaranteed.

The fourth concern is that many DB pension plans are severely underfunded and may fold before their current participants, most of whom are baby boomers, receive a dollar in benefits. Just ask the Pension Benefit Guarantee Corporation (PBGC), which is responsible for ensuring workers' private pensions. To date, it's gotten stuck with the task of paying benefits to over a million participants of 3,000 private pension plans that went belly up. Many of the companies that sponsored these plans were once household names but achieved their last 15 minutes of fame in bankruptcy. The list includes Bethlehem Steel, National Steel, LTV Steel, TWA, Eastern Airlines, Pan American Airlines, Polaroid, Singer, Grand Union, Bradlees, and Caldors. Those companies have already closed their doors and flipped their pension obligations to the PBGC. But what about ongoing concerns that sponsor DB plans? Are their plans in good shape? Nope, nicht, nada, nyet, non, or however you want to say it. As a group they're underfunded to the tune of $350 billion![18]

Today, the PBGC is running in the red and running scared. Since its inception in 1975, it has been socked with $17 billion in claims. And it could soon face another $80 billion in obligations from the current crop of troubled companies. Although the PBGC is a government corporation, it's not backed by the full faith and credit of the federal government and receives no federal tax dollars. This means that the PBGC itself could go broke, leaving in the lurch millions of current and future retires with claims on pension plans that have already failed or will fail in the future.

From a worker's perspective, the really worrisome thing is not that the PBGC will go bust. This seems unlikely since the federal government would face significant pressure to support it. The real concern is that the PBGC guarantees workers only their *accrued pension benefits*—the benefits earned up to the time their plan folds. These benefits are much smaller than the benefits workers would receive if they were to remain employed in the company and the company (and its pension plan) were to stay in business.

If you have a DB plan and are feeling queasy, we hope you don't have a DC (defined contribution) plan as well, because we're now going to raise some concerns about those plans.

There are over 700,000 DC plans covering nearly 56 million American workers.[19] In contrast, there are only 56,000 DB plans, which cover 23 million workers. Unlike DB plans, DC plans are fully funded, so absent fraud, they can't fold. Fraud, however, is well worth worrying about. DC account balances aren't guaranteed by the PBGC or any other federal agency or federal law. If your employer sets up a DC account and doesn't make promised contributions to the account or somehow steals your personal DC contributions, too bad. You can take him to court, and he might go to jail—but your money will be history. Another possible source of fraud is the bank, investment company, mutual fund, or other group that holds your DC account. They can steal your money as well.

This actually happened to one of us (Kotlikoff) who set up a Keogh account through a Chicago bank four years ago. The day after the bank received his $10,000 check and put it in his account, it closed its doors. Actually, the Feds closed the doors as they hauled the bank owners and managers off to jail for stealing depositors' account balances. Kotlikoff's account was frozen for three years while the court figured out how to allocate all the bank's losses over all the accounts, including all the DC accounts. The bank had insurance for its checking account deposits but none for its other deposits. In the end, Kotlikoff lost about 15 percent of his $10,000 as well as all the interest, dividends, and capital gains he would have earned had his money been invested in the way he directed.

So, yes, DC fraud can happen. But Kotlikoff's experience aside, it's highly unlikely. Our big concerns with DC plans and baby boomers number four.

1. We worry that boomers may be overvaluing their DC account balances by ignoring the fact that these funds will be taxed upon withdrawal.

2. We're sure that income taxes are going to rise and worry about boomers' getting hit with particularly high taxes when they start making DC withdrawals.

3. We worry about DC plans turning into tax traps for low- and middle-income boomers because the withdrawal of these funds can trigger the taxation of Social Security benefits (more on this in chapter 8).

4. Our most significant concern involves the investment of DC account balances, specifically the diversification of those balances. As the former employees of Enron will tell you, investing all or most of your savings in your company's stock can be very risky. If your company goes south, you not only lose your job. You also lose your life's savings.

Most DC plans don't permit such investments. But the largest plans, which cover the most workers, do. Indeed, two-fifths of DC participants are in plans that allow their workers to invest in company stock.[20] And participants in those plans have invested 29 percent of their assets in the companies for which they work. The 29 percent company stock figure rises to 43 percent if we're talking about DC participants in companies with 5,000 or more workers.[21]

As we write, over 10.6 million DC participants hold more than one-fifth of their DC account balances in company stock. Of these, 7.6 million participants hold more than two-fifths of the DC balances in company stock, and 5.3 million participants hold more than three-fifths of their DC balances in company stock.

These facts are really quite remarkable. They tell us that the largest and, presumably, most responsible U.S. companies are systematically inducing, enabling, or encouraging their workers to hold huge fractions of their DC portfolios in company stock. This is the last thing an economist or other serious student of portfolio diversification and allocation would recommend.[22]

If so many workers are being duped into holding their own company's securities, we also wonder about the portfolio choices of workers whose companies don't offer company stock as a DC asset choice. Some of these DC participants are so scared by the word *stocks* that they keep most or all of their assets in low-yielding bond funds or money market accounts, whose real return, given inflation, is typically negative. Indeed, almost three-fifths of overall DC account balances are invested in fixed income securities.[23]

Many of those DC participants who do hold stocks in their accounts may panic when the market takes one of its periodic nosedives. The result will be selling at the bottom of the market and, typically, buying at the top—a prescription for a small DC account balance upon entering retirement.

Another concern, and one that we consider at length in chapter 8, is the transaction costs, loads, fees, commissions, and other implicit taxes that DC plan administrators and investment managers impose on DC plan assets. These expenses may seem small, but they can take a huge bite out of retirement income.

A final concern is whether firms will cut back on their contributions to DC plans. Ironically, one of the largest administrators of DC plans, Charles Schwab, recently stopped making contributions to its own DC plan on behalf of its own workers. If Charles Schwab can stop making such contributions, with all the embarrassment that entails, any other firm can stop as well.

Our bottom line, then, is that many of our employers aren't exactly holding our hands as we head toward old age. Some are actually picking our pockets. Those who are trying to do their best to help us save and have a decent retirement can't guarantee they'll be around to ensure that outcome. If you're looking for additional proof, just ask current retirees who had been promised health care benefits by their employers in retirement. Many of those promises were either simply canceled or contravened through various provisions and restrictions. A report from the Employee Benefit Research Institute, for instance, showed that corporate coverage for early retirees declined from 46 percent to 29 percent between 1993 and 2001. During the same period, coverage for Medicare-eligible retirees declined from 40 percent to 23 percent.[24]

Don't get us wrong. Your own 401(k), 403(b), Keogh Account, SRA, SEP, or other form of DC plan may be perfectly safe and secure. But then again, it may not. In this case, you may think about delaying your retirement—the topic to which we now turn.

The Delayed Retirement Cure

Another comforting assumption is that our country can literally work its way out of its aging problems by delaying retirement a few years. This is much easier said than done. Older American men have spent the last half-century working at not working, and older American women have never really worked to a significant degree.

In 1950, 46 percent of males over age 65 belonged to the labor force. Today that figure is 17 percent. The comparable female figures are 10 percent in 1950 and 9 percent today. These figures are incredible when you realize that over the same period, life expectancy at age 65 rose 4 years for males and 5.6 years for females.

Most of the decline in male labor force participation occurred prior to 1980, when the participation rate hit 19 percent. In the past few years, there's been some upward movement in post–age 65 participation rates of both males and females, but it has been very small. The U.S. Department of Labor now projects that the male participation rate will rise from 17 to 18 percent through the end of this decade and that the female rate will stay about the same.[25]

This is hardly the delay in retirement needed to make a difference, particularly given the further projected increase in life expectancy. According to the Social Security Administration, life expectancy at age 65 in the 2030s, when the youngest boomers born in the early 1960s reach age 65, will be almost two years greater than it is today.

Part of the problem in getting people to change their retirement plans radically is that the government isn't telling them how hard they'll be hit down the road. If the government tries to muddle through for another decade without announcing a clear game plan, many boomers will already have retired without having worked and saved long enough to finance their old age.

Another issue to think about is how much more the elderly would have to work to cover large Social Security benefit cuts. Take low-wage earners, for whom Social Security benefits replace almost half of pre-retirement earnings. Ask yourself how many years more they'd have to work to sustain their living standard in the light of a 30 percent benefit cut. The answer, which we've worked out on a life cycle financial planning model discussed below, is *six long years*!

Come again?

It's six years, because Social Security benefits are paid as an annuity and continue right up to one's maximum age of life, which we take to be 95. If the worker's benefits are cut when he or she is age 65, we're talking here about losing the equivalent of 15 percent of earnings every year for thirty years. That turns out to be a big deal, particularly once one takes into account the higher rate of taxation applied to labor earnings than to Social Security benefits.

But what if all workers worked a couple of more years and we didn't cut benefits? Would the additional labor income raise the tax base by enough to make a difference to the fiscal picture? Not really, although the reason is surprising.

Delayed retirement is a win-lose proposition for the economy and the tax base. When workers work longer, they actually save less because they have fewer years of retirement to finance. This reduces capital accumulation, their real wages, and the real wage base. Having run precisely this experiment in the Kotlikoff-Smetters-Walliser model, we can tell you that, on balance, the net impact of delayed retirement on the wage base is negligible, leaving payroll taxes soaring by just as much as with earlier retirement.

Let the Immigrants Come and Pay

Yet another supposed elixir for our demographic and fiscal dilemma is immigration. The notion is that if we just open the gates, millions of new young immigrants will happily pay for the baby boomers' retirement.

Not so fast. First of all, we're at our wit's end trying to keep illegal immigrants out of the country. Last year we arrested over 1 million people trying to enter the country illegally. And we're doing our level best to discourage legal immigrants by confronting them with the dreaded Immigration and Naturalization Service (INS), recently renamed the Bureau for Citizenship and Immigration Services (BCIS). Anyone who has ever had to deal with the old INS or the new BCIS will tell you that joining our country on a legal basis is an experience straight out of Kafka. The Pilgrims would have sailed right back to England had they been forced to deal with the immigration bureaucracy.

Presumably we've constructed this hellish experience because we really don't want a whole lot more immigrants soiling "our" soil. As it is, over 825,000 legal immigrants came to the country in 2002 and another 400,000 or so illegal immigrants did likewise. Almost half of our population increase from one year to the next is due to the arrival of immigrants. That's a lot of immigrants.

We didn't realize this until we checked, but in terms of absolute numbers, immigration is as high as it's ever been for all years except the early 1990s. So is it really likely we'd dramatically expand immigration beyond current levels? Before you answer that question, digest the following. Maintaining the ratio of workers to beneficiaries at the current level (that is, using immigration to fully offset population aging) would require admitting 4 million to 6.5 million immigrants *each year* between 2010 and 2030.[26]

Moreover, bringing in immigrants isn't necessarily going to reduce our fiscal problems. Immigrants don't just work and pay taxes when they come to the United States. They also collect benefits and demand government services. So the real question is whether immigration generates a net fiscal surplus. Professor Alan Auerbach of the University of California at Berkeley and Professor Philip Oreopoulos of the University of Toronto have studied this question.[27] Specifically, they've done an extensive study of the impact of changing immigration on the U.S. generational imbalance and found that the government spends roughly as much on immigrants in terms of additional public goods and transfer payments as it collects from them in taxes. To quote these authors, "The impact of immigration on fiscal balance is extremely small relative to the size of the overall imbalance itself. Thus, immigration should be viewed neither as a major source of the existing imbalance nor as a potential solution to it."

Well, how about the economic benefits to the economy from increased immigration? Like delaying retirement, increasing labor supply by expanding immigration is, economically, a double-edged sword. Letting in more immigrants expands the tax base by expanding labor supply, but it also reduces workers' productivity and wage rates by lowering capital-labor ratios. This induced scarcity of capital serves to reduce the wage-tax base.

That's the story in an economy that's closed to international trade. In an open economy, things look more promising. The reason is that when immigration increases, more capital flows in from abroad to alleviate the capital scarcity. It flows in as foreign investors see that the capital scarcity will lead to higher returns to capital in the country that is expanding immigration. With more capital coming in, the wage rate doesn't fall and the expansion, via immigration, of the labor income tax base is not undercut.

Kotlikoff and Fehr have simulated an immediate and permanent doubling of U.S. immigration under the best-case scenario—a fully open economy. Their simulations show the wage-tax base expanding, but not by much. Over time, the doubling of immigration reduces the payroll tax increase needed to pay the boomers' their Social Security and old age health benefits by less than 2 percentage points. That's far too small a payoff to persuade the public to double the country's immigration rate. So here again we have a political and economic nonstarter.

Voodoo Economics

The expression *voodoo economics* was coined in 1980 by George H. W. Bush when he ran for the Republican presidential nomination against Ronald Reagan. George the First applied the term to Reagan's advocacy of *supply-side economics*—the view that cutting taxes would actually raise revenues by stimulating the economy. This idea that we could have our fiscal cake and eat it too captivated Ronald Reagan, who not only got elected but also succeeded in getting Congress in 1981 to pass major tax cuts.

The intellectual foundation for the supply-side view was furnished by Arthur Laffer, a professor of economics who now works at Yorktown

University in Virginia. One momentous evening in the late 1970s, Professor Laffer took Robert Bartley, the editor of the *Wall Street Journal*, to dinner and drew a curve on a napkin. This curve became known as the *Laffer curve*. It showed that as you raise tax rates, tax revenues first rise, then reach a maximum, and then decline.

This makes sense. If the tax rate is zero, revenues are zero. And if the tax rate is 100 percent, revenues are again zero, because no one will work for free. In between tax rates of zero and 100 percent, revenues will be positive. This point wasn't exactly news to the economics profession or, indeed, to anyone with a modicum of common sense. But for Bartley, it was the equivalent of the second coming. Bartley used the *Wall Street Journal* to spread the word of this amazing discovery, and the idea caught on like wildfire, especially among those paying lots of taxes.

In March 1999, *Time* included Laffer in its cover story on "The Century's Greatest Minds" and called the Laffer curve one of "a few of the advances that powered this extraordinary century." Just think about it. When it comes to physics, you need to be Albert Einstein to be classified as one of the century's greatest minds. But when it comes to economics, all you need to do is draw a completely obvious picture on a napkin, and you're in like Flint.

Almost all economists, whether in the academic or business worlds, denigrate supply-side economics. Part of this, to be honest, is jealousy. If they'd only paid more attention to drawing in kindergarten, they might have beaten Laffer to the punch. But the real reason is that most economists don't think our tax rates, as high as they are, have really discouraged labor supply or saving to the extent needed to achieve the Laffer effect.

Recall that tax revenue is the product of a tax rate and a tax base. In the case of labor income taxes, it's the product of the average labor income tax rate and pretax labor earnings. *For tax cuts to raise revenues, pretax labor earnings have to rise by a larger percentage than the tax rate falls.*

There are two competing forces at play in determining whether pretax earnings rise, stay the same, or fall. On the one hand, workers may say to themselves, "Boy, now that taxes are lower, I can work less and still receive the same after tax pay. I'm going to cut back on my workweek."

Or the other hand, they may say, "Boy, now's a good time to work more and earn more because taxes are lower on every extra dollar I earn." Economists call the first of these reactions the *income effect*. They call the second reaction the *substitution* or *incentive effect*.

Some of the best labor economists in the country have spent their lifetimes measuring income and substitution effects. The broad consensus of these experts is that the two effects are roughly offsetting. This means that if wage tax rates are cut by, say, 15 percent, tax revenues will fall by 15 percent.

When George the First ran for president again in 1988, he sure sounded like a supply sider. He told a packed hall of Republicans at the convention, "Read my lips. No new taxes!" The assembled delegates went wild. But after being elected, George reneged on his promise. This, no doubt, cost him some votes in 1992 when he lost to Clinton, who ran on a platform of "Read my lips. Lots more spending!"

To pay for some of the government's additional spending, Clinton also raised taxes. But to the chagrin of the supply siders, neither George the First nor Clinton derailed the economy with their tax hikes. Indeed, federal income tax revenues, personal and corporate, rose from 9.6 percent of GDP in 1988 when President Bush took office to 12.3 percent when President Clinton left office. And since this period was one of remarkable GDP growth, there is no evidence whatsoever that higher tax rates lowered tax revenues.

Facts are, however, of little consequence when it comes to religion. And unlike his dad, George the Second is a true convert to supply-side economics. Since taking office in 2001, he has, to repeat, presided over three tax cuts. To his and other supply siders' dismay, revenues as a share of GDP haven't grown. Instead, they've shrunk—from 20.8 percent of GDP in 2000 to a projected 16.2 percent of GDP this year.

The president, bless his heart, hasn't bothered to tell anyone who he expects will pay the principal and interest on all the additional official debt he's generating. This year's increment, as previously mentioned, will likely exceed a half-trillion dollars. Maybe the president intends to raise taxes in the future on all those who have enjoyed his tax cuts? In this case, his policy would simply amount to a relabeling game.

But we don't think that's what he has in mind. We think he thinks the economy and revenues will soon start growing like crazy and that the tax cuts will pay for themselves. The president's most recent tax cut, which slashed taxes on dividends, is a case in point. He and his minions argued strongly that the policy would both stimulate the economy and raise national saving.

Now mind you, stimulating the economy requires the public to consume more, while getting the economy to save more requires it to consume less. But, no matter. Economic logic never restrained supply siders in the past, and it's not likely to restrain them in the future. The truth is that these people never met a tax they liked and never met a spending program they really supported—unless it was subsidizing their own business ventures.

Eliminate Waste, Fraud, and Abuse

A final entry in our field of dreams is reducing wasteful federal spending, popularly referred to as waste, fraud, and abuse, or WFA for short. WFA certainly exists. Indeed, those of you who remember Wisconsin's cherished U.S. Senator William Proxmire will recall his Golden Fleece awards, which he used to focus public attention on "wasteful, ridiculous, or ironic use of the taxpayers' money." Senator Proxmire handed out his first Golden Fleece Award in March 1975 to the National Science Foundation for spending $84,000 for a study on why people fall in love. For the next thirteen years, Proxmire presented an award each and every month. Figure 4.1 summarizes the top 10 recipients. We'd rank TV watching lessons as number 1, but don't want to quibble.

The problem with trying to eliminate WFA is not in identifying it. Lists are available, gratis, from any number of Beltway think tanks. They will happily tell you, in chorus, that everything on their lists, like names on the list of the Lord High Executioner in Gilbert and Sullivan's *Mikado*, "never would be missed." Unfortunately, even if we eliminate every single instance of WFA, it would be peanuts compared to the $45 trillion fiscal shortfall we face. Think back to chapter 2's menu of pain. One of the items was a *106* percent immediate and permanent cut in federal

10. Surfing Subsidy

For the Department of Commerce for giving the City and County of Honolulu $28,600 in 1981 to study how they could spend another $250,000 for a good surfing beach. At the time, even a few Honolulu officials protested the grant, saying that local lifetime surfers would be available as volunteers.

9. Basketball Therapy

For the Health Care Financing Administration for Medicaid payments to psychiatrists for unscheduled, coincidental meetings with patients who were attending basketball games, sitting on stoops, etc.—the cost of which was between $40 and $80 million from 1981 to 1984.

8. $2 Million Patrol Car

For the Law Enforcement Assistance Administration for spending $2 million in 1978 on a prototype police patrol car that was never completed. The car was loaded with gadgets and would have cost $49,078 each.

7. Tailhook

The Department of the Navy for using sixty-four planes to fly 1334 officers to the Hilton Hotel in Las Vegas for a 1974 reunion of the Tailhook Association.

6. Tennis Cheaters

The National Endowment for the Humanities for a $25,000 grant in 1977 to study why people cheat, lie and act rudely on local Virginia tennis courts.

5. TV Watching Lessons

The Office of Education for spending $219,592 in 1978 to develop a curriculum to teach college students how to watch television.

4. New Jersey Sewer Museum

The Environmental Protection Agency for spending an extra $1 million to $1.2 million in 1980 to preserve a Trenton, N.J., sewer as a historical monument.

Figure 4.1

Golden Fleece Top Ten. *Note:* These ten were selected by Taxpayers for Common Sense from fleeces awarded between 1975 and 1988. www.taxpayer.net/awards/goldenfleece/topten.htm

3. How to Buy Worcestershire Sauce
The Department of the Army for spending $6,000 in 1981 to prepare a seventeen-page document that told the federal government how to buy a bottle of Worcestershire sauce.

2. Great Wall of Bedford, Indiana
The Economic Development Administration of the Commerce Department for spending $20,000 in 1981 to construct an 800-foot limestone replica of the Great Wall of China in Bedford, Indiana.

1. Tequila Fish
The National Institute on Alcohol Abuse and Alcoholism for spending millions of dollars in 1975 to find out if drunken fish are more aggressive than sober fish, if young rats are more likely than adult rats to drink booze in order to reduce anxiety, and if rats can be systematically turned into alcoholics.

Figure 4.1 (continued)

government purchases. This, of course, means totally eliminating federal discretionary spending (and still coming up short). So if WFA is really, really large—say 20 percent of federal purchases—eliminating it entirely would still make a relatively small contribution to the overall problem.

The problem here is something we might call *political selective hearing*. Talk about "waste, fraud, and abuse" in general terms and most people hear you talking about spending that is unrelated to them or their pet hobby-horse. They feel righteous and safe, which is so warming they'll vote for you. Change the conversation and get specific—saying you're going to save Social Security and Medicare by forbidding the government to pay $49,000 for a police car—and even the dimmest audience will grow restive. Without doing the math, they know it takes a lot of $49,000 police cars to save $51 trillion.

The Price of Hope

We've spent this chapter dismissing ten alleged cures for our demographic dilemma—technological progress, selling government assets, capital deepening, help from abroad, help from parents, help from employers, working longer, immigration, voodoo economics, and reducing waste, fraud, and abuse. In the process of thoroughly dissing these "solutions," we've changed yea into nay and hope into nope.

But we take no joy in this enterprise. There's no freude in our schaden. We don't yearn to be more dismal than other dismal scientists. Nor are we looking forward to telling anybody, "We told you so." On the contrary, our fondest hope is that everything we've claimed in this chapter is dead wrong. We'd love for all the elixirs, antidotes, palliatives, tonics, and magic spells we've denigrated to work precisely as advertised and to transform the coming generational storm into a passing sprinkle.

But the stakes here are far too high to let hope conquer fear and to let wishful thinking perpetuate inaction. There is, in fact, no realistic painless escape from our date with demographic destiny. And as we now point out, that date is much closer than most people seem to think.

5

Going Critical

Every body continues in its state of rest or uniform motion in a straight line, except insofar as it doesn't.
—Sir Arthur Eddington, father of astrophysics

The End Game

Determining when a company is bankrupt is never clear-cut.[1] It requires weighing the company's debts against its ability to generate future profits. The future's a long time, and it's highly uncertain. So there's always the chance that a failing company could turn around. Indeed, with enough hype, even a firm with significant short-term losses can look like a keeper.

Amazon.com is a good example. Billed as the "Earth's Biggest Bookstore," this company went seven straight years without posting a single quarter of profits. No matter. With every report of losses, investors bid up the stock even higher—for a while, that is. In 1999 the stock price peaked at $113 per share.[2] Over the next two years, it plunged to $14. Today, with only a couple of quarters of positive earnings, Amazon is selling around $48 per share.

Creditors are the ones who decide whether and when to pull the plug, and, in the case of Amazon, there's a big daddy—Time Warner—that's filling up the tub with tens of millions of dollars at a pop. Whether this money goes down a sinkhole remains to be seen. If so, Time Warner won't be the first creditor to get snookered into investing too much and too long in a losing proposition. Having bet the farm, creditors are often reluctant to admit to themselves, their business partners, and particularly their spouses that they made a mistake. Moreover, those with the most knowledge about the company's prospects—the managers—have good reason to gild the lily. If the company folds, they lose their jobs.

So there's a natural tendency for creditors to be overly optimistic and for managers to dissemble. This explains why creditors often invest in dying companies and end up shutting them down much later than should be the case. Although the timing of commercial bankruptcy is a judgment call, the outcome is always the same: the company defaults on its debt, and creditors take a hit.

There are lots of parallels between companies that go bankrupt and countries that go broke. First, no one can say with absolute certainty that a country is insolvent. There's always the chance it can pay its bills by increasing its future receipts much more rapidly and its future spending much more slowly. Second, a country's managers—its incumbent politicians—have every reason to embellish the country's fiscal prospects since they too like their jobs. Third, when a country does go broke, it defaults on its debts, be they explicit or implicit.

The real difference between commercial and national bankruptcy seems to be the ability to stop the bleeding. Commercial creditors can haul a company into bankruptcy court. Future generations are in no position to keep current generations from making things worse. The only institution that could possibly declare the U.S. government bankrupt is the International Monetary Fund (IMF), but that will never happen, because the IMF is, to a large extent, a wholly owned subsidiary of the United States and other governments that are going broke. The IMF knows how to go along to get along.

Although there are no formal bankruptcy proceedings, everyone knows when a country is on the ropes. They can see it in the interest rates being charged by international and domestic lenders. Take Brazil. The annual interest rates on Brazilian government bonds are 27 percent—even though its inflation rate is running below 10 percent. That's an astronomical real interest rate of 17 percent! In comparison, U.S. real interest rates are currently less than 3 percent. Brazilian real rates are this high for a reason. Everyone and his brother think the government will default on its debt in the near future.[3] Hence, lenders require a very high interest rate to compensate for this risk.

The key question facing our country is, When will bond traders start looking at the U.S. menu of pain and draw the appropriate conclusions?

The first conclusion is that no politician in her right mind is going to propose ordering any of the menu's entrées or any combination of them. The second conclusion is that future politicians will face tougher choices and be even less willing to bite the bullet. The third conclusion is that absent some miracle cures (proposed in chapter 6), the only way the government can "pay" its bills is literally to print tons of money.

Resorting to the printing press is the time-honored opiate of governments embarked on fiscal suicide. It dates back at least to ancient Rome. Printing money leads, of course, to inflation and, potentially, hyperinflation. If we could take a time machine to 300 A.D., we could visit hundreds of mints located throughout the Roman Empire, all hard at work minting denarii for Emperor Diocletian. The denarii were Roman coins made partly of silver. In the year 300, it took 50,000 denarii to buy a pound of gold. Six years later, after the minting of a lot more denarii, each with less and less silver, it took 100,000 of these pieces of metal to purchase a pound of gold. By 324, it took 300,000. And by 350 it took 2,120,000,000! The denarii was da nada.

Poor Diocletian tried his best to stop inflation, even issuing the Edict of Prices in 301. The edict contained an incredibly long list of prices of goods, services, and salaries that everyone in the empire was supposed to follow for the foreseeable future. But when Emperor Constantine took over in 306, inflation really took off. Indeed, the price rise in the first half of the fourth century appears to literally have been the mother of all hyperinflations.[4]

When inflation takes off, sellers of goods and services, whether they are yesterday's Romans or today's Americans, worry whether the money they get paid will actually be able to buy something of value by the time they get a chance to spend it. That's why they raise their prices during inflationary periods—to ensure they get enough money to compensate for the higher prices of the goods and services they want to buy later.

This same instinct for economic self-preservation can be found among ancient and modern lenders. The higher is the projected rate of inflation, the higher are nominal interest rates. Why? Well nobody wants to lend money and be paid back in coins or pieces of paper whose real value has been watered down by rising prices, so lenders demand higher interest rates to compensate for projected price increases. While it may come as a surprise, ancient Rome had banks. It even had a stock exchange. And when inflation took off, so did Roman interest rates.

Economic Chicken

If financial markets decide a country is broke and its price level is going to inflate, they have a way of ensuring that outcome: They jack up nominal interest rates. This naturally drives businesses nuts. They start screaming at the government to do something. In response, the government starts printing money and injecting it, via the banking system and bond market, into the private sector. The additional money leads to inflation and, voilá, the higher inflation rate assumed by the market turns into a self-fulfilling prophecy.

If the government resists printing money, the high nominal interest rates will turn into high real interest rates. Businesses will realize that they can't count on inflation to water down the real value of their loan repayments. Hence, they'll perceive, and rightly so, that borrowing is expensive. In no time flat, they'll stop borrowing and start laying off workers. The attendant recession will lower tax receipts and put the government into a deeper fiscal hole.

Thus, the private sector and the government find themselves playing a game of chicken. If the government can convince the private sector that it can pay its bills without printing money, nominal interest rates stay down. If it can't, nominal interest rates go up. In this case, the government may be forced to print money a lot sooner than it had planned in order to prevent real interest rates from rising.

In recent years, Alan Greenspan has been extraordinarily adept at playing this game of chicken. He has convinced the financial markets and companies setting prices that inflation was low and would stay low. But as we write, interest rates, particularly long-term rates, are edging up. And there is increasing public discussion of both our short- and long-term fiscal problems. Once the financial markets catch on to the depths of these problems, they will quickly dump their holdings of U.S. Treasury and other bonds. Precisely when the markets will wise up is hard to say, which is why long-term U.S. interest rates could start to soar at any time.

Making Money by Making Money

Whenever and however a government resorts to printing money, doing so helps resolve its fiscal problems in three ways. First, the government gets to exchange intrinsically worthless pieces of paper for real goods and services. The formal economic term for this is *seigniorage*, named after the medieval seigniors. These were the feudal sovereigns who would mint coin, declare it the sole money of their realm, and then use it to buy whatever was for sale. The seigniors got the goods, but their subjects got screwed. Prices rose because more coin was circulating. This reduced the purchasing power of the coin the subjects already had, which is why economists call seigniorage *the inflation tax*.

The second fiscal advantage to inflation is that it waters down the real value of official debt. To see how much this can matter, suppose the government printed enough money this year to raise prices by an extra 5 percent. By how much would this reduce the real value of what the government officially owes? The answer is roughly $200 billion, which is 5 percent multiplied by the roughly $4 trillion in outstanding federal debt. This $200 billion is a big number—roughly a quarter the size of annual individual income taxes and two-fifths of the 2004 budget deficit predicted by the Congressional Budget Office in August 2003.

We've had such low inflation for the past decade that running a 5 percent annual inflation rate may sound highly unlikely, but inflation has equaled or exceeded 5 percent in ten of the past thirty years. In six of those years, it exceeded 8 percent, and in three of those years it exceeded 12 percent!

The point here is that even modest and short-lived inflations can generate significant resources for Washington. And if a higher inflation rate is sustained through time, the growth in prices will compound. How much such sustained inflation devalues real government debt depends on the *maturity structure* of the debt—the amount of time the government has to repay its borrowing. The longer is the debt's maturity, the more time is available for a given rate of inflation to expropriate government creditors.

As an example, consider a thirty-year U.S. Treasury Bond sold today for $10,000 and promising to pay $1,000 in interest every year for thirty years and return the principal—the $10,000—in the thirtieth year. Suppose the annual inflation rate is zero when the bond is sold, but that right after the bond is sold, the annual inflation rate rises to 5 percent. Let's also suppose that this new 5 percent inflation rate is perceived to be permanent.

What happens to the bond's market value, which was $10,000? The answer is that it immediately drops by a third. The reason is that anyone buying the bond realizes that with each passing year, inflation will eat up another 5 percent of the real purchasing power of the remaining payments one receives from holding the bond. In particular, when the $10,000 of principal is received in year 30, it will purchase only $2,314 in real goods and services because after thirty years the price level will have quadrupled, and then some.

Next assume the bond has a one-year, rather than a ten-year, maturity. In this case, the 5 percent inflation rate doesn't do much to help the government renege on its $10,000 obligation. The bond's market value falls by only 4 percent.

The fact that the prices of long-term bonds are much more sensitive to inflation than are short-term bonds explains the typical upward slope of the *yield curve*—the tendency for interest rates to be higher, the longer is the bond's maturity. Since there is more inflation risk in buying long-term bonds, investors in such bonds need a higher risk premium.

Today's yield curve is quite steep, with long-term bonds yielding almost 4 percentage points higher than short-term yields. This suggests that investors are particularly concerned about the risk of inflation taking off. On the other hand, 1965 was the last time nominal interest rates on long-term bonds were this low. This fact suggests that investors expect relatively low levels of future inflation, even if the future rate of inflation is viewed as more uncertain.

Inflation's third and final fiscal function is to reduce the real value of government expenditures. Government transfer payments, like welfare and Social Security benefits, that either aren't indexed to inflation or aren't adjusted for inflation in a timely manner are fair game when it comes to eroding what they can buy. So too is government discretionary spending, the most important of which is paying government workers.

Russia provides one of the most recent examples of the use of inflation to cut real government expenditures. In 1992, Russia's inflation rate peaked at 292 percent *per month*. As it was hyperinflating, the government chose to pay soldiers, state workers, and pensioners with a roughly three-month lag. Rubles that were supposed to be paid in June were received in September. Getting paid with a delay is inconvenient when the price level is fixed, but when it's rising like crazy, getting paid late is the same as being robbed. That's exactly what happened. Today, Russian army officers make only $115 per month, and elderly widows receive state pensions worth only $25 a month.

Multiple Equilibria

The fact that the current and future level of prices (the cost in dollars of a representative basket of goods and services) can have such major consequences for the conduct of fiscal policy provides a deeper reason that interest rates and inflation could suddenly take off. The reason is *multiple equilibria*, a term economists apply to situations in which two or more market outcomes could equally well arise.

As a simple example of multiple equilibria, suppose that for no particular reason, everyone simultaneously gets depressed about the economy. Specifically, suppose everyone comes to believe that the economy is going down the tubes. What will happen? Well, firms, fearing they won't be able to sell their products, will cut back on production and lay off workers. The laid-off workers will reduce their demand for the goods and services sold by firms. So the original belief by producers that demand for their products will be low will in fact turn out to be true. If instead of everyone becoming pessimistic, everyone becomes optimistic, the economy will boom; firms will hire more workers believing, again correctly, that demand for their products will be high. In this simple story, the economy can support two outcomes or equilibria—one bad and the other good.

With respect to our fiscal problems, the potential for multiple equilibria arises because there are lots of different ways to close the fiscal gap. Each of these methods entails a different course of inflation as well as a different path for the underlying real economy. If, for example, the price level were to double immediately, the real value of the government's official debt would instantly fall in half.[5] This would, of course, reduce the fiscal gap as well as some of the pressure on future spending cuts and tax hikes. If, instead, the current price level were to triple immediately, a different equilibrium would present itself, one with even less need for other fiscal adjustments.

Were the government telling us how much it plans to spend and tax in the future, the current and future price level would adjust to accommodate those plans. But if the government isn't formulating such plans, there is nothing to definitively pin down the course of prices and the economy's expectation of its future fiscal affairs. Stated differently, there is nothing to prevent the price level from doubling tomorrow to help resolve a course of fiscal policy that is out of control and apparently up for grabs.

The reality is stark. No one really knows how our government's long-term fiscal difficulties will get resolved. Those who are in the best position to tell us—the president and members of Congress—aren't talking because they don't have a clue, don't think it matters, or couldn't care less. How the economy, including its price level, should respond to this situation is anyone's guess, which is precisely why the price level could jump a hell of a lot at a moment's notice.

Losing Traction

The extent to which the price level might jump depends critically on the extent to which inflation can "cure" our fiscal imbalance. The easier it is for inflation to work its fiscal magic, the lower it needs to be. Unfortunately, addressing America's $51 trillion fiscal gap through inflation won't be easy.

On average, federal debt has a maturity of five years, and a full third of the debt will come due in less than one year. This short maturity structure means that moderate rates of inflation will do very little to reduce the debt's real value. But the important point to keep in mind is that official government debt is the tip of the iceberg. Even if we could inflate away all $4 trillion in federal debt, we'd still be left with a $47 trillion problem.[6]

Social Security, Medicare, and other entitlement benefits account for the lion's share of this red hole.[7] Inflating away these benefits would also be tough sledding because entitlement benefits are either officially or implicitly indexed. And they're indexed not just to inflation but also to labor productivity. This means that when workers become more productive and their real wages rise, real entitlement benefits rise as well.

In the case of Social Security, such *wage indexation* is codified in law. The system calculates the initial benefits of new retirees based on the retiree's *average indexed monthly earnings*, or AIME. The retiree's AIME is formed by inflating her past covered earnings according to the growth in economy-wide average wages between the year she earned the money and the year she reaches age 60. Once workers start receiving their wage-indexed retirement benefits, these benefits are annually adjusted for inflation.

The upshot is that Social Security benefits are very well protected against low and moderate rates of inflation. Nevertheless, *high rates of inflation could substantially reduce real benefits* because the adjustment of benefits for inflation occurs only once a year—on January 1. Consider, for example, a 5 percent monthly inflation rate. With inflation at that level, prices on December 31 would be 80 percent higher than on the preceding January 1. And real Social Security benefits received in December would be roughly half of what they were the previous January.

Mind you, a benefit cut of this or, indeed, any other significant magnitude would cause every one of AARP's 35 million members to march on Washington. They'd start attacking members of Congress with their canes, just like they did Congressman Dan Rostenkowski in 1989. In that year Rostenkowski helped pass a bill providing the elderly with catastrophic health insurance, but he and his colleagues had the temerity to ask the elderly to help pay for this extra goody. According to the *Chicago Tribune's*, August 18, 1989, story, "Congressman Dan Rostenkowski, one of the most powerful politicians in the United States, was booed and chased down a Chicago street Thursday morning by a group of senior citizens after he refused to talk with them about federal health insurance. ... Eventually, the six-foot four-inch Rostenkowski cut through a gas station, broke into a sprint and escaped into his car, which minutes earlier had one of the elderly protesters, Leona Kozien, draped over the hood."

Attempts to cut Medicare would meet the same fate (except the old-sters would be hurling their bedpans). Indeed, the government has utterly failed for four successive decades to bring Medicare growth in line with that of the economy. In 1970, Medicare benefit payments were .74 percent of GDP. Today, they are 2.6 percent of GDP. In 2030, they're projected to equal 4.7 percent of GDP. And in 2075, they're projected at 9.0 percent of GDP. That, by the way, is the same as today's ratio of federal income taxes (corporate plus personal) to GDP!

Medicare's sobering track record is due primarily to the fact that real benefits per beneficiary grew much more rapidly than did labor productivity. So historically, at least, Medicare benefits have been indexed not to the price level plus labor productivity, but to something that grew much faster than these two variables. Going forward, Medicare benefits per beneficiary are projected to grow year after year at a rate that is one-third higher than labor productivity growth. Given the program's history and the way it continues to be structured, this assumption is, to be kind, optimistic.

Why have Medicare expenditures grown so rapidly? The answer is obvious. Medicare participants, which include everyone age 65 and over, are free to see whatever doctors they want, whenever they want, and wherever they want. They're also free to flip 80 percent of the cost of doctor visits and 100 percent of the cost of hospital care to the government, which means to us the taxpayers.

The medical profession, hospitals, and the drug companies may grumble from time to time about the level of Medicare reimbursements, but down deep, they love this system. Imagine running a business where you can tell every customer who walks in the door, "Choose whatever you want, and I'll charge it to the government." Your only concern would be getting customers to come to your shop rather than your competitor's. The trick would be to provide the nicest shopping environment and to stock your store with the very latest, the very best, and the most expensive products available.

In the medical arena, the only caveat to this heavenly business plan is that even the spiffiest medical products and services aren't necessarily all that much fun to consume. A good example here is bypass surgery. If you had clogged arteries in the 1970s, you might have opted for a rather invasive operation in which a surgeon would cut out a vein from your leg, then cut open your chest, then cut out your artery, and then try to keep you alive while replacing your damaged artery with your vein. Lots of potential bypass customers thought about it for all of two seconds and decided to take a pass, even though they could get the operation for free. This meant that Medicare paid for a relatively small number of very expensive operations.

Today, things have changed. The surgeons have developed angioplasty, in which a small incision is made in your groin. Then your clogged artery is gently threaded and expanded with a balloon. Goodbye heart clog, goodbye pain. The good news is that angioplasty costs a lot less than a bypass operation. The bad news is that having angioplasty is tons more fun than having a bypass. It's so much fun that anyone with even mildly clogged arteries is signing up for the experience. Consequently, Medicare is spending more of our money cleaning oldsters' pipes than ever before.

Medicaid is the other major entitlement program whose real benefits could potentially be eroded by inflation. Unlike Medicare recipients, young and middle-aged Medicaid beneficiaries are poor—indeed, very poor. Consequently, they have no money to spend on Washington lobbyists. Older Medicaid beneficiaries are also very poor and live, for the most part, in nursing homes. They too are in no position to start complaining about the quality of their care. Given this, one might presume that Medicaid spending hasn't kept up with economic growth. Nothing could be further from the truth. Over the years, Medicaid spending has grown as fast as—indeed, somewhat faster than—Medicare spending. This growth has occurred under Republican and Democratic administrations alike, but, interestingly enough, the fastest growth has occurred under Republican administrations. *Today, believe it or not, total Medicaid expenditures exceed total Medicare spending.*

The explanation for Medicaid growth appears to be the same as that for Medicare growth. Both programs provide their benefits in kind as opposed to in cash. There's also no straightforward way to limit how much of this free, or nearly free, health care is demanded by program recipients and therefore provided by the all-too-eager-to-comply health care sector.

In recent years there have been attempts to enroll Medicare and Medicaid participants in health maintenance organizations (HMOs) as a means of lowering costs and reducing expenditure growth. But the fact that both programs are now spending more relative to GDP than at any time in the past indicates that the experiment with HMOs hasn't worked.

The reason is that HMOs enroll the healthier Medicare and Medicaid beneficiaries and leave the less healthy and more expensive beneficiaries in the traditional fee-for-service programs. So Medicare and Medicaid end up paying HMOs more to take care of their program participants than those participants would have cost the programs had they not joined an HMO. These programs base their payments to HMOs on the medical costs of the average Medicare and Medicaid participants rather than on the lower costs of those who sign up for the HMOs.

As we've seen, inflation doesn't have much traction (at least in low gear) in wiping out federal debt. It may also be powerless to limit growth in real entitlement benefits. So let's ask another question: Can inflation help out much in reducing real discretionary federal spending? Here again, to the extent that the government is purchasing real goods, inflation is not going to lower their real costs. On the other hand, if the government is willing to get by with lower real services, it could attempt to use inflation to cut the real wages of government workers.

The problem with this approach comes in the form of 600,000 federal government workers who belong to the American Federation of Government Employees, which is part of the 13 million strong AFL-CIO. Having 600,000 federal workers go on strike would quickly dampen any administration's appetite for using inflation to cut real federal workers' wages. In addition, since half of federal discretionary spending is on defense, much of the federal government's payroll represents military wages. Expecting to cut those salaries in real terms at a time when the country is trying to conduct a global war against terrorism seems unrealistic at best, delusional at worst.

The final mechanism by which the government can make money by making money is seignorage, mentioned earlier. The question here is how much of an inflation tax the government can reasonably expect to impose on the economy. To answer this question we need to consider the size of the *monetary base*. The money base is the basic amount of money that the government has printed and injected into the economy in the past either by handing money to people in the form of transfer payments or by buying goods and services.

Today the monetary base totals close to $700 billion. Were the government to print and spend another, say, $70 billion, the monetary base would rise by 10 percent. Other things being equal, we could expect this monetary injection to raise prices by 10 percent. Hence, coming up with $70 billion in real revenues each year would likely come at the cost of a high and also permanent level of inflation. The problem with this strategy is that $70 billion is not much quo if the quid is an ongoing 10 percent rate of inflation.

To see how small $70 billion is, suppose we were able to borrow the $51 trillion that we need to cover our nation's present value budget gap. We'd then have to pay interest on that borrowing. But real interest on the $45 trillion would total roughly $1.7 *trillion per year*—miles higher than $70 billion.

If we were willing to endure even higher inflation, we could print even more money each year. The difficulty with this strategy is that the amount of inflation generated as the government prints more and more money starts rising exponentially. The reason is that when prices rise, people start treating money like a hot potato: They try to use it as quickly as possible. They know that the longer they wait, the higher prices will be and the less their money will buy.

This increases the *velocity* of money—the rate at which money circulates in the economy and accelerates inflation. At some point, as inflation gets sufficiently high, people will stop using dollars altogether. They will either resort to barter, use other currencies, particularly the euro, or use gold and other precious metals as money.

During the 1920s, when prices rose in Germany at the fastest rates ever recorded, workers were literally paid twice a day in wheelbarrows full of money. As soon as they got their wheelbarrow, they'd head off to spend it on groceries and other commodities. If they waited a few hours, their money would be worthless. How fast exactly did prices rise? In the five months leading up to November 1923, prices rose 854 billion-fold! To bring this down to earth, consider the fact that in 1920, the most expensive German stamp cost 4 marks. In 1923, the most expensive stamp cost 50 billion marks.

Things are a bit different these days when it comes to the public's response to hyperinflation. During Russia's recent hyperinflation,

Russians stopped using the ruble altogether and developed elaborate barter arrangements, many of which continue to this day. They also began transacting in dollars, particularly for significant purchases like buying a home.

To summarize, the federal government isn't likely to be able to generate substantial real budgetary resources or savings by printing money. So does this inability to get much traction from printing money mean we don't have to worry about inflation? On the contrary, the fact that so little can be gained via low and moderate rates of inflation makes it more likely that prices will inflate at an extremely rapid clip when they start rising.

This point is important, so let us express it differently to make sure you get it: *The government is going to need the budgetary resources that only high inflation can provide.* Hence, high inflation is going to occur. Indeed, it's likely to occur sooner than later.

The Big Inflexion

Drop grains of sand in a pile on the beach, and your pile will grow until that one extra grain brings the whole thing crashing down. That's nature going critical, hitting an inflexion point. Exactly when your sand pile crashes, or the earth quakes, or the volcano erupts, or the dam breaks is difficult to predict. But one thing is sure—abrupt change *will* occur at some point.

Economies also go critical. When the fiscal pressure gets too high, financial markets start to boil. Interest rates soar, currencies collapse, stock markets plummet. But timing the boiling point is damned near impossible. The reason it's so hard is what we've said before. Governments are infinitely lived institutions. If they act irresponsibly in the short run, there's always the possibility that they can redeem themselves in the long run through a variety of fiscal adjustments.

Take Japan. The country has a huge debt relatively to its GDP. It's aging more rapidly and more significantly than any other developed country, and its implicit debt is massive. Yet long-term interest rates are less than 1 percent. Apparently, the purchasers of long-term Japanese bonds think the country can raise taxes and cut expenditures by enough to survive without inflating. Everything we know about Japan's fiscal and economic position suggests the opposite, but millions of people and thousands of institutions are holding those ten-year Japanese Treasury bonds assuming the yen will retain its value. Part of this belief is, no doubt, mistakenly predicated on the mild deflation now underway. This deflation has overshadowed the fact that the Japanese government has been engaged in massive money creation over the past few years. Indeed, in 2002 for every 100 yen collected in taxes, the government simply printed 30 yen.

Why hasn't this money creation led to inflation? The answer is that Japan's money supply, which ultimately determines the price level, is partly controlled by the banking system, and the banking system is contracting the money supply as fast as the Bank of Japan is expanding it. The government pumps money into the economy, but the banking system expands this *monetary base* by making loans and issuing checking accounts.

In 2002, the Bank of Japan increased the monetary base by 26 percent, but the ultimate money supply, *M1*, which consists of currency plus checking account balances, rose by only 2 percent. How did this happen?

Most Japanese banks are technically insolvent. They are afraid to make new loans or renew existing ones. The same thing happened in the United States in the early 1930s.

When an economy is down in the dumps, it's nice that the government can print money to pay its bills without this action registering immediately in price increases. But once the economy and banking system revive, all that extra base money sloshing around will produce one thing: higher prices via inflation.

When Bad Things Happen to "Bad" Countries

When people drown, they're fine right up to the minute the water level reaches their lips. The same holds when countries get over their heads financially. As the probability that a country can pay its bills through standard means gets smaller and smaller, a seemingly small factor can flip the switch on the economic electric chair. When that happens, the transformation from economic health to economic death is swift and merciless.

Argentina is just the latest example of this outcome. Although it had a much lower debt-to-GDP ratio than Japan, had a currency pegged one for one to the dollar, had a policy of trade liberalization, had privatized every public sector industry in sight, and had been growing at an impressive rate, it also had a bad history. This history included periodic hyperinflations, political instability, defaults on official debt, military coups, and fiscal malfeasance. Consequently, whenever something went wrong around the world, whether it was the Russian government default on its debt, the Asian crisis, or the devaluation of the Brazilian Real, the financial markets remembered that Argentina was Argentina—a country long addicted to the printing press—and jacked up the country's interest rates.

This rise in the interest rates following each external shock reflected the larger risk premium lenders required to lend to Argentina. Part of the risk premium reflected concern about possible debt default by Argentine borrowers, including the government, and part reflected concern about the government's resorting to the printing press to pay its bills. Lenders reasoned that if inflation returned to Argentina, the interest and principal payments they'd receive on their loans would be watered down by price increases, so they set higher interest rates on their loans to protect themselves from that outcome.

Note the multiple equilibria aspect of this. If everyone believes that everyone else believes that Argentina is getting into trouble or could be getting into trouble, everyone raises the interest rates at which they lend to the country. The higher interest rates then put the country into a recession, forcing it to default on its loans and to use the printing press (inflation) to pay its bills. Hence, the original beliefs about default and inflation become self-fulfilling prophecies.

After each external shock, the Argentine government, knowing that its actions would dramatically affect domestic and world opinion about the nature of its equilibrium, kept the peso glued to the dollar. This meant that the high nominal interest rates imposed from abroad became high real interest rates. Argentine companies responded to the high real interest rates by laying off workers, investing less, and generally putting the Argentine economy into a tailspin. The government had played chicken and lost.

As revenues fell, the twelve Argentine provincial governments decided that hard times weren't for them and began printing their own money. The central government was none too happy about this but was too weak to stop the provinces. And realizing that having an additional twelve currencies circulating in the country would dramatically increase the prospect of counterfeiting, they volunteered to print all twelve currencies in Buenos Aires on the government's own machines. Talk about enabling bad behavior!

When economic minister Ricardo Lopez Murphy resigned in disgust in June 2001 after spending all of a week in office, the public started heading for the exit, which in this case was their banks. If they could get their money out and convert it to dollars, they'd be safe. But when everyone came running, the banks closed their doors.

Three years later the economy is ruins. The government has defaulted on its debt. The banks are insolvent. Inflation is raging. The peso has lost roughly 80 percent of its value. Output is down by almost a third. Unemployment stands at 25 percent. The country has seen seven presidents in thirty-six months. And the best-educated members of society are leaving the country in droves.

Who's Next?

Brazil seems to top most people's list for the next country to go critical, but we are taking bets on Japan. The temptation on the part of the Bank of Japan to use the current deflation as an opportunity to print huge quantities of money to buy up most, if not all, outstanding Japanese government debt may become overwhelming. As that occurs, the country could flip from mildly declining prices to rapidly rising prices. Whether Japan wipes out its official debt, its implicit liabilities are so massive and the country is aging so rapidly that things could get very dicey very soon.

Although Japan appears to have the largest fiscal gap relative to GDP of any developed country, a number of other countries are in bad shape—indeed in worse shape than the United States. The list includes Austria, Finland, France, Germany, Italy, Spain, and Sweden. Several of these countries, particularly Sweden, Italy, and Germany, have taken steps in the past couple of years to institute reform of their state pension systems.

The Italian and Swedish reforms seem mostly cosmetic, while the German reform appears to have lowered the long-run payroll tax needed to pay for pensions from 29 percent to 25 percent. That's not just makeup, but even with this reform, Germany is still looking at a 60 percent long-run payroll tax rate to fund the combination of old age pensions, health care, long-term care, accident insurance, and disability.

Yes, you read that right: 60 percent. Add in future income taxes and value-added taxes to pay for the rest of government activities, as well as interest on the ever-rising German official debt, and you've got some pretty unhappy campers. These campers aren't going to accept close to 100 percent tax rates. Nor, as the most recent pension reform indicates, will they accept dramatic reductions in their benefits. Hence, German politicians will have one and only one alternative: printing money. But there's a rub. Germany is part of the euro system and doesn't have complete control of the European Central Bank. As Germany and Italy and France and Spain and Austria push for printing and distributing huge quantities of euros, other EU members may balk.

This is particularly likely if the United Kingdom eventually joins the EU. The United Kingdom is in much better long-term shape than are other countries in the European Union. Thanks here go to Margaret Thatcher, who set in place a policy of holding fixed the real level of pension benefits per beneficiary even as overall British living standards rose. That policy plus the willingness of the Brits to live with a cheap but substandard health care system makes all the difference to their long-term prospects.

The particular message here is that trying to protect ourselves from an increasingly worthless dollar by buying euros may be jumping from the pot into the frying pan. The general message is that, like the United States, Japan and the European Union are very likely to melt down. Whenever Japan and the EU go critical, the repercussions for the United States will be enormous. Just as Russia's default, Brazil's devaluation, and the East Asian crisis killed off Argentina, a Japanese or EU meltdown could push the United States over the brink.

Economic Purgatory

Mention Argentina these days, and U.S. bankers cringe. In the past three years, they've written down billions of dollars in bad loans to the Argentine government and to Argentine companies, and they are still counting the losses. The banks that were hurt the worst were Citigroup and Fleet, which lost $2.2 billion and $1.2 billion, respectively.

Should we feel sorry for them and Argentina's other creditors? Probably not. After all, they'd been burned before and knew what they were getting into. What's more, the interest rates they charged the Argentines included a very healthy risk premium. This risk premium is worth dwelling on. It's part of the ongoing economic penance facing countries that establish themselves as serial defaulters.

When it comes to economics, history matters, particularly credit history. A country can have the best leaders and the best policies, but if it has been bad in the past, it won't be trusted when the going gets tough. Lenders will realize that default could be just one or two administrations away. They'll tag the country with that potential in thinking about their prospects for repayment.

Default can take many forms. It can be explicit, as in the government's declaring it's just not going to pay back what it officially owes (e.g., Russia and Argentina). It can be implicit, as in the government's running inflation and wiping out the real value of nominal obligations. Or it can be done with taxes, as in the government's taxing away the principal plus interest received by creditors on their loans.

Job applicants with criminal records know how tough it is to get a job. And countries that have made a practice of defaulting on their debts know how hard it is to get a loan on reasonable terms. Invariably the country ends up borrowing on unfavorable terms, which then encourages default for both psychological and economic reasons. If you're being forced to pay huge sums for years for the privilege of being bad, why not exercise the option? It gives you a chance to torment your tormentors and to save a few bucks, at least in the short run.

In the case of former fiscal malfeasants who really want to stay clean, the path to recovery is long and painful. Such countries are forced to live with usurious interest rates for years. They must also take radical steps to get out from under their economically suffocating commitments.

The big danger for countries that are trying to go straight is that they will opt for minor rather than major surgery. For example, they may make minor cuts in pension and other benefits when only major cuts are consistent with long-run solvency. Alternatively, they may cut just enough to ensure that every generation from now to kingdom come will be stuck paying very high taxes.

As the Russians have shown in treating their current elderly, coming clean is brutal business. It means recognizing the zero-sum nature of generational accounting and sacrificing the welfare of one generation to benefit all future generations. But spreading the pain condemns the economy to endure perpetual sky-high tax rates, periodic bouts of rampant inflation, and continual exposure to runs on the country's currency, securities, and financial institutions.

The lesson for the United States in all this is that ongoing economic purgatory (what economists call a *bad steady state*) rather than simple short-lived economic hell may be its long-run destiny. It's hard to believe that any American administration would have the courage to dramatically cut, if not eliminate, the Social Security and Medicare benefits of a contemporaneous older generation in order to dramatically lower the fiscal bills facing all subsequent generations.

We certainly don't advocate such a policy. We understand full well just how many older people literally depend on these programs for their survival. But this concern about half-measures is real. Countries can and do get trapped in bad long-term positions from which they can't escape because they can't stomach the sacrifices needed for full recovery. The United States, Japan, and most of Western Europe appear headed for just such economic purgatory.

Ironically, it's Russia and the other members of the former Soviet Union that have the best long-term prospects from a fiscal perspective. They have so thoroughly wiped out the real value of their fiscal obligations that they are in a marvelous position to outgrow them. Of course, if future growth in Russia and its former clients is matched step by step with expanded intergenerational redistribution from young and future generations to the current elderly, they will end up in the same hole from which they are now trying to climb out.

Approaching Full Boil

The menu of pain should give U.S. bond traders lots of pause. It says our current policies are completely unsustainable. It also suggests that expecting future governments to try to fix things is whistling "Dixie." If we aren't prepared, for example, to raise federal income taxes by 69 percent in the near term, do we really think a future government will be prepared to raise income taxes by an even higher percent?

Each passing year will bring us closer and closer to 2008, when the oldest baby boomers become eligible to collect Social Security retirement benefits and are out in full force to vote in the presidential election. That event is going to make a big impression on the public's collective conscience. So will the drip, drip, drip of information that will be coming out about our long-term fiscal woes.

As time moves on, the government will find it can no longer suppress the truth about the coming generational storm. Every economist inside and outside of academia will shortly begin to realize that this issue represents the major American economic dilemma of the twenty-first century.

As we all know, our country loves a good worry, and if there's nothing to worry about, we can always rely on the media to come up with something. But when the media sink their teeth into a real problem, they generally don't let go. True, there's no sex involved, but we're talking here about a problem that confronts *every American*. This problem pits the old directly against the young and the rich directly against the poor.

Any day now, bond traders, who, truth be told, can be as thick as bricks, may start to react to our official deficit that is now running at almost 5 percent of GDP. Another flash point could be Alan Greenspan's retirement. Greenspan has told the bond market what to think for so long that it's largely forgotten to think on its own. His exit could prompt a reappraisal of the financial and fiscal landscape.

The sequence of events might run like this. Greenspan leaves. The dollar slides. Long-term interest rates rise. The Congressional Budget

Office issues a warning about U.S. fiscal sustainability. The International Monetary Fund comes out with a similar report. Long-term interest rates rise some more. Inflation picks up owing to higher import prices, which is due to the weaker dollar. Long-term interest rates move into the double-digit range. The stock market tanks. The Federal Reserve prints money to lower rates, but this raises long-term rates even further. The economy moves into recession. Deficits hit 7 percent of GDP. Inflation hits double digits. The government cuts taxes in a desperate attempt to stimulate economic activity. Japan and the EU look shaky. And we're off to the races.

6

Changing Course

They who have been bred in the school of politics fail now and always to face the facts. Their measures are half measures and make-shifts, merely. They put off the day of settlement indefinitely, and meanwhile, the debt accumulates.
—Henry David Thoreau, "Slavery in Massachusetts"

Fixing Coordinates

It's far too late to escape the coming generational storm, but there's still time to get out of its direct path and avoid the full brunt of its impact. Doing so will require major sacrifices, real statesmanship, and new ideas. But first it requires convincing the country that we're facing a grave economic danger. Absent that consensus, even the best reform plan will end in a stalemate, with the Republicans pushing in one direction and the Democrats pushing in the other.

The previous chapters were relentless in clarifying our current position. We're $51 trillion in the red and making matters worse by cutting taxes, expanding Medicare benefits, and growing the government sector, particularly the military, much faster than the economy as a whole. Reversing the recent Bush II income tax cuts, eliminating the new Medicare drug benefit, or cutting back on military spending are political nonstarters. The only real hope lies in reforming the Social Security and Medicare programs. According to The Treasury Papers, the combined unfunded liabilities of these two programs account for almost all of our now $51 trillion red hole.

To be fair to these programs, we need to repeat the message of chapter 3 that the measurement of the liabilities of any particular government program is economically arbitrary. Use different fiscal labels, and the two programs can be said to account for a much smaller, and even negative, portion of the $51 trillion shortfall. Stated differently, the measure of the fiscal gap (the $51 trillion) is independent of the choice of labels, but its breakdown as between different programs is not.

If that's the case, why pick on these programs? If you rule out raising taxes (meaning what the government calls "taxes") and limiting discretionary government spending, the only other option available, short of printing money and increasing our national debt, is cutting transfer payments (actually, what the government calls "transfer payments"). Social Security and Medicare are the federal government's largest transfer programs. Moreover, reforming both of these programs is long overdue, notwithstanding their tremendous success over the years in assisting the elderly.

In this chapter we provide simple, sensible, and responsible plans to reform both Social Security and Medicare. But before presenting each proposal, we do two things. We lay out the case for structural reform and describe the proposals being advanced by the two political parties.

This *Is* Your Father's Oldsmobile

Social Security is almost seventy years old. It was established in 1935, smack dab in the middle of the Great Depression. Things were a lot different then. Life expectancy was a lot lower than it is today. Gross domestic product was down by a quarter. One in four workers was unemployed. Half of all Americans were living in poverty. A third of the banks were insolvent. Prices were falling. Stockbrokers were jumping out of windows. Millions of Americans were visiting soup kitchens. And nobody was happy.

The elderly were in the worst shape of all. Their financial wealth was wiped out by the collapse of the financial markets and by widespread business failures. They had no pensions to rely on and were too old to work. Letting them starve was not an option, so President Franklin Roosevelt proposed and the Congress enacted the Social Security System.

The program's primary objective—securing the economic welfare of the elderly—was and remains a perfectly laudable goal. But the program had very serious design flaws from the start, and we're not talking here just about its pay-as-you-go method of finance. These problems have been exacerbated over the years through an incredible array of patchwork provisions and piecemeal reforms. This process has left us with a system that is so complicated that only one or two human beings on earth fully understand its details.

The *Social Security Handbook*, which is supposed to clarify Social Security's 2,528 separate rules for paying taxes and receiving benefits, runs for hundreds of pages. But talk to the benefit experts at Social Security's administrative offices in Baltimore, and they'll just shake their heads about the accuracy of that document. For certain questions, there may be only one old hand still knocking about Social Security's massive administrative building who knows the answer.

One might expect or hope that the actual computer code determining benefits would clarify what's what. But that code is written in an ancient computer language that today's geeks no longer speak. It's also apparently *very* poorly documented, and the original programmers are long gone.

The net result is that we have a black box handing out Social Security benefits with very limited human oversight. A few years back, the box was discovered to be making a big error in calculating survivor benefits. From one day to the next, the government realized it had underpaid beneficiaries (many of whom had already died) over a billion dollars— big change in anyone's accounting.

The main concern, however, with Social Security's inscrutable black box is not that it makes mistakes. The big problem is that it systematically provides benefits to certain individuals who neither need nor deserve this support, that it generates major work disincentives, that it leaves workers with little idea of what they are getting in exchange for their tax contributions, and that it cannot guarantee the payment of the benefits it calculates. Fixing these equity, incentive, information, and risk problems as well as securing Social Security's finances are objectives that any reasonable person should support.

When it comes to Social Security, however, our politicians aren't particularly reasonable. For their part, the Republicans have a sure-fire way to repair Social Security: *eliminate it*. Their idea has two parts. First, let workers direct a portion of their payroll tax contributions to a private account, which they would then be free to invest as they like in our tried, but not necessarily true, financial market. Second, phase out benefits provided by the old system. The end result is that Social Security benefits would be replaced by withdrawals of income and principal from private accounts.

This "privatization" of Social Security wouldn't affect current retirees or, presumably, workers now in their early 60s who are just about to retire. But most of the boomers and those coming after them would all see their Social Security benefits cut. The precise phase-out formula is not something the Republicans like to talk about too loudly, but one prominent plan that emerged from President Bush's Commission on Social Security Reform entails switching from wage- to price-indexing Social Security benefits.[1] This modification would keep the average level of benefits per beneficiary fixed in today's dollars. Consequently, average Social Security benefits wouldn't keep pace with the economy-wide growth in real wages, so over time, Social Security retirement benefits would replace a smaller and smaller share of preretirement earnings. Today's teenagers, for example, would pay the same Social Security payroll taxes throughout their working lives, but their retirement benefits would be only 40 percent of what they would receive under the current system. That's a pretty nasty hit.

Retiring Social Security in this manner may seem inconceivable, but, as mentioned, the Brits have been doing precisely this for years thanks to Margaret Thatcher. Her decision in the mid-1980s to price-index government pensions, coupled with the country's long-standing practice of keeping a lid on the state-run health care system, explains why the UK is in the best long-term fiscal shape of any major EU nation. This may also explain why the UK has so far declined to adopt the euro. Doing so would entail adopting the inevitable inflationary "solutions" of current euro participants, which are in much worse long-term fiscal shape.

In contrast to their Republican colleagues, Democratic politicians view Social Security's potential "privatization" with abject horror. Social Security is, after all, their proudest domestic achievement. The idea that anyone would dare discuss Social Security's demise is, by itself, a huge shock. After all, the Democrats have spent over fifty years siccing the

AARP's 35 million elderly voters on anyone who even breathed the words "Social Security reform." This is why Social Security is called the *third rail* of politics. Touch it, and you get a one-way ticket out of Washington.

Mind you, the Democrats are well aware of Social Security's structural problems. They've thought about them carefully for a very long time and have come up with the perfect solution: *do nothing*. Their rationale is that opening the door—even an inch—to any type of reform would give their opponents a chance to toss out the baby with the bathwater.

Both the Republicans and Democrats do, however, agree on one thing: how to deal with Social Security's long-term insolvency. Their answer is simple—*play the stock market*. The Democrats want to invest Social Security's relatively small trust fund in the market and use the high returns they project to pay a large share of the baby boomers' benefits.

The Republican plan leverages the stock market in a much more subtle manner. The Republicans assume that workers will not only invest their new accounts in the stock market, but they'll also make such a killing that they won't notice that the government has wiped out most of the benefits they have accrued under the old system. As for paying off current and near-term retirees, the Republicans claim that the somewhat reduced payroll taxes that workers will continue paying under their scheme can be maintained indefinitely and will cover, in present value, the costs of winding down (via price indexing) the old system.[2]

The really cool thing about proposing the stock market as a miracle cure is that neither party has to ask any voter to make any sacrifice to deal with our $51 trillion nightmare.

But there's one catch to this brilliant solution. *The stock market is extremely risky.* Any adult who's been awake over the last decade can tell you that. Between January 1, 1997, and January 1, 2000, the value of the S&P 500 increased by 97 percent! Over the next three years, it fell by 38 percent!

If the stock market were a sure bet, the government wouldn't need to waste time with either the Republican or Democratic plan to "save" Social Security. Uncle Sam could simply borrow huge sums of money and invest it in the stock market. The much higher return in the stock market would more than cover the interest payments needed to service this debt.

And the government would turn a huge profit that could be used not only to pay the baby boomers their old age benefits, but also to buy up everything on the planet.

How can the Democrats and Republicans get away with recommending what amounts to a leveraged buyout of the American economy? The answer is through an accounting practice that would make the former managers of Enron blush.

Here's what Republicans and Democrats do in "costing out" their plans. They assume, in effect, that if you take a dollar in cash and use it to buy stock, you immediately end up holding assets worth more than a dollar. That's nonsense. Stocks have a market value, and if you buy a dollar's worth of stocks, you have an asset worth $1.00, not $1.10 or $1.50 or, indeed, anything more than $1.00.

But the Democrats and Republicans don't use market prices to value the holdings of stocks in their Social Security reform plans. Instead, they discount the expected future income stream from stocks at the government's long-term bond rate. This means that they are discounting a highly risky income stream using a safe rate of return; that is, they are failing to adjust for risk in their choice of the discount rate.

This procedure leads to $1 of stock being valued at roughly $3. Imagine a corporate annual report overstating the value of company assets by a factor of three, and you can see what our leaders are up to.

Of course, the Democrats and Republicans don't actually make these bogus calculations on their own. They force the Social Security Administration to do it for them, knowing that the public trusts the professionals in this organization to tell them the truth. Little does the public know that these professionals are being forced to engage in accounting practices far more fraudulent than anything Arthur Andersen ever did for Enron.

Making Sausage

In addition to being unbelievably complex and providing workers with little idea of the return they'll receive on their payroll tax contributions, Social Security has structural flaws that make the system highly inequitable and inefficient. The most serious of these problems involve dependent and survivor benefit provisions, which provide nonworking spouses retirement and survivor benefits completely for free, based on the earnings histories of their working partners. Retirement and survivor benefits are also available to working spouses if they aren't eligible to collect higher benefits based on their own earnings records.

To get the picture, consider two married couples: Bob and Karen Whitney and Charlie and Lauren Cochran. All four spouses are age 35, and all four started work right after college. Each year Bob and Charlie, who are both car salesmen, earn $75,000 and pay $9,300 in Social Security payroll taxes (including the employer contribution). Karen works a grueling nighttime shift as a nurse's aide in a nursing home, earning $20,000, on which she pays $2,480 (including the employer contribution) in Social Security payroll taxes. Although Lauren could earn as much as Karen, she chooses not to work. Instead, she spends her days playing golf at the public course.

Here's a question for you. Compared with Lauren, how much additional Social Security benefits will Karen receive for the $2,480 she pays into Social Security year after year for all forty-four years of her working life? Think this over carefully.

Ready for the answer? It's zip, nada, rien, gar nichts, not one red penny. Why's that? Because while Bob is alive, Karen will be able to collect more retirement benefits as a dependent spouse than she'll be able to collect based on her own history of contributions (covered earnings). This dependent retirement benefit is half of the retirement benefit Bob receives. And when Bob dies, Karen will be able to collect as a survivor 100 percent of the benefit that Bob would otherwise have enjoyed.[3]

Lauren is a bit lazy, but she's no dummy. In deciding not to work, she realized that there wasn't much economic gain to taking a job because of all the extra taxes she'd have to pay. She understood that the 12.4 percent combined employer-employee Social Security "contribution" is a tax, pure and simple. She also realized that the 2.9 percent combined employer-employee Medicare "contribution" represents another tax, pure and simple, because she'll receive Medicare benefits regardless of whether she ever contributes to that system.

When Lauren thought about working, she added the 15.3 percent pure FICA tax to the additional federal and state income taxes she'd have to pay for the pleasure of working eight hours a day, seven days a week, fifty weeks a year, for forty-four years and realized that the extra $20,000 per year would raise her family's annual living standard by less than $7,000. Meanwhile, poor Karen is cleaning bedpans at three o'clock in the morning under the illusion that all those FICA payments that show up on her monthly paycheck are going to raise her Social Security and Medicare benefits.

Lauren was able to play the system because of special insider information: her golfing partners told her it didn't pay to work. For Karen to get things right, she'd have to spend a fair amount of time learning Social Security's benefit provisions and then unlearning them. We say "unlearning" for the following reason. Social Security goes to considerable lengths to persuade workers like Karen that they actually are getting something back in return for their payroll taxes when nothing could be further from the truth. What Social Security does is to describe the benefits Karen receives as partly coming from her own contributions and partly coming from Bob's contributions. The reality, however, is that if Karen were to contribute nothing, she'd get precisely the same benefit. Stated differently, every dollar of benefit Karen earns based on her own contributions reduces by a full dollar the benefits she receives based on Bob's contributions, so the benefits she earns based on her own contributions are, in effect, subject to a 100 percent marginal tax.

In addition to the clear equity and information problems raised by this example, there is huge economic inefficiency. Lauren ends up wasting her life beating up on little white balls when she could be contributing to society. When Karen and Lauren meet at the local Dunkin Donuts at 7:30 A.M. every morning—with Karen heading to bed and Lauren heading to the first tee—neither is very happy. Karen is exhausted and depressed, and Lauren is fully rested and depressed. If Karen could earn more on an after-tax basis for all her effort, she could afford to take it a bit easier. And if Lauren could earn more after taxes, she'd go to work and get some real fulfillment out of life.

We picked this example to put Social Security's treatment of secondary earners into the starkest relief. Were Karen to earn $30,000 rather than $20,000, her Social Security contributions wouldn't constitute a 100 percent tax when it comes to retirement benefits, but rather a 72 percent tax; by working she'd end up with 28 percent higher retirement benefits than Lauren. On the other hand, her contributions would still represent a 100 percent tax when it comes to survivor benefits: she'd end up with the same survivor benefits as Lauren.

In pointing up these problems in the way Social Security provides survivor and retirement benefits to secondary earners, we don't mean to suggest that secondary earners don't need protection. What we do mean is that this protection is very poorly structured and is being provided at a potentially very large efficiency cost.

Many secondary earners are also economically abused by Social Security when it comes to divorce. Let's return to Charlie and Lauren. So far, we've pretended that the two are happily married and planning to live together until they meet their maker, but in fact, Charlie and Lauren can't stand each other. Charlie keeps yelling at Lauren to get a job, and Lauren keeps screaming that it doesn't pay for her to do so and that she has a job—taking care of their home and cooking them meals. They've been having this argument with increasing vitriol for the past ten years, and to make matters worse, Charlie has been having an affair with Karen.

As we write, it's one day shy of Charlie's and Lauren's tenth wedding anniversary, and the two hate birds are sitting in Lauren's lawyer's office signing divorce papers. Lauren's lawyer is very bright. He just graduated from Boston University Law School, one of the finest law schools in the country. But he slept through the family law class that discussed Social Security benefits, so he missed the point that divorcees can collect dependent and survivor benefits based on their ex's earnings record *if and only if* their marriage lasts ten or more years. If the couple gets divorced even one day before ten years are up, the divorcees forgo all claims to benefits based on their former partner's pre- as well as postdivorce earnings history. So when Lauren signs those papers, she's signing away her claim to thousands of dollars of future benefits—benefits that can pay for lots of greens fees.

Most troubled couples approaching their tenth anniversary would get a lawyer smart enough to schedule the divorce signing a day or so after their anniversary or, if he's really cynical, on his clients' anniversary. But what about those people who can't wait ten years to get divorced. What about those who are married, say, seven years and can't take it a minute longer? Those people end up with no divorcee benefit protection whatsoever. If one spouse has been staying home caring for the kids, while the other has been working and establishing a Social Security earnings record, the house spouse will have nothing to show in terms of Social Security benefits for all the time he or she spent changing diapers, cleaning the house, buying groceries, chauffeuring the kids to hundreds of play dates, and making three square meals day in and day out for years.

Yet another equity problem with the existing Social Security System is that in paying out its benefits exclusively in the form of annuities (income streams that are paid for as long as the recipient lives), it discriminates against those with short life expectancies. Take today's 22-year-old black males. They can look forward to dying at age 70, a scant three years after they start receiving their normal retirement benefits. White 22-year-old males, on the other hand, can expect to live through age 76 and collect benefits for an additional six years. That's a huge difference. For 22-year-old females, the difference in life expectancy between whites and blacks is five rather than six years, but that's still enormous.

And speaking of inequality, consider the fact that men die a lot younger than do women, particularly when you factor in both sex and race. The difference in expected longevity between a 22-year-old white woman and a 22-year-old black man is eleven years. While the two may earn exactly the same amount each year and pay precisely the same Social Security payroll taxes, the white female can look forward to receiving benefits for fourteen years, while the black male can look forward to receiving benefits for only three years. Moreover, this discussion abstracts from income-related differences in life expectancy. Poor 22-year-old black men will live shorter lives, and rich 22-year-old white women will live longer lives, on average, than the typical members in their groups.

An important mitigating factor, however, is that Social Security provides its benefits on a progressive basis, so low-income workers with shorter life expectancies will be treated somewhat better by the system than high-income workers with longer life expectancies. Since minorities earn much less than whites, on average, this factor greatly reduces the degree to which the system discriminates against minorities.[4] Still, in fifty years, when the majority of America's workers are short-lived blacks and

Hispanics and the majority of America's elderly are long-lived whites, the majority "minority" workers may balk at supporting the majority "majority" retirees.

A final concern about the structure of the current Social Security system is that those who go to work relatively early in life receive no additional compensation for the fact that they pay their payroll taxes much sooner than those who go to work relatively late in life. The old saying "time is money" is nowhere more apt than when it comes to the timing of tax payments.

Paying the government, say, $1,000 right now is a lot different from paying it $1,000 in five years. If the payment is made now, the government can invest the money and end up, including accumulated interest, with more than $1,000 in five years. How much more? If the real (inflation-adjusted) return the government can earn on its investments is 3 percent, $1,000 received today will be worth $1,159 received in five years. Hence, the government would much prefer to receive $1,000 today than in five years. (Incidentally, one straightforward investment for the government to make if it receives the money today is simply to buy back $1,000 of government bonds held by the public. In five years it will have $1,159 less in outstanding debt than would otherwise be the case.)

Of course, the gain to the government of getting its payroll taxes up front is the loss to the worker of having to pay them early. The reason, to repeat, is that Social Security provides no interest credits for early tax payments. All else equal, the high school graduate who goes to work at age 19 and works for, say, forty years, is disadvantaged relative to the college graduate who goes to work at age 23 and also works for forty years. To understand the potential magnitude of this effect, let's assume that both workers initially earn $87,000, which is the 2003 maximum level of covered earnings, and that their earnings keep pace with inflation. Consequently, the two pay $10,788 in Social Security payroll taxes, measured in today's dollars, each year of their working lives.

Now if we accumulate at a 3 percent real interest rate the amount contributed by the high school graduate by the time he reaches his normal retirement age of 67 and do the same for the college graduate, the difference in their accumulated tax payments at age 67 is 12.5 percent or $119,877. Stated differently, were the high school graduate credited for paying her taxes early, Social Security would have to give her an additional $119,877 at retirement. That's almost a year and half's salary!

The icing on the cake when it comes to Social Security's poor treatment of early contributors is that the program completely ignores contributions made to the system prior to age 22 when it comes to calculating Social Security retirement benefits. Whether this matters when it comes to calculating these benefits depends on the length of the worker's career and whether her or his pre–age 22 earnings are particularly high. But the fact that contributions prior to age 22 are treated as irrelevant to the calculation of retirement benefits is a clear statement that the designers of this system had no regard for the time value of money.

To summarize, the current Social Security system has a host of serious efficiency, equity, and information problems. Like sausage, no one really wants to know how it's made. Were Social Security a minor program, we wouldn't need to worry that its ingredients are bad for our economic health. But the program is huge and about to get a whole lot bigger. After almost seven decades of adding pig snouts, horsehair, and chicken toes to the Angus ground beef that started out in our mixing bowl, it's time to change recipes for this meatloaf.

If It's Broke, Fix It!

Social Security has significant structural problems that would justify reforming the program even were its finances in great shape, but its finances are in horrible shape. Indeed, paying promised Social Security benefits through time requires roughly a 33 percent immediate and permanent Social Security payroll tax hike.

Recall that this financial assessment comes courtesy of the bowels of the 2003 Trustees Report of the Social Security Administration—specifically, the highly cryptic table (IV.B7) tucked deep inside the report. The table reports the present value of Social Security's fiscal gap—the difference between the present value of all its projected future benefit payments and the sum of all its projected future payroll tax receipts and the current value of the so-called Social Security Trust Fund. The projections underlying these present values aren't truncated at seventy-five years, so they indicate the true long-run costs and receipts of the program. Except for this one table, the Trustees Report focuses exclusively on the 75-year unfunded liability of the system. The reason is obvious: the long-run fiscal gap is *three times larger* than the seventy-five-year gap![5]

Clearly, financial reform of Social Security is imperative, and structural reform is long overdue. Combining the two reforms makes perfect sense. If the public is going to be asked to make a major sacrifice, it should also get a system that is equitable, efficient, and easily understood. Any reasonable reform of Social Security must satisfy the following five basic conditions.

1. Resolve the system's long-term financial problems
2. Fix the system's structural problems
3. Be more equitable and efficient than the system it replaces
4. Deliver income security for the elderly, survivors, and dependents
5. Be acceptable to both sides of the political aisle

The Personal Security System

We call our proposal the *personal security system—PSS* for short. We think that this is the system most Social Security experts would choose were we able to set up the system from scratch. The title should appeal to Republicans, but as you'll see, there are many social (dare we say socialistic) elements to this system. So if you're a Democrat, hang in there. Anyway, here's the plan in the following box. See what you think.

The first thing to notice is that the plan is short. Its eleven provisions fit on a postcard, which seems to be the attention span of most politicians. The second thing to see is that the plan shuts down, at the margin, the retirement or Old Age Insurance (OAI) portion of Social Security. Current retirees continue to receive their full OAI benefits, and current workers receive, *in retirement*, all the OAI benefits owed to them as of the date of the reform. But once the reform is implemented, the accrual of additional OAI benefits is history. This is what we mean by shutting down the system at the margin. We pay off what we owe, but that's it. We don't incur any further obligations.

The Personal Security System

1. The accrual of additional Social Security retirement benefits is eliminated.
2. Current retirees and current workers receive their accrued Social Security retirement benefits.
3. Social Security's Old Age Insurance (OAI) payroll tax is eliminated and replaced with equivalent compulsory contributions to PSS accounts.
4. A new federal retail sales tax is used to pay off the accrued retirement benefits owed under the old system.
5. Workers' PSS contributions are shared fifty-fifty with their spouses.
6. The government contributes to PSS accounts on behalf of disabled and unemployed.
7. The government matches PSS contributions on a progressive basis.
8. All PSS balances are invested in a single market-weighted global index fund of stocks, bonds, and real estate.
9. The government guarantees the real principle that workers contribute to their PSS accounts.
10. Between ages 57 and 67, workers' PSS balances are gradually sold off and transformed into inflation-protected pensions.
11. If a worker dies prior to age 67, any remaining PSS balances would be transferred to PSS accounts of the worker's heirs.

So what exactly would current workers receive from Social Security in retirement benefits in exchange for their past contributions to the system? They'd receive exactly what they'd get under the current system if the current system were maintained but they simply stopped working and hit the beach for the rest of their lives. In this case, they'd show up at retirement with zeros in their Social Security earnings records indicating they'd had no covered earnings since the time they hit the beach. Under our proposed reform, current workers would have zeros entered in their Social Security earnings records from the date of the reform onward. So in retirement, they'd receive the Social Security retirement benefits accrued as of the reform, but nothing more.[6]

For workers close to retirement, their accrued Social Security retirement benefits are very close to what they'd receive under the current system. But for today's young workers in their 20s and 30s, their accrued Social Security benefits are fairly small. This means that over time (actually, over about forty-five years), the aggregate amount of Social Security benefits that will need to be paid each year will decline to zero.

The next thing to see is that the plan doesn't mess with either survivor (SI) or disability (DI) benefits. It also leaves in place the payroll taxes needed to finance these two programs. Workers would continue to make SI and DI contributions, and they and their survivors would continue to receive precisely the same SI and DI benefits as under the current system.[7]

Provisions 3 and 4 in the plan deal with funding a new retirement saving system and paying off accrued OAI benefits over the next roughly forty-five years. Provision 3 eliminates the OAI payroll tax, but requires workers to contribute the money they'd otherwise pay in OAI taxes to PSS accounts. Provision 4 introduces a new federal retail sales tax to pay off OAI benefits during the transition. Since the total amount of OAI benefits needed to be paid would gradually decline to zero, this retail sales tax, which would start out at roughly 12 percent, would also phase out through time, although not to zero (as discussed shortly).

Before you start screaming that a sales tax is regressive and will hurt the poor, remember what we told you in chapter 3. Sales taxes are in part wealth taxes because when rich people spend their wealth to buy caviar, BMWs, yachts, and facelifts, they end up spending part of their wealth on taxes. Also, realize that the elderly poor who are living solely off of Social Security will be completely insulated from the effects of the retail sales tax. The reason is that when the tax raises consumer prices, the Social Security benefits of the poor and everyone else will be automatically adjusted for a simple reason: by law, Social Security benefits are indexed to inflation.

So what about the young and middle-aged poor? They'll have to pay the sales tax, but they will be spared having to pay the OAI payroll tax. If you're a diehard liberal and are worried we're pulling a fast one on the working poor, ask yourself whether you think a minimum wage worker would prefer to pay (A) 12.4 percent of her wages in Social Security payroll taxes now, with the prospect of that tax rate doubling through time, or (B) whether she'd prefer to pay a 12 percent sales tax now, with the sure knowledge that that the sales tax rate will decline through time to around 3 percent as the accrued retirement benefits owed by the old Social Security system are paid off and head to zero.

We figure you'll opt for B, particularly when you realize that the reason we can spare poor workers higher future taxes and, indeed, can lower the taxes they face through time, is that *today's and tomorrow's middle class and rich elderly will be shouldering a much bigger fiscal burden than is now the case.*

This is the really nice thing about a sales tax. Apart from the elderly poor, the tax hits everyone—old and young, and rich and poor. This is much different from the payroll tax that it would replace, which is paid only by young and middle-aged workers and is paid only up to a ceiling, which, as we write, is $87,000. Because of this ceiling, the nation's 2.1 million millionaires and 57,000 super-richies—those with more than $30 million in assets—pay a pittance of their annual incomes in OAI payroll taxes. But these people sure do know how to shop, and everything they buy, including playoff tickets, would be subject to the new federal retail sales tax.

Provisions 5 and 6 are designed to protect nonworking spouses, spouses who are secondary earners, the disabled, and the unemployed. The idea is that every American adult would have a PSS account. Married workers would have to split the contributions fifty-fifty with their spouses, so each would end up with an equal-sized PSS account. The government would contribute on behalf of the disabled and the unemployed, so these people too would end up with secure retirements. Thanks to provision 5, spouses who don't work and spouses who work but earn a lot less than their partner receive the same retirement income. In addition, divorced spouses walk away with their own accounts.

Provision 7 calls for the government to make matching contributions to PSS accounts on a progressive basis. The new retail sales tax would finance these matching contributions as well as cover contributions on behalf of the disabled and unemployed. That's why it would never fall all the way to zero. The current OAI system provides benefits on a progressive basis. The government's matching contributions would be structured to ensure the same degree of progressivity in the new PSS system as under the current OAI system.

Provisions 8 and 9 indicate that PSS account balances would be invested in the global financial market, but that the government would insure the downside of this investment: it would guarantee that workers never lose the principal that they invest in their accounts. The worst they could experience is a zero real rate of return. This means that all workers would hit retirement with account balances equal to at least the value of their past contributions adjusted for inflation.

A critical feature of our plan is the requirement that all account balances be invested in a single security—a global index fund of stocks, bonds, and real estate. Yes, we know that many Republican Congress members think workers should be able to invest personal account balances any way they'd like. And yes, we agree that the freedom to make a killing on the market or lose every penny you own is a cherished American right when it comes to private saving. But we aren't talking here about a private saving system. We're talking about replacing an outmoded, inequitable, and inefficient compulsory public saving system with an alternative compulsory private saving system, but one that's modern, equitable, and efficient. But just as with the existing OAI system, the entire raison d'être of the PSS will be to ensure that American workers have solid financial support in their old age.

Many readers may take issue with the proposed requirement that all PSS assets be invested identically in a market-weighted, global index fund. But consider the alternative. With complete investment discretion, Joe Sixpack and Sally Corona Light might make precisely the same contributions to their PSS accounts each year, but end up with vastly different living standards in retirement because Joe took his uncle's stock tips and lost his shirt and Sally selected a diversified portfolio that yielded a good return. On the other hand, were Joe to accidentally make a killing, Sally would feel she was an idiot to have played it safe. She'd also feel vaguely mistreated. After all, she'd made the same contributions as Joe, but he ended up living the life of Riley, and she ended up scrimping on her prescription drugs.

Government-mandated retirement income security means different things to different people, but it surely doesn't mean that Uncle Sam drives Joe and Sally over to the local casino, gives them the same amount of money, points to the slot machines, and says, "Good luck securing your retirement." No Democrat who deserves the name will ever agree to turning Social Security into a crap shoot. On the other hand, no Republican who deserves the name believes that Social Security should continue to be run as a Ponzi scheme or chain letter that steals from the young to give to the old, and then placates the young by promising to give them a share of the future loot.

Provisions 8 and 9 reconcile the minimum requirements of both political parties. The Republicans get a fully funded retirement saving system that's invested in the market. The Democrats get a system that is equitable, as they define equity, and that protects workers from the downsize risk of investing in volatile financial instruments.

One reason to include provision 8—investing all PSS balances in a single global index fund—is that our friends on Wall Street aren't going to like it one bit. They've been dreaming for years about the prospect of reaping huge fees, loads, and commissions from investing Social Security contributions for America's workers. Under our plan, our Wall Street buddies won't get their fat little hands on any of our money.[8] Instead, a single computer, situated in the Social Security Administration, would be programmed to buy and sell securities to ensure that the share of each security in the PSS global index fund always equals that security's share of the total value of the global financial market. The Social Security Administration would also take care of all the PSS paperwork, including sending workers annual reports about their account balances.

Are we being too restrictive in not letting workers have some choice and control over their portfolio allocations? We believe not. Economic theory indicates that all households should be highly diversified in their asset holdings. We are recommending the most diversified portfolio available. Giving workers the option to switch between different securities or even large classes of securities, like stocks and bonds, will lead them to try to time or play the market even were they permitted to make trades only once or twice a year. And the transactions costs of allowing such gambling will eat up too much of the available return.

By providing a lower limit of zero on the real return workers can earn, the proposal provides what amounts to portfolio insurance for the PSS accounts. We believe the cost to the government of providing this insurance will be very low. But its inclusion in the plan is imperative to raise the comfort level of those scarred and scared by the short-run volatility of financial markets.

What's the rationale for including foreign stocks and bonds in the PSS index fund? It's diversification. By investing abroad, the fund will lower the riskiness of the return of the PSS index without lowering its average return. What we have in mind here is that the fund would invest in all major internationally traded securities. We're not talking here about holding shares of the Almalty stock market. (Almalty is the capital of Kazakhstan.) What we're talking about is investing in the Amsterdam, Frankfurt, Hong Kong, London, Paris, Tokyo, and other major foreign stock and bond exchanges. Who would decide what constitutes the global index fund? We'd leave that decision to the Social Security trustees, who would ultimately be responsible for overseeing the new PSS system. In making that decision, they'd have to weigh the transactions costs of purchasing foreign securities against the diversification advantage. But the trustees' discretion would be very limited. They'd have to include in the global index fund all financial instruments marketed on all of the major stock and bond markets.

The plan's tenth provision involves the sale of each participant's account balances starting at age 57 and continuing each day for ten years until the participant reaches age 67. By liquidating PSS balances in this very gradual manner, there is much less risk of selling when the market is temporarily low. The sale would be organized by the Social Security trustees, and participants would receive inflation-projected pensions (annuities) starting at age 62 reflecting the proceeds of all account balances sold prior to age 62.[9] Each year between ages 62 and 67, the amount of annuities provided to the participant would be increased based on that year's sale of the participant's remaining holdings of the global index fund.

The trustees would provide the annuities to all members of an age cohort on equal terms given the cohort's life expectancy. In providing these annuities, the trustees would invest the proceeds from the sale of the participants' global index funds exclusively in long-term inflation-indexed government bonds. This will permit the annuities that are provided to incorporate a 2 to 3 percent real return in addition to the return due to the mortality rates of cohort members.

The final provision specifies that all nonannuitized PSS account balances are bequeathable. So if a participant dies at age 55, his spouse or designated heirs would inherit his entire account balance. If a participant dies at, say, age 63, her spouse or designated heirs will inherit her remaining account balances—the funds not yet annuitized.

So What's Not to Like?

Now that you've seen the plan, do you like it? We hope so, because it seems to us to be the only reform that could possibly make sense. If you haven't made up your mind, maybe our recapping the plan's key features will help.

The plan is progressive (it helps the poor). It protects spouses. It protects divorcees. It protects the disabled. It protects the unemployed. It protects minorities and others with early death rates. It provides everyone with the same return. It puts everyone in the market. It limits the downside risk of investing in the market. It minimizes transactions costs. It keeps investment bankers and insurance agents from getting their paws on our money and reducing our investment returns. It provides everyone with the same annuity deal. It limits the market risk of annuitizing one's assets. It ensures ongoing, inflation-indexed income for the elderly as long as they live. It achieves maximum portfolio diversification. It precludes huge Social Security payroll tax hikes. And it distributes the burden of paying off benefits owed by the old system fairly and squarely.

In short, it's a really great idea that everyone, even the politicians, seems to be willing to accept right up to the point where we mention the bit about paying off the Social Security benefits owed under the old system. This is where the politicians in particular start getting queasy. Here's their reaction:

Introducing a new tax is political suicide. What's to ensure the retail sales tax rate will actually decline through time? Can't the market yield on the fund cover the costs of the old system? How can workers afford both to pay the new tax and contribute to the new accounts?

Here's our response:

We're eliminating an old tax at the same time we introduce a new tax, so relax about this being a tax hike. The retail sales tax could be entered into the Constitution, for all we care, to make sure it's not used for extraneous purposes. No, the market yield on the fund is risky, so there is no guaranteed excess return on the market that can be used to pay transition costs. Workers who are already saving outside of Social Security in, say, a private account or through a 401(k) plan, can choose to reduce that other saving in response to the establishment of PSS accounts. And workers who aren't saving anything outside of Social Security need to do so, and the compulsory contributions to PSS accounts effectively compel that outcome.

Have we convinced you? If not, this may do the trick. Of the fiscal gap reported in The Treasury Papers, $7.2 trillion is attributable to Social Security's unfunded liability, again using the government's fiscal accounting labels. This figure includes the unfunded liabilities of the survivor and disability programs. Consequently, the PSS plan wouldn't reduce the fiscal gap by the full $7.2 trillion, but by more like $5 trillion. Still, that's a tenth of our problem, and every trillion dollars in this business counts for a lot.

Whether we've sold you on the PSS plan or not, it's now time to rescue Medicare and then Medicaid (medical assistance to the poor). Repairing those programs is absolutely imperative. They are both runaway freight trains that on their own can fully bankrupt the country.

Diagnosing Medicare

According to The Treasury Papers, Medicare has a $43.6 trillion unfunded liability![10] This is over four-fifths of the $51 trillion fiscal gap.[11] The reason the Medicare liability is roughly six times larger than Social Security's is not due to major differences in the present values of their projected future benefit payments. Medicare's projected benefits are larger than those of Social Security, but by only one-fifth. The big difference is that the 12.4 percent Social Security payroll tax is much larger than the 2.9 percent Medicare tax. In the Treasury Papers' fiscal gap accounting, Medicare is allocated none of the general revenue finance used to finance a good chunk of its benefits.

Whether or not you like this measure of Medicare's fiscal gap, here are three options to come up with $37.6 trillion and eliminate it. First, we could raise federal income taxes, immediately and permanently, by 57 percent. Second, we could raise payroll taxes, immediately and permanently, by 79 percent. Third, we could immediately cut the current level of real Medicare benefits by 83 percent and let benefits grow at their projected rate thereafter.

None of these seems too attractive, and none seems likely to be legislated. So what about simply reducing the growth rate of Medicare benefits? That way, no one loses anything he or she currently has. This does seem like the most attractive alternative, particularly because Medicare benefits per beneficiary are projected to grow much faster than real wages.

Recall that Social Security benefits are wage indexed, so the benefits per beneficiary grow at exactly the same rate as real wages. In the case of Medicare, we're essentially talking about a system in which benefits are effectively super-wage-indexed or over-waged-indexed or uber-wage-indexed or however you'd like to say it. ("Growing like nuts" works too.) Historically, real Medicare benefits per beneficiary have grown three times faster than real wages![12]

The reason for the excessive growth is that Medicare basically pays for whatever medical bills the elderly incur. We say "basically" because there are deductible and copayments, but for many of the elderly, these out-of-pocket costs are covered by supplementary insurance policies that they've purchased. Consequently, we have a system in which millions of old people can receive as much medical care as they'd like without having to pay a penny at the margin.

Imagine telling the elderly they could go to any restaurant they'd like and send Uncle Sam the bill. They'd quickly learn that eating out is the ticket. Then they'd learn that eating in the most expensive restaurants is the way to go. Then they'd learn that having the most expensive restaurants deliver breakfast, lunch, dinner, and snacks to their homes makes good sense. Then the restaurants would learn that the finer the meals they prepare, the more customers they'd get regardless of what they charge. Overnight, the fast food restaurants that decorate most of Florida would turn into gourmet vendors of foie gras and champagne.

This is, of course, a bit of an exaggeration when it comes to Medicare. For most of the elderly, seeing the doctor isn't the greatest fun in the world. And, right now, Medicare doesn't cover prescription drugs, forcing many poor elderly to choose between buying pills or buying food.

But if you have to see a doctor and the doctor's costs are covered by Medicare, why not see the best? Better yet, why not seek several expert opinions? And why not have the latest and most expensive medical tests preformed? And why not encourage the medical equipment makers to come up with better and more expensive devices? And why not ask the government to pump billions into medical research to produce new procedures, tests, and therapies for you and your fellow oldsters to consume?

Here's the Beef

Now that you see the problems with controlling Medicare expenditures as the system is currently structured, your next question is most likely to be, "How much money can be saved by limiting excessive Medicare growth?" The quick answer is "a lot," but before we give you some hard numbers, we need to remind you of one unpleasant fact.

The Treasury Papers *already* assume a much slower growth rate of benefits per beneficiary than the historical rate leads us to believe will be the actual case. The assumed growth rate of Medicare benefits per beneficiary is only 1 percentage point, not the historical 2.7 percentage points, above the assumed growth rate of real wages. This assumption is incredibly optimistic given that there's been no fundamental structural change in Medicare to justify it. But it's the assumption being made by the actuaries at the Centers for Medicare and Medicaid Services (CMS), the federal agency that administers Medicare.

To see how important Medicare growth is to the overall fiscal gap, let's assume that CMS is off by just .5 percent in its projected growth rate; in other words, let's assume that Medicare benefits per beneficiary grow at a rate that is 1.5 percentage points above the growth rate of real wages. In this case, both the Medicare unfunded liability and the fiscal gap rise by $13.4 trillion, or by almost a third of the gap![13]

The good news here is that just as there is lots of money to be lost from excessive growth, there is lots of money to be saved by eliminating it. Indeed, allowing benefits per beneficiary to grow only with labor productivity would reduce the gap by about $17 trillion. If we add this to the $5 trillion we believe our PSS proposal would save, we're talking about eliminating about half of the fiscal gap. We'll discuss how to come up with the rest of the money, but for now, let's return to the critical question of how to limit Medicare's growth.

"Curing" Medicare

The U.S. government has tried for years to slow Medicare spending. They've tried a lot of different things. They've tried limiting how much they'd reimburse doctors and hospitals for particular procedures. They've tried giving doctors and hospitals fixed amounts of money based on the patient's medical problem. And they've tried to get Medicare participants to enroll in HMOs.

None of this worked very well for very long. In 2001, the last year with solid data, real Medicare benefits per beneficiary grew by a staggering 8 percent. Real wages in that year hardly grew at all. Since lowering real Medicare benefit levels once they've been increased is well nigh impossible, everyone now collecting Medicare and everyone who will ever collect Medicare got a big bonus for free in 2001. In particular, all 77 million baby boomers can expect 8 percent higher levels of real Medicare benefits when they retire.

The root of the Medicare growth problem is the program's fee-for-service structure. This stands for the fact that health care providers can charge Medicare a fee when they provide Medicare participants a service. One might think that capping the fees would limit total expenditure, but doctors and hospitals simply change the classifications of the services they provide to ones that provide higher fees. Or they schedule more visits. Or they order more expensive tests. Or they do all of the above.

Getting out from under the fee-for-service system is essential to resolving the excess Medicare growth problem and, when you think about it, saving the country. Congress was on to this solution when it tried to give the HMOs fixed sums to take Medicare beneficiaries off the government's hands. The notion was that HMOs would have every incentive to limit unnecessary medical care because, at the margin, they'd have to pay for it. The hope was that HMOs would introduce enough competition in the medical sector that Medicare would also save money on participants who remained in the traditional fee-for-service program.

Things didn't work out as expected. To repeat, the HMOs realized what Congress was up to and sought out the healthiest Medicare participants, and the least healthy Medicare participants realized that joining HMOs would mean facing restrictions on their access to care, so they stayed away. The result was that the government, which based its payments to the HMOs on the latest average Medicare costs per beneficiary, ended up overpaying many HMOs for taking on the relatively healthy and inexpensive Medicare beneficiaries who actually signed up.

In the case of HMOs that accidentally got stuck with a particularly sick and expensive bunch of Medicare beneficiaries, the solution was simple: ask the government for more money. The government refused, so these HMOs simply kicked their Medicare patients out the door and stopped taking in new ones. In recent years, half of the HMO programs established by private companies to enroll Medicare participants have closed. In so doing, they told 1.1 million Medicare beneficiaries to get lost.[14]

Having failed miserably to enlist the private sector to keep it from spending ever more on Medicare, the government is in the process of repeating its mistakes. But this time, the government plans to provide a larger bribe to HMOs to enroll Medicare recipients.

This is part of the new prescription drug benefit bill passed in November 2003 which, according to George Will, represents "the largest expansion of the welfare state since the Great Society 40 years ago."[15]

The Treasury Papers, anticipating the passage of a Medicare prescription drug benefit, included $6 trillion of present value costs for the new program. But according to Treasury Papers authors Gokhale and Smetters, the drug benefit actually legislated raises that figure to $12 trillion and the fiscal gap from $45 trillion to $51 trillion!

The only possible explanation for this lunacy is that the administration and members of Congress are themselves on drugs (the kind that will never be covered). Mind you, we agree 100 percent that the elderly need prescription drug insurance. And we think it should be a key part of Medicare. What we don't agree with is engaging in a major expansion of Medicare when the government is completely broke, when it has no idea how to pay for the Medicare program we've already got, and when the elderly who are to receive this insurance aren't being asked to pay the premiums necessary to cover its costs.

Getting Real

It's time to get real. There is no way that we can maintain Medicare's fee-for-service method of paying the elderly's health care bills. We can't maintain that program in full, and we can't maintain it in part. Doing so will always leave the system open to *adverse selection*, which is economist speak for gaming insurance systems. In this case, private insurers running HMOs will try to enroll the healthy oldsters and ditch the unhealthy ones.

But closing down the fee-for-service program (traditional Medicare) and simply handing each oldster a fixed sum of money, in the form of a voucher, with which he or she can purchase health insurance, is also no solution, again because of adverse selection. The insurance companies will force people who want to join their plans to reveal their health status and charge an arm and a leg to those with expensive-to-treat preexisting medical conditions. And if potential enrollees refuse to take a medical test or hand over their records, the insurance companies will assume the worst and charge them for the unknown risk they pose. Either way, those elderly who need health insurance coverage the most will be least able to afford it.

There is only one way out of this. Fortunately, it's amazingly simple. And the credit goes to Dr. John Goodman, the director of the National Center for Policy Analysis (NCPA).[16] Yes, we know that the NCPA is a conservative Republican think tank. But unlike most other politically oriented think tanks, this one actually thinks.

Goodman's idea is embedded in our proposed Medicare reform, which we dub the Medical Security System (MSS). In our proposal, which we summarize in the box on the next page, we close down the fee-for-service program and provide all Medicare participants with vouchers, but we make those vouchers *individual specific*. Participants would receive a voucher each year, say on October 1, to use to purchase insurance coverage for the following calendar year.

The size of the MSS voucher would be based on the participant's current medical condition. Hence, a perfectly healthy 67-year-old might get a voucher for $6,000, whereas an 85-year-old with pancreatic cancer might get a voucher for $100,000. Because those people in the worst

---

The Medical Security System

1. The traditional fee-for-service Medicare system is discontinued.
2. Medicare participants receive vouchers to purchase health insurance coverage.
3. Voucher amounts are participant specific and depend on the participant's health status.
4. New vouchers are issued annually, and participants can change plans annually.
5. Insurers/HMOs cannot deny coverage or delay service.
6. Insurers/HMOs must provide basic coverage, including prescription drug benefits.
7. Insurers/HMOs are free to market additional coverage at additional premiums.
8. Government sets voucher amounts to limit per capita MSS growth to that of real wages.

---

medical shape would have the largest vouchers, insurance carriers would be just as happy to have them as customers as their healthy contemporaries. Stated differently, the size of the voucher would be set to account for the higher expected cost of participants with preexisting medical conditions. So insurance companies could expect, on average, to make just as much money covering sick people as healthy ones.

From a cost perspective, the key thing to bear in mind is that the government can establish the values of the vouchers each year such that the total MSS expenditure on vouchers per beneficiary grows only as fast as real wages. As we've indicated, this could slice $20 trillion or so off the fiscal gap without any elderly recipient feeling he or she had been hurt. Indeed, they wouldn't be hurt. Their real medical benefits would continue to rise, but not as fast as in the past. Instead of worrying about the future collapse of the system, they could rest assured that the MSS would be able to pay its bills through time. Finally, they'd realize that no matter how sick they got in the future, they would always have a voucher big enough to purchase insurance coverage, and their insurance company would always want to provide them coverage.

The government would have to collect up-to-date records about participants' medical records. But given current computer technology, establishing such a system seems straightforward. And because the government would maintain this information, one could be confident that it would be kept confidential and provided only to insurance carriers at the request of the MSS participant. We realize this is easier said than done, but think about the confidentiality of income tax returns. We can't think of anyone, other than Richard Nixon, who has, in recent memory, illegally received access to an American's income tax return.

All insurance carriers that wished to enroll MSS participants would be required to provide a basic set of benefits, including prescription drug coverage. But the insurers would be free to sell additional coverage at premiums they would set for these additional services.

The Medicaid Bonus

After Social Security and Medicare, the largest federal government transfer program is Medicaid, which pays for medical care to the poor, including the poor elderly. In the case of the poor elderly, Medicaid pays for nursing home care and picks up bills left unpaid by Medicare.

Total Medicaid and Medicare expenditures are quite close in magnitude, but the federal government covers only about three-fifths of Medicaid's costs. The rest is paid by state governments under matching arrangements. These arrangements differ across states. In some states, like Mississippi, the federal government matches the state government's Medicaid expenditures on a roughly four-to-one basis. In others, the matching rate is one-to-one. The two programs have experienced and are projected to experience quite similar growth rates.

Like controlling long-term Social Security and Medicare spending, getting Medicaid spending under control is critically important. Medicaid is not only helping bankrupt the federal government, it's the key cause of the burgeoning red ink in most state government budgets. As in the current Medicare system, Medicaid is structured to ensure that the federal government has no ultimate control over the total amount it ends up paying for the program. In Medicaid's case, the states know that the Feds will reimburse them between fifty cents and eighty cents on every dollar they spend on health benefits for the poor. This artificially lowers the costs to the states of expanding Medicaid. In addition, in most states,

Medicaid is still run on a fee-for-service basis, leaving participants free to use as much of the available medical system's services as they'd like with no need to worry about the costs associated with that usage.

The nice thing about the MSS proposed to replace Medicare is that it could equally well be used to replace Medicaid. The federal government, in conjunction with the state governments, could simply provide each Medicaid participant with an individual-specific voucher each year that the participant would use to purchase health insurance.

Talk about killing two birds with one stone!

Getting to Yes

If you've kept count, you know that even if we implement the two proposals here advanced for Social Security and Medicare reform we'll still be left with a roughly $26 trillion fiscal gap. How do we intend to close that?

If we were selected to serve as president and vice president, we'd do three things. First, we'd extend our MSS reform to Medicaid. This would save another $10 trillion. Second, we'd eliminate all three of the Bush tax cuts. This would shave roughly $9 trillion off our $26 trillion target. The third thing we'd do is limit federal discretionary spending to 6 percent of GDP, which is the ratio of federal spending to GDP that prevailed when Bush the Second took office. Since this spending is now running at 7.4 percent of GDP, we could save another $8 trillion in present value through this channel. These three steps would more than cover the remaining $26 trillion fiscal gap.

So, yes, there *is* a way out of the morass. It involves fundamental reforms of Social Security, Medicare, and Medicaid; the enactment of a new retail sales tax; the elimination of the unaffordable tax cuts; and restraining discretionary spending. None of these steps will be easy, but each is essential if we hope to preserve the American dream for our children, grandchildren, and generations to come.

Unfortunately, knowing our political system, there is every reason to believe that our politicians are going to miss this opportunity to save our ship of state. In this case, it's critical that we look out for ourselves and our own families. So don your life jacket and follow us to chapter 7!

7

Grab Your Life Jacket

The best things in life are free, but sooner or later the government will find a way to tax them.

—Anonymous

Did You Read Your Warning Letter?

If you work and are 25 or older, the Social Security Administration sends you a letter once a year. It's called your "earnings statement." In addition to showing your earnings record, the letter estimates what you will receive in benefits when you retire. It provides a figure for early retirement at age 62, another if you retire at your "full" retirement age of 65 to 67, depending on your year of birth, and still another if you delay your retirement to age 70.

Most people skip the introductory letter and go straight to the benefit estimates on page 2 or their earnings record on page 3. That's too bad because they miss a tough and explicit warning about possible future benefit cuts. Here's how the most recent letter, signed by Social Security commissioner Jo Anne B. Barnhart, reads:

About Social Security's future . . .
Social Security is a compact between generations. For more than 60 years, America has kept the promise of security for its workers and their families. But now, the Social Security system is facing serious future financial problems, and action is needed soon to make sure that the system is sound when today's younger workers are ready for retirement. Today there are almost 36 million Americans age 65 or older. Their Social Security retirement benefits are funded by today's workers and their employers who jointly pay Social Security Taxes—just as the money they paid into Social Security was used to pay benefits to those who retired before them. Unless action is taken soon to strengthen Social Security, in just 15

years we will begin paying more in benefits than we collect in taxes. Without changes, by 2042 the Social Security Trust Fund will be exhausted. By then, the number of Americans 65 or older is expected to have doubled. There won't be enough young people working to pay all of the benefits owed to those who are retiring. At that point, there will be enough money to pay only about 73 cents for each dollar of scheduled benefits. We will need to resolve these issues soon to make sure Social Security continues to provide a foundation of protection for future generations as it has done in the past."[1]

This is not a warning from the Cato Institute, the Washington, D.C.–based libertarian think tank that has been critical of Social Security for decades. Nor is it a message from the Heritage Foundation, the National Taxpayers Union, or any number of conservative organizations that have devoted much of their research to the goal of privatizing (read eliminating) Social Security.

This is a message from Social Security—the government organization that mails the checks. They are telling us that the benefits promised could be cut in the future because there won't be enough money to pay them.

They are telling us, loud and clear: *this is not a drill.*

What can we do to protect ourselves, especially if no corrective action is taken?

In the sections that follow, we worry with you about the likelihood and impact of higher taxes, rising inflation, and benefit cuts. We also provide some commonsense financial advice on how to protect yourself from what's coming both here and in the following chapter.

Who Can't You Trust?

Perhaps the real future of Social Security and Medicare is in Area 51, the reputed Roswell, New Mexico, location where our government "hid the truth" about alien visitors. When Third Millennium, a nonprofit group devoted to generational equity, did a survey of young workers in 1994, they found that more young people believed in flying saucers than believed they would receive Social Security benefits.[2]

In fact, the truth isn't quite so harsh.

What all of us will have to deal with is a future of political weasel wording that will take obfuscation to new levels. While politicians of both persuasions continue pledging to "save" Social Security, they are doing it in a very uneven way. For the past thirty years, members of both parties have worked hard to secure the benefits of *current* retirees. What they don't tell you is that they secure today's benefits by reducing the benefits of *future* retirees. All of this can be, and has been, shown using generational accounting. Witness earlier chapters in this book.

It's also possible, however, to see how the coin is being clipped by more conventional means—by taking existing legislation and calculating how it will cause future benefits to be drastically reduced.

Not *may*, mind you, *will*. Remember, we're talking about *existing* legislation. This is not speculation.

Economist Alicia Munnell, for instance, calculates three certain ways that today's 30-somethings will get a worse deal than current retirees:[3]

• The extension of the age for full retirement
• The rising cost of Medicare Part B premiums
• The taxation of Social Security benefits

While these are all implicit reductions, she's also willing to make a reasonable guess at how much future benefits may be explicitly reduced to close the funding gap coming our way.

You should know that we haven't chosen Munnell from a random pool of economists. She is the director of the Center for Retirement Research at Boston College and she has been a student of Social Security and public retirement systems for her entire career as a researcher, including her stint as director of research at the Federal Reserve Bank of Boston. Using the same "replacement rate" measure that the Social Security trustees use, Munnell estimates that while today's midrange earner can expect Social Security benefits to replace 41.2 percent of her earning power, current legislation will reduce the replacement rate to 30.5 percent by 2030. That's a 26 percent de facto cut in retirement benefits. Table 7.1 shows her estimates for retirement at ages 65 and 62.

Here's how the pieces fit together:

The Rising Retirement Age for Full Retirement Benefits
The age for collecting full retirement benefits started to increase in 2000. The traditional 65 years will slowly rise to 67 by 2022. This may seem minor, but it amounts to a benefits cut for anyone who retires earlier

Table 7.1
Social Security: As certain as a flying saucer—but it won't go as far

Development	Income replacement rate in 2030	
	Age 65	Age 62
Current rate, unadjusted for retirement age change	41.2%	33.0%
After retirement age change	36.5	29.2
After Medicare Part B Premium	33.2	25.9*
After personal income tax	30.5	23.7
After 10 percent benefit cut to eliminate financing gap	26.9	20.8

Source: Alicia Munnell, Center for Retirement Research, Boston College.
Note: Figures show estimated Social Security benefits as a percentage of pre-retirement earned income for a medium-income worker.
*Medicare eligibility begins at age 65.

than the new full retirement age. Currently, about 40 percent of all workers retire by age 62. About 70 percent retire by age 65.

How big will the cut be?

According to Social Security Administration figures cited by Munnell, a low-wage earner who retires at the traditional age of 65 will see benefits decline from 55.5 percent of earned income to 49.1 percent in 2030. A maximum earner will see the replacement rate fall from 27.3 percent to 24.0 percent.

Rapid Growth of Medicare Part B Insurance Premiums

At age 65, retirees are eligible for Medicare health insurance. The premium for Medicare Part B, the insurance that covers doctor bills and other services, is automatically deducted from retirement benefits. Over the past ten years, Part B premiums rose at a slower rate than retirement benefits.

In the future, the monthly insurance premium is expected to rise much faster than the monthly retirement benefit. In 2003, for instance, the cost of the Medicare insurance premium rose 12.4 percent—*four times faster* than the retirement benefit. A person who retired at age 65 in 2000 paid about 6 percent of his or her retirement benefits for the insurance premium. In 2020, when the same person is 85, the insurance premium will take 10.6 percent of retirement benefits. Similarly, a person retiring in 2030 can expect Medicare premiums to absorb 9.1 percent of their benefits at age 65—but 13.6 percent twenty years later.

The Taxation of Benefits

Today, about 20 percent of retirees pay some income taxes on their Social Security benefits. The income thresholds for taxing the benefits, however, aren't indexed. As a consequence, even middle-income workers are likely to pay taxes on future benefits. "A 15 percent personal income tax on half of the benefits will reduce replacement rates by another 7.5 percent compared to today," Munnell observes.

Sadly, the reductions probably won't stop there. Examining Social Security's seventy-five-year financing shortfall, she assumes retirees will pay half the cost of putting the system in balance. She estimates an additional 10 percent benefit cut in the future. That would take the replacement rate for a medium income worker down to 26.9 percent—*a 35 percent reduction in benefits from today.*

Notice there has been no mention of a corresponding reduction in taxes.

Of course, that last reduction is a speculative number. There is a long list of ways the system could be "adjusted" to make the numbers work. The payroll tax could be increased. The retirement age could be raised again. *All* benefits could be subject to income taxes. Eligibility for retirement benefits could be means tested. Whatever the route chosen, only one thing is certain. The changes will be well oiled and slippery. Members of both parties will still be swearing they have "saved" Social Security when its recipients eat more cat food than the nation's cats.

Something You Can Count On—Death and Higher Taxes

In America, taxes are changed constantly. They are reduced. They are reformed. They are indexed. They are tweaked. They are manipulated to provide incentives for one thing and disincentives for another. They are used to encourage our saving. They are used to subsidize home ownership and to underwrite long-term care. Hardly a year goes by without a piece of tax legislation. As it approaches law, it is touted, discussed, analyzed, blessed, and cursed.

Today, your estate tax will depend more on the year in which you die than on the size of your estate—if you have the luxury of an estate to worry over. Worse, the Jobs and Growth Tax Relief Reconciliation Act of 2003 made future tax rates about as uncertain as possible. The current law states that the tax cuts we enjoy in the next couple of years will be eliminated by the end of the decade. Of course, no one believes this to be Congress's true intent. Everyone believes these sunset provisions were included in the bill to make future deficits look artificially small. Still, the law says that rates will go back up.

Another key element of uncertainty involves the alternative minimum tax (AMT). Originally designed to make sure the rich didn't escape all their tax obligations through tax shelters and other loopholes, the AMT is indexed for neither inflation nor real income growth. So unless it is modified, much of the middle class will end up paying the AMT in short order. Again, everyone expects the AMT to be amended, but until that happens, no one can say for sure what taxes will prevail in the near term, let alone the long term.

In spite of this profound shiftiness, revenue collected by the federal government has been remarkably stable over a very long stretch of history. Don't trust us on this—check the figures for yourself by visiting the "Historical Tables" portion of *The Budget of the United States Government for Fiscal Year 2004*.[4] There, on pages 23 and 24, you'll find the receipts, outlays, and surplus or deficit of the U.S. government expressed as a percentage of our gross domestic product. While receipts climb steadily from 1930 to 1943, rising from 4.2 to 13.3 percent of GDP, they are remarkably stable from 1944 to the present.

How stable?

With the exception of 1949 and 1950, receipts vary in a range of less than 5 percentage points. They have ranged from a wartime high of 20.9 percent in 1944 to a post–Korean conflict low of 16.1 percent in 1959. If you want the statistics, government receipts averaged 18 percent during the fifty-eight years, with a standard deviation of only 1.27 percent.

That means government collections were between 16.7 and 19.3 percent of GDP two-thirds of the time. They exceeded 19.3 percent only in eight years. The years were 1944 and 1945 (World War II), 1969 (Vietnam), 1981 (major recession), and 1998 through 2001 (the bubble years of capital gains and stock options). During that period, the highest tax rate on high earners ranged from a low of 35 percent (the present) to a high of 94 percent (1944–1945). The payroll tax has ranged from a low of 1 percent in 1944 (employee) to a high of 7.65 percent (the present). Basically, our friends in Washington have been experimenting on us for a long time, but the total tax take has remained pretty stable. Indeed, it isn't difficult to start thinking of 20 percent of GDP as the practical limit on federal tax receipts. But 20 percent of GDP is miles below the level of taxation that we need to deal with what's coming.

In thinking about the need for future tax increases, we also have to realize that the revenue base won't be expanding in the future anything like it did in the past. In the 1960s, according to Department of Labor data, the labor force grew faster than the population. The same thing happened in the 1970s, the 1980s, and the 1990s. The primary driver for this forty-year surge was the flood of women into the workplace.

In 1960 men held two of every three jobs. By 2000 the sexes were near parity: men held 53 percent of the jobs and women 47 percent. During those forty years, the participation rate of men fell from 83 percent to 75 percent. The decline was easily offset by the participation rate for women. It rose from 38 percent to 60 percent.

Viewed as a competition for jobs, women won. In the half-century from 1950 to 2000, the labor force grew from 62.2 million to 140.9 million—an increase of 78.7 million, roughly the size of Germany's current population. The participation of women grew from 18.4 million to 65.6 million, an increase of 47.2 million. Women, in other words, won six positions while men landed only four.

Writer George Gilder, in his pre-telecosm period, was so worried about this phenomenon and its impact on the delicate psyches of American men that he wrote a book about it. *Sexual Suicide*, a title that makes one think of Woody Allen's preoccupation with sex and death, was published in 1973.[5] The dust jacket warns us of "the dangerous social, economic, and political effects of the so-called sexual revolution, particularly the programs of the women's liberation movement."

Priapic angst aside, the flood of women workers was about as good as it gets for government revenues. The number of workers—read taxpayers—rose faster than the population. Better still, since most of the new workers were women, they paid their full share in taxes but increased the long-term liabilities of government very little.

Why?

Simple. As we've seen, in the *Leave It to Beaver* notion of social structure used in the creation of Social Security, men weren't just the primary earners. They were the *only* earners. Women were scheduled to receive Social Security retirement benefits based on the earnings record of their husbands. Policy called for them to receive half the benefit of their husbands while the husband was living. After his death they would receive the larger of the two benefits—all without paying a cent in payroll taxes.

Then Rosie the Riveter joined the labor force. She earned less than her husband, but she paid full freight in payroll taxes. Her retirement benefits increased slightly over not working—at least while her spouse was alive and retired—but she paid the full rate for payroll taxes. Basically, *she paid for benefits she was already scheduled to receive.* It is difficult to imagine a more positive environment for government revenues.

Today, this trend is reversing completely.

In the first decade of the twenty-first century, the labor force will grow about as fast as the population. In the 2010s, 2020s, 2030s, and 2040s, the labor force will grow more slowly than the population. The boomers, always the bulge in the python, will be retiring. They will be leaving the workforce, making way for their children—of whom there are relatively few.

While the civilian labor force grew at a 1.6 percent annual rate from 1950 to 2000, it will grow at only 0.6 percent annually from 2000 to 2050. In population studies, that's a *major* shift.

So the natural flow of revenue will be down. The natural flow of expenses will be up. Examining and projecting the federal share of the economy over a 125-year period ending in 2075, the Congressional Budget Office found that Social Security, Medicare, and Medicaid combined cost 7.6 percent of GDP in 2000. They will *more than double* to 16.7 percent of GDP by 2050.[6]

Nor will it end there. By 2075 the combined cost of promises made long ago will hit 21.1 percent of GDP. If that figure grabs your attention, it should. Relative to GDP, it's higher than *all* government revenue collections in *any* past year. At the peak of World War II, 1944, the federal government collected a record 20.9 percent of GDP in taxes.

And what about the rest of government? You know, things like defense, government departments like Justice and Health and Human Services, and the cost of interest on the national debt?

Well, it all depends.

In fiscal 2000 our Social Security, Medicare, and Medicaid promises took 7.6 percent of GDP. All other government expenditures except interest took 8.5 percent of GDP. Interest took another 2.3 percent. That's a total of 18.4 percent compared to revenues of 20.8 percent. The combination meant a (rare) surplus of 2.4 percent. Three years later, the economy is in recession, we're in a war, and revenues have fallen to 17.1 percent of GDP. Expenditures have surged to 19.9 percent. So now we have a 3 percent of GDP deficit.

And what about the future? All we can be certain of, according to the Congressional Budget Office, is that government spending, driven almost entirely by Social Security–related promises, will rise dramatically. *The result will be fifty years of pressure to raise taxes.*

There is, of course, an alternative. Run big deficits. Borrow the necessary money from our generous friends all around the world. Speculating on exactly that assumption—that federal revenue collections would remain around 19 percent of GDP as expenditures rise, creating an ever-growing deficit—the Congressional Budget Office projected that federal *outlay*, as a percentage of GDP, would double by 2075. If we actually took that route (what a psychiatrist would call complete denial), net interest on the national debt as a percentage of GDP would exceed what we currently pay for Social Security, Medicare, and Medicaid combined sometime after 2060.[7]

How will it actually work out?

No one knows. We can only be certain that every year in the next seventy-five will be a year our government is looking for new revenue sources. Some of them will be called taxes. Many won't. Members of both parties will spend their time thinking about the urgent need to raise revenue. If you make any money and can fog a mirror, you'll be a candidate to pick up part of the bill.

Table 7.2
If you earn more than $27,682, you may be rich (only your congressman knows for sure)

Percentiles ranked by AGI	Adjusted gross income threshold on percentiles	Percentage of federal personal income tax paid
Top 1%	$313,469	37.42
Top 5%	128,336	56.47
Top 10%	92,144	67.33
Top 25%	55,225	84.01
Top 50%	27,682	96.09
Bottom 50%	<27,682	3.91

Source: "New IRS Data on Income Tax Shares Now Available: Tax Share of Top 1 Percent Climbs to 37.4 Percent," Joint Economic Committee, October 24, 2002.

"Not to worry," you say. "They'll go after the rich people."

There are two problems with that idea. First, everyone defines "rich" as someone who has more money than she does. This is convenient and natural. We all know that the only just and proper tax is one paid by someone else. When you look at the actual numbers, however, you encounter two awkward facts: people with more money than others are already paying most of the taxes. Worse, *you* probably look rich to the government. (Hard to believe, isn't it?)

Consider the reality of income taxes (table 7.2). In 2000, the bottom half of all taxpayers were those with adjusted gross incomes under $27,682.[8] Their share of the income tax bill was small, only 3.9 percent, and their average tax rate was also low, only 4.6 percent. They're not rich because they are in the bottom half of the income distribution.

But do you think people with incomes over $27,682 consider themselves rich? Somehow, we doubt it. "No," they'll say, "if you want to tax the rich people, tax the top half of the top half—the people in the top 25 percent."

They, however, earn incomes starting at $55,225, and most of them don't even know they were already in the top 25 percent, a group that pays 84 percent of all income taxes. They pay these taxes from the 67 percent of all income they earn, while paying at an average rate of 19.1

percent. "No," they'll say, "you're not really rich until you're in the top 10 percent of the population. Tax them!"

Those with incomes of $92,144 have a pretty good idea that they're doing better than most people. Their kitchen pantries, however, are strangely bereft of Beluga and few own any of the $8,000 watches advertised so persistently in the *New Yorker*. They're also highly aware that the top 10 percent pays 22.3 percent of income in taxes on average.

They point out a practical problem. While the top 10 percent collects 46 percent of the income, there is no way you can raise their taxes enough to collect the money needed. Remember, we're talking about taking another 20 percent of GDP.

"No," they'll say, "we can't carry this burden alone, this has got to be a very broad tax."

And so it will go, right up to the 99 percent of the earners who will point their fingers at the fat cats in the top 1 percent of the earnings distribution. Trust us, they will be nominated by acclaim. Unfortunately, they already pay 27.4 percent of their income in taxes on their 20.8 percent of all income. More important, even if government taxed it all away, it wouldn't be enough money. More important still, earners in the top 1 percent didn't get there by being less creative than their government. The income that appears at a 35 percent tax rate won't show up for a 90 percent tax rate.

When the future comes, Washington will discover that *everyone* is "rich." Our tax system will work to put people with very pedestrian incomes into fat cat tax brackets. Skeptics should consider the taxation of Social Security benefits, which has remained un-indexed to inflation since the early 1980s.

Realizing that major future tax hikes are virtually guaranteed has a way of concentrating the mind, particularly if one has lots of tax-deferred retirement accounts that are scheduled to be withdrawn *exactly when taxes are being raised*.

The 401(k) Tax Trap

Today's brain twister quiz: You have 75 cents in your pocket. A friendly person comes to you and asks if you would trade your 75 cents for his 54 cents. Should you do it?

If you answered yes, you're a devoted participant in a 401(k) plan.

Here's how the magic shrinkage happens. You're a well-paid employee approaching retirement. You're in the 25 percent tax bracket. You want to put as much aside for retirement as possible. Your government is encouraging you to do so—it recently raised the amount you can contribute. So you contribute the maximum amount allowed to your 401(k) and, if possible, to an IRA.

This means you put aside 75 cents of future purchasing power. (The $1 you put aside was taxable. If you had paid taxes and saved it in a taxable account you would have put aside 75 cents.)

The following year you retire. You and your spouse collect $25,400 in Social Security benefits. You'll take the other income you need from a combination of a corporate pension (remember those?) and your qualified plan accumulations.

No problem, right?

Wrong. While you can withdraw all the money you need, there is a good chance that some of it will, in effect, be taxed at rates approaching 50 percent. *The 75 cents of purchasing power you set aside only a few months earlier will become only 54 cents of purchasing power, all through the magic of qualified plans.*

This happens because every worker faces a barrier reef of added taxes. While Social Security benefits are tax free if you have little or no other income, the benefits become taxable as your income from other sources increases. Cross the reef—the fixed threshold of $34,000—and every $1,000 of outside income will cause $500 of Social Security benefits to be *added* to your taxable income. Instead of paying the expected $150 on that $1,000, you'll pay $150 plus an additional $75, for a total of $225. The extra $75 is the 15 percent tax on $500 of Social Security benefits that became taxable. Suddenly you are losing 22.5 percent of each dollar taken from your old 401(k) plan.

And that's just the start.

The burden gets stiffer when your marginal tax rate in retirement is 25 percent. At that income level, there is a good chance that $850 of Social Security income will become taxable for each additional $1,000 of other income. So the additional $1,000 of income will trigger $250 of normal income tax, plus an additional $212.50 on the $850 of Social

Security benefits. The total is $462.50. That's a marginal tax rate of 46.25 percent on each dollar taken from your retirement accounts (before the 2003 tax cut the burden was 50 percent).

Presto, some of the 75 cents of purchasing power you put aside last year has become only 54 cents of purchasing power! (Table 7.3 shows the federal income tax obligation and how it rises with other income.)

While couples with taxable incomes over $311,950 are currently taxed at our highest official tax rate of 35 percent, the provision for the taxation of Social Security benefits works to create a 46.25 percent tax rate for people with one-fourth the income—provided they are old enough to collect Social Security.

Before you start to cry for the retired, you should know that having a high marginal tax rate doesn't mean that your *absolute* tax bill is larger. A working couple with the same cash income would pay more in taxes, not counting payroll taxes, at each of the above levels of income. The difference—and it's a big one—is that the retirees pay at higher *marginal* rates for additional dollars of income that come from their tax-deferred retirement plans.

As a consequence, 85 cents of purchasing power while working can become 77.5 cents of purchasing power when it has been put through a qualified plan. At still higher levels of income, 75 cents of purchasing power while working becomes 54 cents of purchasing power—when it's put through a qualified plan.

This little bit of tax torture can be traced to the administration of Ronald Reagan. His budget director, David Stockman, contributed the diabolical part. He suggested that the income thresholds not be indexed. As a result, the tax on benefits bites at lower levels of real income every year.

Republicans, however, can't take all the credit. In 1991, during the Clinton administration, the second level of taxation was added. While the Republicans were satisfied with taxing up to 50 percent of Social Security benefits, the Democrats raised the bar and set the maximum at 85 percent. This tax is truly bipartisan.

This isn't the best way to encourage people to save for their retirements. In the conventional view, one of the benefits of qualified plans was that they allowed workers to protect income from taxation during

Table 7.3
Hitting the hump: How a retiree hits the 50 percent tax bracket

Other income	Federal income tax	Social Security taxable	Tax increase	Marginal rate	Total cash income	Net new cash	Cumulative net cash
$33,600	$3,424	$7,962	$278	27.8%	$59,016	0	0
34,600	3,701	8,812	277	27.7	60,016	$723	$723
35,600	3,979	9,662	278	27.8	61,016	722	1,445
36,600	4,256	10,512	277	27.7	62,016	723	2,168
37,600	4,534	11,362	278	27.8	63,016	722	2,890
38,600	4,811	12,212	277	27.7	64,016	723	3,613
39,600	5,089	13,062	278	27.8	65,016	722	4,335
40,600	5,366	13,912	277	27.7	66,016	723	5,058
41,600	5,644	14,762	278	27.8	67,016	722	5,780
42,600	5,921	15,612	277	27.7	68,016	723	6,503
43,600	6,199	16,462	278	27.8	69,016	722	7,225
44,600	6,533	17,312	334	33.4	70,016	666	7,891
45,600	7,033	18,162	500	50.0	71,016	500	8,391
46,600	7,532	19,012	499	49.9	72,016	501	8,892
47,600	8,032	19,862	500	50.0	73,016	500	9,392
48,600	8,531	20,712	499	49.9	74,016	501	9,893
49,600	9,031	21,562	500	50.0	75,016	500	10,393
50,600	9,314	21,604	283	28.3	76,016	717	11,110
51,600	9,584	21,604	270	27.0	77,016	730	11,840
52,600	9,854	21,604	270	27.0	78,016	730	12,570

Source: Authors' calculations using Intuit TurboTax 2002.
Note: Shows the calculated federal income taxes to be paid for each additional $1,000 over a worker's pension of $33,600 a year and Social Security benefits of $25,416 based on 2002 tax rates. It assumes the standard deduction is used because the net deductible expenses are less than the standard deduction.

their most highly taxed years and move it to their retirement years, when they would be taxed less. Instead, a $75,000 retirement income is taxed at higher rates than earned incomes over $300,000.

In fact, the higher tax rates have a truly perverse effect. While higher-income earners enjoy lifetime tax savings and a lifetime increase in consumption by using qualified plans, lower-income workers will pay more in lifetime taxes, and their lifetime consumption will be reduced. This happens because Social Security benefits and the taxes levied on those benefits are a smaller part of the retirement income for higher-income earners.

Here is what Kotlikoff found while exploring this issue with Jagadeesh Gokhale and Todd Neumann, both economists at the Federal Reserve Bank of Cleveland. A couple with earnings of $50,000 a year at age 25 and a 6 percent real return on their 401(k) contributions could expect to see their lifetime taxes increase by 1.10 percent while their lifetime spending was reduced by 0.39 percent—not exactly what you hope to accomplish by saving in a 401(k). If the taxation of Social Security benefits was eliminated, however, the same couple would see their lifetime taxes reduced by 2.24 percent and their lifetime spending increased by 0.50 percent. The change is shown in table 7.4.

Examining different income levels and rates of real return of 4, 6, and 8 percent, they found that couples with incomes of $25,000 to $50,000 would experience *higher* lifetime taxation and *lower* lifetime spending,

Table 7.4
How much the 401(k) tax trap costs a young $50,000 a year couple

Condition	Taxes	Spending
Under current law	+1.10	−0.39
Eliminate SS benefit taxation	−2.24	+0.50

Source: Jagadeesh Gokhale, Laurence Kotlikoff, and Todd Neuman, Does Participating in a 401(k) Raise Your Lifetime Taxes?, 2002, (www.econ.bu.edu/kotlikoff).
Note: Estimated lifetime change in taxes and spending for a 25-year-old couple with starting income of $50,000, assuming a real return of 6 percent on contributions. A 6 percent real return is about what a 60/40 equity/fixed income portfolio earns.

Table 7.5
Percentage change in lifetime taxes and spending from 401(k) participation

Real return age 25 earnings	4 percent		6 percent		8 percent	
	Taxes	Spending	Taxes	Spending	Taxes	Spending
$25,000	−2.70	0.29	1.66	−0.36	9.37	−1.60
$50,000	−3.34	0.70	1.10	−0.39	6.38	−1.73
$100,000	−5.23	1.95	−2.40	0.89	0.84	−0.35
$150,000	−5.87	2.81	−2.44	1.15	0.38	−0.18
$200,000	−8.32	4.33	−5.19	2.62	−2.56	1.24
$250,000	−8.97	5.14	−6.55	3.58	−4.23	2.22
$300,000	−8.43	5.10	−6.71	3.84	−4.50	2.31

Source: Jagadeesh Gokhale, Laurence Kotlikoff, and Todd Neuman, Does Participating in a 401(k) Raise Your Lifetime Taxes?, 2002, www.econ .bu.edu/kotlikoff.
Note: A 6 percent real return is about what a 60/40 equity/fixed income portfolio would return; an 8 percent real return is somewhat higher than the real return on a 100 percent equity portfolio; and a 4 percent real return is a small premium over the 3 percent real return on a 100 percent fixed income portfolio.

largely owing to the taxation of Social Security benefits in retirement. (The figures are shown in table 7.5.)

As a practical matter, if your family income is $150,000 or under, current tax law gives completely perverse results for investing in qualified plans: the higher your return, the greater the increase in your taxes and the bigger the reduction in your lifetime spending! Without an employer match, 401(k) plans are a losing deal for most workers.

The bottom line here is very simple. For all the talk in Washington (from both parties) about encouraging people to save for their retirement, workers who saved diligently are already retiring into tax traps. They are paying at higher marginal rates in retirement than they paid while working—and this is happening *before* the pressure to increase taxes really hits.

We're going to need a Plan B, particularly when the driving power of inflation is considered.

Planning for Inflation

Governors of the Federal Reserve, our nation's central bank, seldom make speeches that shock or surprise people. It's not part of their job description. But on November 21, 2002, one governor, Ben S. Bernanke, gave a speech that shocked everyone who heard it.

Addressing the National Economists Club in Washington, D.C., he spoke about deflation and all that the Federal Reserve Bank could do to combat it if it occurred. He made it clear that deflation was not an option. Our government could, and would, print as much money as needed to keep our economy in mild inflation.

"Like gold," he said, "U.S. dollars have value only to the extent that they are strictly limited in supply. But the U.S. government has a technology, called a printing press (or, today, its electronic equivalent) that allows it to produce as many U.S. dollars as it wishes at essentially no cost. By increasing the number of U.S. dollars in circulation, or even by credibly threatening to do so, the U.S. government can also reduce the value of a dollar in terms of goods and services, which is equivalent to raising the prices in dollars of those goods and services. We conclude that, under a paper-money system, a determined government can always generate higher spending and hence positive inflation."[9]

To be sure, the path our Fed governor was describing is unorthodox, just as deflation is unusual, but it should assure us that our government would meet any problem with flexibility. Printing lots of money is just another way of being flexible.

Query: If taxes aren't increased and money is borrowed to fulfill promises, what's the fastest way to reduce the burden of that debt?

Answer: Use the "technology" suggested by Ben Bernanke. With a gigantic future obligation to be realized—the $51 trillion Gokhale and Smetters calculated—taxes can't be raised enough to pay the bill. And borrowing the money would make financing World War II look like child's play.

The "solution" may be to do all three: tax more, borrow more, and print enough money to water down the real value of the debt and reduce its burden on the economy. Create some inflation. Will this ever be announced as a specific policy of the government?

Table 7.6
Treasury inflation protected securities: How the real after-tax return falls as inflation rises

Consumer price index	Gross yield	Less taxes	After-tax return	Real after-tax return
0	2.50	0.63	1.88	1.88
1	3.50	0.88	2.63	1.63
2	4.50	1.13	3.38	1.38
3	5.50	1.38	4.13	1.13
4	6.50	1.63	4.88	0.88
5	7.50	1.88	5.63	0.63
6	8.50	2.13	6.38	0.38
7	9.50	2.38	7.13	0.13
8	10.50	2.63	7.88	−0.13
9	11.50	2.88	8.63	−0.38
10	12.50	3.13	9.38	−0.63
11	13.50	3.38	10.13	−0.88
12	14.50	3.63	10.88	−1.13
13	15.50	3.88	11.63	−1.38
14	16.50	4.13	12.38	−1.63
15	17.50	4.38	13.13	−1.88

Source: Authors' calculations; assumes 25 percent tax rate.

No way.

But the coming economic environment probably will be characterized by higher taxes, heavy government borrowing, inflation, and interest rates that produce a negative real return. If the real return isn't negative *before* taxes, it most certainly will be negative *after* taxes.

Is this possible?

Absolutely. While investors enjoyed positive real returns on fixed-income investments from 1981 onward, real returns on government long- and intermediate-term bonds were negative for the five, ten, fifteen, and twenty years ending 1980. Over the fifteen-year period Intermediate Government bond holds lost purchasing power at a 1.2 percent annual rate. And that was before taxes.[10]

Make the inflation rate high enough and even the much-praised TIPS, Treasury Inflation Protected Securities, will have a negative real return *after* taxes. A TIPS priced to produce a 2.5 percent real return, for instance, will have a zero *after-tax* real return if inflation rises to over 6 percent. Table 7.6 shows how the real return after-tax return declines as inflation rises. It's also a reason we favor putting TIPS (and mutual funds that invest in TIPS) into Roth IRA accounts. Do that and you'll never have to deal with the taxation of inflation adjustments—you'll get a safe, real return.

Under the conventional assumption of a lower tax bracket in retirement, an IRA account is a good choice. If your future tax rate is the same, an IRA and a Roth IRA will be equally beneficial. But with uncertainty over future tax rates, a Roth IRA is a better choice because the taxes are paid up front.

How high will future tax, inflation, and interest rates be?

Any answer is a guess.

What's important is that legislation is already in place to reduce Social Security benefits and make them subject to taxation. Even a modest inflation rate may negate the benefit of 401(k) and IRA saving for many workers. Needless to say, no one in political office has ever owned up to cutting benefits.

While government will be bringing us lower benefits, higher taxes, and more inflation, we still haven't recognized the invisible monster gnawing at the feet of our proud "free agent" nation—the expense of supporting the retirement-investment complex. That's where we'll start looking at what we can do—in investments and personal decisions—to defend ourselves.

8

Securing Your Future

I never been in no situation where havin' money made it any worse.
—Clinton Jones

Financial Malpractice

Tax hikes, benefit cuts, and inflation can transform our retirement dreams into financial nightmares. Unfortunately, as we've been pounding into your head, thanks to the government's phenomenal fiscal malfeasance, the occurrence of each is a question of when, not if.

Is there anything we can do to protect ourselves? Our answer is a firm yes. As detailed below, we can start saving like mad, invest in securities that are insulated against inflation, and hold assets whose return is not taxed. But the first and most important thing to do is to preserve what we've already got—and that's harder than it sounds. There is an entire industry—the financial services sector—whose primary goal is to separate us from our money. Avoiding this industry's financial malpractice is step one in our self-help guide.

What do we mean by "financial malpractice"? We mean the enormous burden placed on our savings by "the retirement-investment complex"—the bankers, insurance agents, brokers, mutual fund managers, financial advisers, and employers sponsoring retirement plans—all of whom purport to be our friends.

We believe that what generally passes for "financial planning," "investment advice," and "portfolio management" can be as dangerous and destructive as taxes and inflation. We don't expect you to take this on faith. We're going to show you what we mean by measuring the impact of financial malpractice on your retirement assets.

We believe that conventional financial services can do more harm than good—like the person who goes to emergency room for a broken arm but dies of a hospital-acquired staph infection, much of the "treatment" offered by the retirement-investment complex represents a major threat to the survival of the investing public. Patients who accept a common placebo would lead financially healthier lives.

What we call financial malpractice is rooted in three different issues:

- False promises
- Wrong targets
- Excessive fees

Let's start with *false promises.*

Until only a few years ago, virtually every financial planner and investment adviser in America routinely led themselves and their clients astray by making simple projections of saving and investment. Many still do.

What they did was take a savings rate, assume a return on investment, and project forward, showing the attentive client how a regular investment plan was going to turn their nest egg into enough money to buy, say, Rhode Island and retire in grand style by age 59.

Retirement was just as simple. The adviser took the amazing accumulation from the first step, assumed a rate of return on retirement assets and a withdrawal rate, and showed that the client could live well, dramatically increase her family's net worth, and still leave the kids enough money to make a real mess of their lives.

Brokers with financial planning hats did this kind of exercise. So did insurance agents: They loved to show gigantic accumulations and years of tax-free retirement living from big life insurance policies.

Even Peter Lynch, the legendary manager of Fidelity Magellan Fund who went on to become an icon of branding, led the public astray. In a column for *Worth* magazine, Lynch offered "the 7 percent solution," telling readers a portfolio that was 100 percent stocks would return a reliable 10 percent a year and therefore allow retirees to withdraw 7 percent a year.[1] Forever.

This, unfortunately, is wrong. Simple projections don't take the variability of returns into account. While the ups and downs of stock and bond prices aren't much of a problem while we are accumulating money—and might, from a tax perspective, even be an advantage—the uncertainty of asset prices can be fatal when the same portfolio is being tapped for living expenses.

What Lynch didn't recognize, or at least didn't discuss, was something biologists call "the extinction problem"—the notion that some setbacks are so great that a species may never recover. Portfolios, like birds and fish on the endangered species list, have the same problem: Draw on them more than a certain amount, and a bear market can mean extinction.

This is not hyperbole. If you retired in the late 1960s or early 1970s and thought you could draw 7 percent a year, adjusted for inflation, from your portfolio, your portfolio died before you did.[2]

Fortunately, this false promising is no longer universal. Nobel Prize–winning economist William Sharp introduced the idea of uncertain returns with his Web-based investing service, Financial Engines.[3] Mutual Fund vendor T. Rowe Price has a calculator on its Web site that allows you to test portfolio survival under different withdrawal conditions.[4] Today, any planner who can't talk Monte Carlo simulation—a probabilistic approach that incorporates the variability of investment returns—is way behind the curve.

Sadly, that doesn't mean simple projection has disappeared. With an army of nearly 70,000 National Association of Securities Dealers registered representatives and nearly as many insurance brokers and agents—virtually all called "advisers" or "consultants" instead of salesreps—you can be certain that many professional financial planners remain as reluctant to discuss uncertain returns today as Peter Lynch was in 1995.

Wrong Targets

The financial services industry has started to recognize the impact of uncertainty in the past ten years (aided immeasurably by the bear market of 2000–2002). But it continues to force you to plan for yourself by asking you to specify your own retirement spending targets. This is the toughest part of the entire financial planning exercise, which may be why the industry offers no help. It's also the most dangerous part. If you set your future spending target too low, you'll end up being advised to save too little and buy too little insurance. If you set your target too high, you'll be told to save too much and buy too much insurance. We only go around once and can't really afford to engage in financial target practice. Nonetheless, traditional financial planning still operates on this basic, let's-throw-it-at-the-wall-and-see-if-it-sticks model.

The result is a lot of poor advice from software and planners. Some people are advised to spend far more than they should and others to spend far less than they can. Moreover, conventional advice leads to fixed recommended saving rates, as opposed to saving rates that vary with one's changing circumstances. Consequently, the traditional approach tells people to save when they should spend and to spend when they should save. These programs also provide little guidance about where to save. But *where* you save and invest—in a 401(k) plan, a Roth IRA, a taxable account, or even in home equity—may be as important as how much you save and invest.

We think the industry can do better.

It has long been recognized that most people try to level out their consumption over their lifetimes, making an effort to avoid reductions in consumption that are forced and large. No one wants to live on a Spam and ramen noodles diet in old age or to scrimp like crazy when young in order to start partying at age 80. Today, we have both the microcomputer power and the software to do a complete life cycle analysis of income, spending, taxes, and saving. Although there is no perfect planning tool in an uncertain world, we believe investment managers and financial planners can finally start planning for their clients rather than the other way around. We also think many individuals and families can kiss their planners goodbye and start planning for themselves.

There's a brand new software program that does this life cycle planning, called ESPlanner. ESPlanner, which is short for Economic Security Planner, is available at www.esplanner.com and is designed for both individual households and financial planners to use.[5] Codeveloped by one of us (Kotlikoff), ESPlanner helps you and your spouse, if married, or partner, if partnered, "smooth" your living standard over your lifetimes. Smoothing your living standard means maintaining your lifestyle over time. In smoothing your ride, ESPlanner doesn't ask you to set your own future spending target. Instead, it finds the target on its own using an advanced mathematical technique, called *dynamic programming*. Mathematicians, engineers, and economists use dynamic programming routinely, but ESPlanner represents the first commercial use of this technique in financial planning. Its recommendations are a major improvement on the deprivations, forced marches, or misplaced euphoria that come out of financial planning as currently practiced.

In smoothing your living standard, the program takes into account your household's current and future composition, the fact that two can live more cheaply than one, all the future taxes you'll pay and Social Security benefits you'll receive, and fully integrates all your off-the-top spending on housing, college tuition, bequests, and the 1952 Jaguar. The program also does Monte Carlo simulations that show how your investment choices affect the variability of your living standard in all future years.

What's the Difference?

Essentially all of the conventional tools engage in target practice. Virtually all add one financial project on top of another without integrating them over a lifetime. Most fail to adjust for changing household demographics. And most do a very crude job when it comes to calculating taxes and Social Security benefits. As a consequence, recommended savings rates and life insurance can be wildly high or way too low even for households with very simple financial plans and circumstances.

If you're feeling you've just read a commercial, we apologize. Our goal here is not to sell you ESPlanner (although it's a good idea to buy it), but to convince you that taking traditional financial planning advice can be highly dangerous to your financial health. As an example, we invite you to visit the TIAA-CREF Web site and use its life insurance calculator. Andrew Carnegie established TIAA-CREF in 1918 to help teachers save and insure. It's one of the most reputable financial institutions in the country. But its life insurance advice is the equivalent of throwing darts. Its life insurance calculator asks for your current income and then tells you to buy six to ten times that amount in life insurance. In other words, it takes your income, multiplies it by six and ten, and then provides this life insurance range.[6]

The difference between six times your income and ten times your income is huge. If you need ten times your income and buy only six times, you've made a major financial mistake and are leaving your kids and spouse or partner at major risk. If you need six times your income and buy ten times, you're going to be spending years taking bread out of the mouths of your children to enrich TIAA-CREF or whatever other insurance company you use. Second, you may well need a lot less or a lot more than six to ten times your current income in life insurance. How much you really need depends on a host of factors, none of which the TIAA-CREF calculator solicits.

So what does this nonprofit company, established through the tremendous generosity of Andrew Carnegie, governed by a board with impeccable credentials, think it's doing providing this advice? Hard to say for sure, but we think the company is trying to sell you life insurance rather than really help you plan your finances.

Excessive Fees

This is a big one. Problems with goal setting and projections are minor compared to the problem caused by how most financial service firms charge for their "expert" advice. The business model for most financial services firms is quite simple: They want to earn a 2 percent return *on your money*. Many hope for a good deal more. That's simply too much, yet it's common for both accumulating and distributing portfolios.

You can understand this by considering two simple examples. One is for an accumulating portfolio such as a 401(k) or 403(b) plan. The other is for a portfolio in distribution, which is what you do when you retire.

Suppose you are 25 years old and earn $30,000 (see table 8.1). You want to save and invest so that you can retire at age 67. You decide to save 10 percent of your income each year and invest it in a 70/30 portfolio of domestic equities and fixed income securities, a mix that described the typical employee retirement account early in the bear market. We're also assuming that inflation averages 3 percent and your income rises 1 percent faster than inflation.

How much will you accumulate by age 67, the current age for "full" retirement? *It depends how much you pay in fees.*

If you could invest at virtually no cost, the 70/30 portfolio would have an annualized average return of 9.29 percent. If expenses whittle 2 percentage points a year off your return, you'll earn, on average, only 7.29 percent.

Table 8.1
The real cost of investment service—more than taxes

Return	Accumulation	Growth	Adviser drain	Adviser drain as percent growth	Adviser fee
9.29%	$2,168,526	$1,837,267	0	0	0.00%
9.09	2,061,192	1,729,933	$107,334	5.84%	0.20
8.89	1,959,791	1,628,532	208,735	11.36	0.40
8.69	1,863,983	1,532,724	304,543	16.58	0.60
8.49	1,773,448	1,442,189	395,078	21.50	0.80
8.29	1,687,884	1,356,625	480,642	26.16	1.00
8.09	1,607,004	1,275,745	561,522	30.56	1.20
7.89	1,530,543	1,199,284	637,983	34.72	1.40
7.69	1,458,247	1,126,988	710,279	38.66	1.60
7.49	1,389,878	1,058,619	778,648	42.38	1.80
7.29	1,325,212	993,953	843,314	45.90	2.00

Source: Scott Burns, *Dallas Morning News*, "The Real Cost of Long-Term Money Management," November 27, 2001.
Note: These calculations assume a 25 year old with a starting salary of $30,000 and career earnings that exceed 3 percent inflation by 1 percentage point annually. The assumed return is that of a 70/30-equity/fixed income portfolio. The worker saves 10 percent of income and retires at age 67.

Let's assume, for argument's sake, that you hit these averages each year. At the 9.29 percent return, you'll accumulate an impressive $2,168,526, which equals 22.3 years of your final salary. That's more than enough to sustain your net standard of living in retirement, without Social Security benefits. At the 7.29 percent net return, however, you'll accumulate only $1,325,212—only 13.4 years of final salary. While investment expenses will have taken only 21.5 percent of your return each year, the cumulative impact will be a 38.9 percent reduction in your final nest egg. That's higher than our highest tax rate—the 35 percent rate reserved for the top one percent of all earners.

Does our comparison of this 2 percentage point cost of investing with a zero cost of investing overstate the case?

Not by much. Today, many 401(k) plans offer a choice of low-cost index funds that typically have expenses of about 0.2 percent a year.

Even that cost is being challenged. Barclay's Global, the leader in the development of exchange-traded funds, offers basic index choices in the Exxon-Mobil 401(k) plan at costs of 3 to 7 basis points.

Yes, you read that right: annual fees of 3 to 7 basis points. In nonfinancial language, that's three one-hundredths of 1 percent (0.03 percent) to seven one-hundredths of 1 percent (0.07 percent). That's less than *one-tenth* that charged by the largest and most popular mutual funds used in defined contribution plans. The large funds, in turn, cost about half as much as smaller or more highly marketed funds cost. To be sure, 3 to 7 basis points isn't free, but it's close.

Similarly, while the largest 401(k) plans typically use funds with annual expenses under 1 percent, small 401(k) plans routinely have expenses around 2 percent a year. Teachers' retirement plans, which are dominated by variable annuity products, regularly cost over 2 percent a year. While salesreps proclaim the brilliance of this or that portfolio manager or the wonders of the research staff, it remains that as a group, mutual fund managers, brokers, financial analysts, and financial planners *are* basically the market because they do so much of the total market's investing and trading. Indeed, mutual funds alone hold almost $7 trillion of Americans' assets. By definition, they cannot all beat the market. Indeed, as a group, money managers must underperform a low-cost market index fund by the amount of their loads, fees, commissions, and other "expenses." The reality is that management "talent" is temporary and fluky, while fees are permanent and regular.

One indication is a recent study of long-term returns in equity mutual funds. Of the 306 domestic equity funds that have survived over the past twenty years, the Vanguard 500 Index fund ranked forty-sixth. That means it was in the top 15 percent of its surviving competitors over the period. The ranking can change from year to year, but it is consistently better than average.

As this is written, the passive index has done better than 79 percent of managed large cap funds over the past fifteen years.[7] In the three-year period ending June 30, 2003—the bear market—the 500 Index did better than 54 percent of managed large cap funds. The Vanguard Total Market Index fund, which incorporates the entire domestic stock market, did better than 63 percent of all competitors. This is important: index funds are supposed to do relatively poorly in bear markets because they have little or none of the cash that acts as a downside cushion for the typical managed fund.

And that's just the *accumulation* side.

Now let's suppose you are retired. You change your portfolio to a more conservative 50/50 mix of equities and fixed income. And you want to spend 4 to 5 percent a year from your portfolio for a period of thirty years.

What are the odds your portfolio will survive that long? *It depends on your investment costs.*

If your investment costs are 0.18 percent and you take 4 percent a year, you have a 100 percent chance that your portfolio will survive at least thirty years. Raise the withdrawal rate to 5 percent, and the odds sink to 84 percent.

At higher investment costs, the survival rate is lower. Why? The portfolio doesn't know, or care, whether the money withdrawn is for you or the financial services industry. Raise your total withdrawal rate, and you will reduce your survival odds. Take 5 percent a year for yourself and let the investment manager take 2 percent a year, and there's only a 53.4 percent chance you'll outlive your money. (Table 8.2 illustrates the impact.)

While some financial advisers and sales reps will advise clients about the impact of high withdrawal rates for personal consumption,[8] we don't know of any who add their fees into the equation. It should also come as no surprise that the "advisers" who sell the most expensive

Table 8.2
How fees reduce portfolio survival rates in retirement

Investment expenses	4 percent personal withdrawal rate	5 percent personal withdrawal rate
0.18%	100.0%	84.0%
1.00%	96.9	70.2
2.00%	83.2	53.4

Source: www.retireearlyhomepage.com.
Note: This assumes a portfolio that is 50 percent domestic equities, 50 percent five-year Treasuries, and that the annual personal withdrawal is increased by the inflation rate each year.

investment products—such as the variable annuity salesreps who buy radio time to tout their high-commission product—regularly tell their customers that a 7 percent personal withdrawal rate is absolutely safe. Add the 2 percent annual cost, and the total withdrawal rate is 9 percent. That reduces the survival odds to only 19.1 percent.[9]

If investment fees can cut your accumulation by over 40 percent and then reduce the odds of portfolio survival in retirement by more, the financial services industry is as much a problem as inflation or taxes.

Depressed? We don't blame you.

Fortunately, there are remedies. The field of low-cost index investments is growing very rapidly. An increasing number of offerings are complete portfolios, turning your retirement saving into one-stop shopping.[10] The first such fund out of the gate was the Vanguard Balanced Index Fund. Modeled on a typical pension portfolio, it invests 60 percent of its assets in the Vanguard Total Stock Market Fund and 40 percent in the Vanguard Total Bond Market Fund. Run at a cost of only 22 basis points (0.22 percent), it has done better than 75 percent of all comparable managed funds over the past five and ten years. You can invest in funds of this type in your spare time, at home.

We believe index investing should be your first step toward coping with the coming generational storm. It's certainly the easiest. For the moment, just start thinking about investment expenses. Recognize that you've got a choice to make.

Odds are that it will be a very simple choice. You can opt to protect yourself and look for low-cost investments—or you can help a salesrep make her Mercedes payment. Lest you think we're being nasty, consider this: At the peak of the bull market the average stockbroker made $200,000, about the same as the compensation of medical school professors in the top 10 percent of their profession.

Before we take the next steps, we need to paint an unconventional picture of our assets.

Remember the Basics

Most media and public attention is focused on financial assets. But our future the welfare depends on a portfolio of four different kinds of assets: *implicit* assets, *financial* assets, *household* assets, and *personal* assets.

Implicit Assets

An implicit asset is a promise of future income, including in-kind income. The three most important implicit assets are Social Security, Medicare, and employer-provided pensions.

With Social Security, we pay payroll taxes in exchange for a promise of future retirement, disability, and survivor benefits. We also pay payroll taxes in exchange for a promise of medical care when we are retired or disabled. Those promises are implicit assets to us and implicit liabilities to the government.

Social Security and Medicare are the largest assets most Americans have. As we've indicated, they represent a government commitment to deliver trillions of dollars in goods and services to current and future retirees. But comprehending trillions of dollars is not easy. A better way to grasp what these programs mean is to absorb the following two facts. *Fact 1 is that two-thirds of all older Americans get at least 50 percent of their income from Social Security retirement benefits and have most of their health care paid by Medicare.*[11] With the average retired couple now receiving about $1,400 a month in Social Security benefits,[12] a figure that is adjusted for inflation every year, they would need a portfolio of $600,000 invested in twenty-year Treasury Inflation-Protected Securities to have the same income. Valued as an inflation-adjusted life annuity, the couple would need to invest about $420,000. Either way, the implied value of Social Security retirement benefits dwarfs the financial assets of most Americans. According to data in the 2001 Survey of Consumer Finances done by the Federal Reserve, for instance, only one household in four has a net worth of conventional assets over $400,000.[13]

To get the same $1,400 monthly income working as Wal-Mart greeters at $8 an hour, before payroll taxes, the same couple would have to put in nearly 2,300 hours of work each year.[14] Since neither of these examples considers state or local income taxes, we're understating the implied asset value of Social Security.

Fact 2 is that the in-kind income future retirees will receive from Medicare will exceed the value of their Social Security benefits. This reflects the extraordinary growth in Medicare benefits per beneficiary that the government projects will continue through the indefinite future.

Defined benefit pensions—the lifetime income guarantee many corporate employees and public school teachers still have—are another implicit asset. Like Social Security, the worker receives a lifetime retirement income based on her years of service, income, and age at retirement. Although the worker can't sell this asset, she receives the income that direct ownership of assets entails. While this implicit asset is important for those who will "own" it, defined benefit pension plans are rapidly becoming an endangered species. Private pensions are a troubled sideshow in the circus of American retirement security.

The problem we face—the coming generational storm—is an implicit asset problem. Raw demography is creating promises of implicit assets faster than the underlying economy is growing. To cope, we'll need to compensate with the other three assets.

Financial Assets

We are deluged with information about the condition and prospects of financial assets. These assets include stocks and bonds, mutual funds that invest in the same, bank deposits, money market funds, shares in real estate companies, annuity contracts, and the cash value of life insurance policies.

With the decline of corporate pensions and rising worry about Social Security, we are urged to accumulate financial assets so we'll have the money to pay our bills when we can no longer work. Over the next few years, contribution limits for existing retirement plans—401(k), 403(b), IRA, and Roth IRAs—are being expanded so that workers can put more money away. Those age 50 and over will be allowed to put away still more.

In which asset class should we invest? The battle rages and will continue long after everyone reading this book is dead.

Much less attention is paid to the *containers* that hold our financial assets. We can hold financial assets in taxable accounts, in accounts that defer taxation to the future such as 401(k) and related qualified accounts, in accounts that eliminate future taxation such as Roth-IRAs, and in a variety of insurance-based containers such as tax-deferred variable annuities and cash-value life insurance.

We believe the choice of container is nearly as important as the choice of financial assets. Why? *Because we need to control two things: investment expenses and taxable events.* With existing legislation that will make the taxation of Social Security benefits commonplace and increasing pressure to raise taxes, we believe individuals and families need a portfolio of containers to hold their financial assets. As you saw in chapter 7, some people need to place some of their savings in Roth IRA accounts rather than place everything in their employer-provided 401(k) account.

Household Assets

Financial assets represent claims to the stock of capital needed to produce the goods and services we consume. We employ household capital in the business of "Home, Inc." to do much the same. We own houses to provide shelter services. We own cars to provide transportation services. We own washers and dryers to provide the services of the Laundromat, lawnmowers to displace the labor of outside yard crews, TV sets to economize on entertainment, and so on.[15]

While many purchases of household assets are less than economic— witness the $12,000 stove hood, the $5,000 refrigerator, and the $7,000 outdoor grill—each can trace its origins to practical economics. It is possible to buy a home that will deliver shelter services more economically than a rental unit. Similarly, if you make regular use of a car, it makes sense to own rather than rent.

The largest and most important of these assets is a house or condo. Because they are acquired with tax-deductible interest loans, can be owned debt free, throw off housing services that aren't subject to taxation, and have no taxes due when sold for a capital gain (unless your gain exceeds $500,000), *we believe home ownership may be one of the best ways to reduce the impact of a decline in Social Security benefits and an increase in taxation.* We'll show you how and why later in this chapter.

Personal Assets

University of Chicago Nobel Laureate Gary Becker and other respected economists have long made reference to the *human capital* embedded in people—the capital of knowledge, education, and skill. *Health capital,* on the other hand, receives much less attention, but it's one of our most important personal assets.

We regularly give our health lip-service, but we don't do enough to preserve it. Major advances in public health characterized the past century. Sewer and water systems reduced common diseases; antibiotics turned tuberculosis and other deadly diseases into oddities; attention to safety reduced accidental deaths and injuries in the workplace and in transportation.

In *this* century the biggest lever on health is our personal habits. How we take care of ourselves will affect more than our life expectancy. We also affect our years of health and our years of infirmity.

Pay attention to what keeps us healthy, and we'll enjoy longer lives with less infirmity. Be inattentive and wait for health in a pill, and we're still likely to live long lives—but with much more infirmity.

No, we do not offer health as a cure to the coming generational storm. But when you consider that Medicare is projected to cost as much as Social Security retirement benefits cost today by 2070, when the newborns of 2000 may retire, improved geriatric health is a gigantic opportunity. Keep reading, and we'll show you exactly how great an opportunity it is.

For individuals, attention to personal health is simple survival: The more we do to maintain and preserve our health, the less we'll be affected by the almost sure collapse of our medical delivery system over the next three or four decades. For those who will retire into that embattled environment, attention to personal health is essential.

Now let's see what we can do with our household, financial, and personal assets to offset the inevitable losses we're going to suffer in our implicit assets. Using ESPLanner, we'll start by showing how home ownership decisions may completely offset losses caused by Social Security benefit reductions.

Buy a House

Conventional thinking on home ownership is dead wrong.

It tells us to become home owners because of the tax deductions and the leverage of long-term ownership. In fact, millions of home owners have no tax benefits from ownership because their itemized deductions are less than the standard deduction.[16] Worse, the leverage of long-term ownership can be deadly—witness the multitudes of home owners who were "upside-down" in Colorado, Oklahoma, and Texas after the oil bust of the 1980s and the home owners in Los Angeles who were in the same condition in the early 1990s, and the condo owners in San Francisco who experienced the same thing after the Internet implosion a few years ago.

The process of acquiring and paying for a house is a lot harder and more uncertain than real estate agents would have us believe. More important, the largest benefit of home ownership—its return in shelter services—starts the minute you buy your house, no matter how you finance it. Unfortunately, we often don't see this return because we are blinded by the mortgage payments. The value of the shelter services return becomes clear when you compare the cash income needs of two couples.

Skeptics should consider the retired couple who lives down the block. You know their income is less than yours and always has been. But they live on the block, live well, and worry a lot less than you do.

Why?

They own their house free and clear. While you have to pay employment and income taxes on what you earn, much of their income never even shows up on their tax return because it is "imputed"—it's income in service, not cash. The service they receive is tax sheltered. You receive the same service income, but it is offset by mortgage payments.

If today's retirees are better off because they have invisible income, tomorrow's retiree–home owners will be even better off. In the high-tax, high-inflation world that is coming our way, the worst income to have will be taxable income. The best income will be "imputed." Imputed income won't be taxable, and it will be rising with inflation.

That's what home ownership gives us: tax-free invisible income in shelter services. It avoids the wedge of taxation.

You can understand this by comparing two home owners—a young couple who recently bought a median-priced home with a large mortgage and a retired couple who owns an identical twin house a few doors down (table 8.3). We've chosen a home valued at $140,000. The young couple carries an extra $8,568 a year in mortgage payments and is surprised to find that their itemized deductions don't exceed the standard deduction. As a consequence, their federal income tax bill isn't reduced.

Table 8.3
Comparing two home owners

Item	New home owner	Retiree
Mortgage	$8,568	$0
Real estate taxes	2,800	2,800
Insurance	700	700
Utilities	2,800	2,800
Maintenance	1,400	1,400
Total	16,263	7,700
First-year tax deductions . . .	9,400	NA
. . . versus Standard deduction	9,700	NA
Tax-reducing deductions	0	NA
Tax savings @$25%	0	NA
Net cost	16,263	7,700
Income taxes to deliver	5,421 (@25%)	1,359 (@15%)
Employment taxes @7.6%	1,796	NA
Pretax total cost	23,480	9,059
Tax wedge	7,217	1,359
The invisible benefit	NA	14,421

Source: Authors' calculations using 2004 tax tables.
Note: This example assumes a home valued at $140,000, financed with 5 percent down and a thirty-year mortgage at 5 percent. While residents of high-tax states may have greater tax deductions due to state income taxes, all owners see their deductions decline as the mortgage is paid down.

In order to deliver the $16,263 net annual cost of shelter, they will have to earn an additional $5,421 to cover their income taxes at 25 percent and $1,796 to cover their share of payroll taxes at 7.65 percent. So they'll need to earn $23,480.

The retirees who own their house free and clear don't itemize their deductions because they total less than the standard deduction. But their out-of-pocket expenses are so low they can easily be in a much lower tax bracket—15 percent instead of 25 percent—and they aren't paying any payroll taxes. As a consequence, they need an income of only $9,059 to support their house—$14,421 less than their mortgage-paying neighbors. To be sure, some portion of the difference is saving by the mortgaged home owners.

Both the new (mortgaged) home owner and the retiree enjoy an imputed income in shelter services. The difference is that the mortgaged home owner secures his shelter services by making mortgage payments, which increases his need for cash income. While the mortgage is being paid off, the home owner benefits from inflation because it reduces the value of the fixed sum he must pay off.

Having an imputed income for an essential service—shelter—and no related debt allows the retired home owner to have less income to tax. It also allows him to pay tax at a lower rate on the income that is needed. If, as we believe, the future is filled with rising income and payroll taxes, home ownership will become the canonical tax-benefited investment.

Nor do the benefits end at simple ownership. Since capital gains up to $500,000 are tax free under current law, home ownership may become the single best tool for maneuvering through the mine fields that lie ahead.

You can understand how this works by considering the example of Mr. and Mrs. Middle, a median-earner home owner couple. Using ESPlanner, we've examined how they can use ownership decisions to reduce the impact of coming reductions in Social Security benefits.

Can You Muddle, Mr. and Ms. Middle?

Joe Middle thinks of himself as a worrywart. At age 35, he's earning $28,000 a year. Like many other workers who didn't go to college, he's seen some nice years of income increases since he started working. He says it was because he's reliable and willing, nothing more. Today he feels as if he's topped out and is wondering if his future income will do any better than keep up with inflation. His wife Mary earns $14,000 a year. "I have a job," she says, "Maybe other people have careers but I'm not one of them."

Together, the Middles earn $42,000 a year. That just happens to be the median income in the United States. Half of all households earn less. Half earn more.

What makes the Middles different from other Americans? It's their caution. It was a struggle to put together the down payment for a home, but they did it. They bought a $100,000 house with $10,000 down. They have a $90,000 mortgage at 5.5 percent for thirty years. Aside from a small car payment, they have *no* other debts. No credit card debt. No student loans. No home improvement loans. Nada.

Unusual? Very.

The average American household has 6.5 credit cards with an average balance of about $8,000.[17] At an interest rate of 18 percent, the interest cost alone is $1,440 a year, entirely undeductible. That's nearly three weeks of wages, before any taxes, for the average worker.

The biggest impediment to buying a house for most first-time buyers is their back-end ratio—the portion of income committed to obligations like car loans, credit cards, personal loans, and student loans. If those monthly payments total over 8 percent of gross income, most mortgage lenders start reducing the amount of money they'll let you borrow for a house.

The Middles have a back-end ratio of 4.6 percent—very low. You get an idea of how rare they are when you consider that many two-earner households have two cars with matching loans. You might also think about the monthly payments on the average new car: nearly $500.[18] This means you need an income of nearly $75,000 a year if you're going to drive just one average new car and keep your back-end ratio at 8 percent.

The Middles have two children but aren't making any plans for sending them to college. If they go, they'll have to finance it on their own. The Middles, meanwhile, are saving for their retirements. Mary saves 5 percent of her income in an IRA. Joe saves 6 percent of his income in a 401(k) plan with a 50 percent match. This puts them way ahead of most people with the same income.

Are they saving the right amount?

We can find out by using ESPlanner (table 8.4). The program indicates that when the Middles retire, Social Security will be providing $23,632 of the $31,432 they spend every year. Do the math, and 78.4 percent of their total cash spending in retirement will come from Social Security. Only 21.6 percent will come from their savings.

Fortunately, they will pay no income taxes once they retire. Their house will be owned free and clear. It will provide them a very valuable noncash income in shelter services. Their shelter expenses are limited to taxes and insurance, which run $3,000 a year (stated in current dollars).

Table 8.4
The Middles: Where their income comes . . . and goes

	Income	Spending	
Social Security	$23,632	$28,432	Consumption
Savings	7,800	3,000	Shelter
Taxes	0	0	Taxes
Total	31,432	31,432	Total

Source: Authors' calculations using ESPlanner software.

Their other shelter expenses, like utilities and repairs, are in their consumption budget.

You don't have to think about their circumstances very much to realize how vulnerable they are to the coming upheaval in Social Security. And they won't be alone. According to Social Security Administration figures, Social Security provides 82 percent of income for the bottom 40 percent of all older Americans. It provides 64 percent of income for the middle 20 percent. And, to repeat, Social Security provides at least 50 percent of income for nearly two-thirds of all older Americans.

Unless the Middles sell their house, any adjustment to lower Social Security benefits will have to come out of their nonhousing consumption spending.

So if Social Security is providing 83 percent of that consumption spending ($28,432/$31,432) and Social Security is cut 27 percent, the Middles will take a 22 percent hit.

They will lose $6,380 of their $28,432 of nonhousing consumption.

Will they survive?

Of course they will. We forget, quite regularly, that many families in the less developed world could live for a year on what the average American family spends on cable TV or cell phones. What the Middles are facing, since so much of their standard of living comes from Social Security, is a drop that will be a hardship if they are healthy—and a disaster if they are not.

What can they do?

There are four options that we can calculate. There's also a fifth option to play by ear.

1. Assuming perfect foresight, they can adjust their current standard of living downward and save more for the (distant) future. They can accept a somewhat lower standard of living for their entire lives.

2. They can restore their Social Security benefit level by delaying retirement. This will do double duty, increasing their savings as it increases their Social Security benefits.

3. They can downsize their house—assuming there is a market when millions of people are trying to do the same thing. The sale will increase their savings, and the downsized house will cost less to operate. They can downsize early, as soon as the kids are grown. Or they can downsize late—after their Social Security benefits are cut.

4. They can move in with their kids, if the kids will let them. This will increase their savings by the equity in their home and eliminate home operating expenses. For reasons cited in chapter 1, we don't think this is a very realistic option.

And what's that mysterious fifth option? Moving to a lower-cost location, combining lower real estate costs with a generally lower cost of living. This could mean something as conventional as moving from Connecticut to Sun City, Arizona, or taking the train to Sarasota, Florida. It could also mean moving to an RV park in Apache Junction or Yuma. It could even mean leaving the country for a new, really cheap, life in Mexico or Costa Rica.

Here's what happens when you work through the changes (table 8.5).

Perfect Foresight

Suppose, unlike every other American, the Middles knew for certain that Social Security benefits would be cut by 25 percent from what they were promised? How much would they have to reduce their lifetime consumption? Intuitively, you can guess that the number is somewhere between zero and the 22 percent we just showed.

Using financial planning software, we calculated that consumption spending has to fall from $28,432 to $24,433. That's a *lifetime* decline of 14 percent. The good news is that the Middles can get there by saving more while they're working (which forces them to consume less) and then using their savings to keep their lifetime consumption at a sustain-

Table 8.5
How the Middles can respond to a 25 percent Social Security benefits cut

Situation	Consumption	Housing	Total consumption
No change	$28,432 (100%)	$3,000	$31,432
Taken by surprise	22,052 (–22%)	3,000	25,532
Perfect foresight	24,433 (–14%)	3,000	27,432
Delay retirement	26,646 (–6%)	3,000	29,646
Downsize home late (in 33 years)	28,111 (–1%)	1,500	29,611
Downsize home early (in 17 years)	28,913 (+2%)	1,500	30,413
Live with kids for free	29,430 (+4%)	0	29,430

Source: Authors calculations, ESPlanner software.

able level. The bad news is that they're going to be out $4,000 of real purchasing power *every year for the rest of their lives.*

Delay Retirement
Since perfect foresight is in short supply, it's more likely the Middles will do an ad hoc adjustment, like retiring later. If Joe works two more years and retires at age 69 instead of 67 and his wife retires when he does, their lifetime consumption will be $26,646 a year. That's 94 percent of what they would have had without a Social Security crack-up. Ask the Middles, and we'll bet they're more upset about the additional two years of work than the lost 6 percent. But remember, they must pay *both* prices.

Downsize Home
Selling a family-sized home and moving to a smaller one, perhaps a condo or town home, would allow the Middles to retire on their schedule and would get them closer to their original lifetime consumption. It's a good strategy because it works. Retirees are already doing it.

Moving to a smaller home liberates equity in the first home, adding to savings. It cuts costs at the same time. It even allows some people to free themselves of lawn care.

The only question about the strategy is *when* to do it. If the Middles wait until Social Security benefits are cut, a lot of houses will be going on the market at the same time. Single-family homes will be a glut on the market. Condos and town homes will be in short supply. We think the odds favor selling early rather than waiting for the last minute. That again requires some degree of foresight.

Live with the Kids for Nada

The Middles could always try the extreme sport version of home downsizing. They could give up home ownership altogether, by asking if they could move in with their children, taking over the grandkids' rooms. The financial results would be great. Social Security can cut benefits 25 percent—and so what? The Middles would see an increase in spending power.

In some families this might work, but we wouldn't bet the ranch on it. Remember that smaller families mean fewer kids. Worse, the kids will be so burdened with taxes they may be less than enthusiastic about having their parents live with them.

Where's the sackcloth and ashes? Where's the big disaster of a Social Security crack-up?

It's there. First, it's one thing for a few families to suffer a loss of purchasing power. It's another when it happens to *everyone* who is receiving Social Security benefits. We're talking millions of people. If you think Wal-Mart is crowded today, just wait until this hits.

The devastation gets more serious when you start thinking about the specific circumstances of other Social Security retirees. Here's a list:

• The Middles expect to enter retirement with no debt. This means they can be very flexible. Most people won't have such flexibility. They'll have car loans and credit card debt. They may still have a home mortgage or a home equity loan. Whatever debt they have, it means a portion of their income is committed.

• About half the population will have smaller Social Security benefits. They'll have less room for making cuts.

• The reduction of retirement benefits is in addition to the squeeze on benefits all recipients will experience from the rapid rise of Medicare Part B premiums.

• A handful of ongoing prescriptions will have the same effect as a monthly payment for a home mortgage, credit card debt, or car loan.

Now look up the income scale. If you're better off than the Middles—about half the population will be—you'll still have worries:

• If you have debt of any kind, the fixed nature of the debt can make your squeeze as tough as what's coming for the Middles.

• On the other hand, a combination of household assets (your home) and personal assets (your ability to be flexible about shelter) can be used to offset most or all of the coming failure of our implied assets.

How will the reduction in benefits actually happen? We don't know. There are, however, some very basic ground rules for coping. You need to save 'til it hurts, pay taxes up front, hoard some gold, and learn to eat broccoli. When you've done all that, you should think about quitting your job.

Save 'til It Hurts

In the world of wishful thinking, we would not have to save. Instead, we would spend every dime we earned and borrow more. Then on our last day of gainful employment, we would visit a Seven-Eleven, wait in the usual line to buy a lottery ticket, and "invest" $1 in a single ticket. Days later, we would respond to the notice of winning with sublime calm and grace, certain that whatever we won, it would carry us through our last days in style.

Sadly, the real world doesn't work that way. What we all face is a delicate balancing of how long we save, how much we save, how much our investments earn, and how long we live after we stop working. Change any one of those factors (not to mention inflation and taxation) and we'll need to change all the others. Worse, they change constantly.

All love the most powerful lever because it doesn't involve pain or discipline. It is *return on investment*. Indeed, it's so powerful we call it "the magic bullet" of investment return. Did your life expectancy rise? Fine—solve it with a higher return. Had trouble saving regularly? No problem—just earn a high return. Got a late start with saving or lost a bunch in a messy divorce? Not to worry; we'll solve the problem with a high return.

Table 8.6
The magic bullet of investment return

| | Life expectancy at age 65 | | |
Real Return	12.6 years (1935)	17.6 years (2000)	20.6 years (2040)
0%	24%	31%	34%
2%	17	22	25
7%	6	8	9

Source: Scott Burns, *Dallas Morning News*, "The Magic Bullet of Investment Return," Nov. 17 and 19, 2003.
Note: This chart shows the percentage of income that must be saved to provide a sum equal to the number of years of life expected at age 65. In each case, the amount of income to be replaced has been reduced by the amount of income saved. As a consequence, the amount that can be consumed rises rapidly with real return. The model used did not consider rises in living standard due to productivity or rising costs due to inflation. Compensating for each of these factors would require a somewhat higher saving rate.

Needless to say, Wall Street loves the magic bullet. The investment-retirement industry extracts billions in fees every year solely on claims of better guns and magic bullets.

You can get an idea of how powerful the magic bullet is by taking a look at table 8.6. It shows what percentage of your income you would need to save to replace the spending power that remained at three different levels of real return and three different levels of life expectancy. Back in 1935, with a life expectancy of 12.6 years at age 65, you would have had to save 24 percent of your earnings to finance your retirement if your savings earned nothing.

That's not a pretty picture, is it?

Raise the return to 7 percent (the real return on equities according to Ibbotson Associates data) and the world improves: You need to save only 6 percent of income. Better still, your spending rises from 76 percent of income to 94 percent of income. The difference is called the Consumer Society. Without the magic bullet, our consumer society would not exist.

Today, with a life expectancy of about 17.6 years at age 65, you'd need to save a whopping 31 percent of income if you received no return, 22 percent if you received the 2 percent real return on most inflation-protected government bonds, and 8 percent if you could count on the historic real return on equities. Most people don't invest 100 percent of their savings in equities. Most people don't save 8 percent of their income. And most people don't get the historic return on equities. (Remember our earlier section, Financial Malpractice?)

That leaves us in a pickle. We have every reason to believe that inflation will reduce real returns in the future, that taxes on investment returns will be higher, and that nominal investment returns may be lower. The net result is that we all need to save more.

Exactly how much do you need to save?

We can't be certain. All we can do is identify the ballpark—somewhere between 8 and 25 percent of income if we exclude Social Security retirement benefits. If you were expecting that Social Security retirement benefits would replace about 40 percent of your income in retirement, this means your savings rate could be anything from 4.8 percent of income to 15 percent of income.

Oops! Social Security benefits are likely to be cut, aren't they? And Medicare insurance premiums will take more and more of the income.

So we'll have to adjust our savings upward. Just as a consortium of Democrats and Republicans has now assured us that no one in America will ever have any basis for tax planning—thanks to our Guess-a-Year Estate Tax and our Phase of the Moon Income Tax—all we can know for certain is that we'll have to save a lot more.

What's our best bet? If you're saving less than 10 percent of your income, excluding any employer match, you're living dangerously. Twice that rate wouldn't be excessive—the worst that will happen is that you'll have the resources for an earlier retirement or expensive medical care.

Impossible, you say? We don't think so. Ironically, the thing that saves us may be the thing that has caused us so much worry: consumer debt. *Every dollar currently committed to the repayment of existing debt is a dollar that isn't being used for current consumption.* Pay off the debt, incur no new debt, and most Americans can double their saving rate. Some could triple their saving rate. (Yes, and some could increase their savings by an infinite amount, switching from spending more than they earn to earning more than they spend.)

How does this work? Simple. Just as Quicken offers tools for planning debt reduction that work by focusing a constant amount of payments on a diminishing number of debts, the dollars used to repay a variety of debts can then be used to increase retirement savings. (Basically, it's all saving, but the first part is used to repay debts.)

We think there is major potential here, but it requires a sea change for American consumers. We have to go from being consumers who ask, "What's the monthly payment?" (paying billions in interest) to being a debt-free nation.

Expect no help from your credit card company, your banker, or any vendor in America.

Pay Caesar Up Front

A great deal of financial planning hinges on a single assumption: When you retire, your taxes—and your tax *rate*—will be lower. With that in mind, you are urged to save as much as possible today, preferably in pretax plans such as IRA and 401(k) accounts. If you do that, the conventional wisdom goes, you'll be trading high taxes today for low taxes tomorrow. You'll also enjoy tax-deferred compounding during all the years in-between.

That assumption is still true for most people, but not for reasons anyone would greet with enthusiasm.

Most people *will* retire to lower tax rates because they will retire to a much lower income, and the bulk of it will come from Social Security. Without income from other sources, that Social Security income will remain tax free, enabling most Americans to retire to the tax bracket we all covet: zero.

Here's the math. With a standard deduction of $9,700 for a couple in 2004, an additional $950 for an elderly couple, and personal exemptions of $3,100 each, a couple filing a joint return can have $16,850 in dividend, interest, pension, or other income, in addition to Social Security benefits, before they pay a dime in income taxes. After that, the first $14,300 of taxable income pays at only 10 percent.

The hard part is that Social Security benefits plus $16,850 to $31,150 of other income isn't a lot of money. Those who successfully retire to a low tax rate usually retire to a loss of purchasing power. Since, as we indicated earlier, Social Security provides at least half of the income received by about two-thirds of older Americans, we can safely assume that two-thirds pay little or nothing in income taxes.

Not so with the remaining third, which is where most people want to be. For those who are successful at saving and building tax-deferred assets, the future holds a series of tax traps:

• As your income from all sources increases, you increase the probability that your Social Security benefits will be taxed as well as your other income.

• As inflation increases both your Social Security benefits and your other earning assets, you will encounter the tax on Social Security benefits at lower levels of real income.

• If you defer retirement to accumulate more assets and increase your Social Security benefits—as many are planning to do since the 2000–2002 bear market—you will (again) increase the odds you will be taxed at higher rates.

Worse, all of this is how things are *today*. The tax cuts we were given in 2001 and 2003 will come back to bite us between 2012 and 2018 as baby boomers retire in droves and the Social Security Administration starts to make noise about its cash situation. As benefit commitments exceed payroll tax income, they will want to receive the interest on the Treasury securities held in the Social Security Trust Fund in cash. Then they will want to sell some of their Treasury securities.

Unfortunately, the Treasury may still be borrowing money from the global public. This will give our government three choices: print money to redeem the Trust Fund Treasuries, creating inflation; issue new Treasuries to the public to replace the Trust Fund Treasuries, providing the public is saving enough; or raise taxes enough to redeem the Treasury securities with new tax revenue. There will be great pressure to increase both the payroll tax and the income tax.

This won't be a temporary problem. Although it will be particularly intense during the next thirty years, it will be a problem for the remainder of this *century*. As a consequence, we believe active savers won't be able to assume that future tax rates will be lower. The more successful you are as an earner and saver, the greater the odds are that you will pay taxes at higher and higher rates when you take money from qualified plans.

That's one reason we're enthusiastic about home ownership: it offers shelter, tax savings, inflation protection, and flexible tax-free access to equity in a basic necessity.

But it won't be enough. Even if you downsize, your shelter investment won't be large enough to provide the portfolio you need in retirement. So we make a simple suggestion: *pay taxes today.* Build assets that can be accessed in the future without creating what the Internal Revenue Service calls a "taxable event."

This means saving after-tax income in Roth IRA accounts and in conventional taxable accounts such as bank savings accounts, brokerage accounts, and mutual fund investments. It means avoiding (or reducing) forms of investment that reduce your taxes today by deferring them into the future. This means limiting your 401(k) contribution to the amount that captures your employer match. It means putting additional savings in a Roth IRA instead of an IRA. It means avoiding tax-deferred annuities, particularly the heavily marketed, high-expense contracts that dominate the industry.

We know this won't be easy. The entire investment industry knows that tax phobia is one of its best allies. Tax phobia sustains the sale of tax shelter schemes of all kinds. Tax phobia blinds investors to the actual benefits and qualities of the investments. Thousands of elderly investors who pay little or nothing in taxes own tax-free bonds that provide no spendable benefit to them—but they do it simply for the joy and magic of "tax free."

Today, many people feel artificially well off. They look at their 401(k) balances and forget that the government has, in effect, a lien on every account. For two-thirds of the population, that lien will be zero. But for the other third, the lien can be nearly 50 percent, not counting state income taxes.

Real money is money you can spend. It is not pretax money. It is money that you can access without creating a taxable event or with little in tax consequences.

What do we have in mind?

Everything ordinary and taxable. One of the best opportunities is in low-cost, tax-efficient index funds. Taxes on their dividend income have just been reduced to 15 percent. Capital gains distributions will be taxed at the same rate, and most won't have a taxable capital gains distribution for years because they have capital loss carry-forwards from the bear market of 2000–2002.

Suppose that you had a choice of two investments that earned 10 percent a year. One was an equity mutual fund. The other was a variable annuity wrapped around the same fund. The return from the naked equity mutual fund would be taxable each year at the current 15 percent rate. The return from the variable annuity, after being reduced by a 1 percent of assets annual insurance charge, would be tax deferred until you made a withdrawal.

What would the magic of tax deferral do for you?

Answer: nothing. The insurance charge, though lower than the 1.12 percent industry average, and the difference between a 15 percent tax rate today and a 25 percent tax rate tomorrow destroys the benefit of tax deferral. While the pretax accumulation in the tax-deferred annuity, before any withdrawal, is always larger than the accumulation in the currently taxed fund, the after-tax spending power in the variable annuity is lower than the after-tax spending power in the naked mutual fund in every one of the twenty years projected (table 8.7). Measured as a percentage of net gain for the mutual fund, tax deferral reduces the assets available to the investor by over 18 percent in the tenth year and 16 percent in the twentieth year. (The declining disadvantage shows that tax-deferred compounding counts for something, but not much.)

Needless to say, if the mutual fund return isn't 100 percent taxed each year, as our example is, or if the withdrawal tax rate is 35 percent instead of 15 percent paid earlier, things look even worse for the variable annuity investor.

As you can see, there is a real benefit for paying some taxes today.

Become a Gold Bug: Build an Alternative Portfolio

A dollar doesn't buy much these days. It will buy still less in the future.

How can we say this when the recent worry was deflation, when the prices of many goods appear to be declining?

Table 8.7
The twenty-year variable annuity disadvantage

Year	Variable annuity pre tax	Less variable annuity tax liability	Equals variable annuity after 25% tax	Mutual Fund, all taxes paid	Mutual Fund advantage
1	$10,900	$225	$10,675	$10,850	$175
5	15,386	1,347	14,040	15,037	997
10	23,674	3,418	20,255	22,610	2,355
15	36,425	6,606	29,819	33,997	4,179
20	56,044	11,511	44,533	51,120	6,587

Source: Scott Burns, *Dallas Morning News*, "The New Math of Variable Annuities," August 19, 2003.
Note: This chart compares an investment of $10,000 in a variable annuity and taxable mutual fund with a gross return of 10 percent annually. The variable annuity return is reduced by a 1 percent annual insurance expense, but all taxes are deferred. The mutual fund is assumed to distribute all of its 10 percent return each year. As a consequence, taxes are paid each year, and the mutual fund has no deferred tax liability.

Simple. We say this because the United States is doing all the things that mark an economy soon to be wracked by inflation and a weak currency:

• We're running a large federal deficit, however it is calculated.

• We're cutting taxes so the deficit will be larger for a longer period of time.

• We're running a record trade deficit. It continues to increase in spite of a weak economy.

• We're no longer a creditor nation. We owe billions around the world.

• Our government doesn't seem to care.

• We have implicit liabilities out the gazoo.

Our response—and we're serious—is to develop an interest in gold and build an alternative portfolio that will provide some protection from inflation and a declining currency.

The U.S. dollar has been the world's reserve currency for over sixty years. That's one reason it is referred to as "almighty." When other governments need to hold a currency as a reserve, they hold dollars. It's also the reason some say we have "dollarized" the world.

When things go seriously wrong—as in the former Soviet Union and the vast area of the world some call "Chaos-Stan," or any other place where people worry about their government's currency—what happens? The only currency that counts is the dollar. When push comes to shove, everything, including oil, is priced in dollars.

Most of us give this absolutely no thought. In fact, the reserve currency status of the dollar provides us with two enormous economic benefits. The first is a global interest-free loan from anyone, anywhere who holds paper dollars. This includes governments holding currency reserves, citizens who prefer holding dollars to rubles or pesos, tyrants who take flight, and every successful criminal organization in the world. All of them hold our currency and receive no interest.

This is no minor matter. Our currency in circulation is now approaching $700 billion. Nearly half of it has been out of the country for years. That means we have what amounts to a $300 billion loan, interest free, from the rest of the world. Nice work if you can get it.

The second economic benefit is what some call the reserve currency *premium*—the dollar has an advantage over other currencies in the exchange markets simply because it is the world's reserve currency. If we lose our position as the world's reserve currency, we will lose *both* of those benefits. The price of imported goods will rise immediately. A flood of dollars will come home, buying everything that isn't nailed down and much of what is nailed down. Our standard of living, which depends on low-cost imported goods, will decline.

In effect, we've been running a great scam on the rest of the world for decades. We import more goods than we export, leaving dollars to accumulate around the world. Some are used to finance crime, some to protect citizens of other countries from their own currencies, and some as currency reserves by other governments.

We also run a convenient federal deficit. The deficit produces a constant supply of new U.S. Treasury obligations, some of which are purchased by foreigners and foreign governments with their excess dollar holdings. For most of the past twenty years, such purchases have been good for foreigners because we were in a long-term bull market for

Treasury bonds. Our notes and bonds were providing high real returns. They rose in value.

The operative word, however, is *were*.

Today, U.S. interest rates are near historic lows, real returns are low to negative, and we are exporting record quantities of dollars. Our trade deficit is running at a $500 billion annual rate. The euro area, meanwhile, is running a surplus of nearly $100 billion. Japan's trade surplus is nearly $100 billion. China is also running a large trade surplus. All three areas import the bulk of their energy, which is priced in dollars.

In the late 1970s, as petrodollars piled up in Saudi Arabia and inflation headed for double-digit rates in the United States, the Saudis made noises about seeking a more secure currency. Nothing happened because there was no place to go. The euro didn't exist. The yen was seen as not quite big enough to replace the dollar. China was still communist, barely starting its shift to a capitalist economy. Basically, there was no alternative to the dollar. That's one of the reasons the price of gold soared, peaking at $800 an ounce in 1980. Gold is the currency without a government. Given the dismal history of government around the world, many think this quality makes gold superior to any paper currency. Others simply wish for a government willing to back its paper with something more substantial than . . . more paper.

Divide the amount of U.S. currency in circulation in 1980 by U.S. gold reserves, and you find that a gold-backed dollar would require gold to be priced at $800 an ounce.

Do the same math today,[19] and U.S. gold reserves[20] would have to be worth about $4,600 an ounce for us to have a gold-backed currency. That's nearly twelve times the current market price of gold.

Is that the "true" value of gold? We don't know. Besides, that's the wrong question. The important question is the reverse: *What's the true value of the dollar?*

This isn't 1980. The euro exists. China is a capitalist nation with a trade surplus, huge reserves, and an established role as the low-cost producer for the world. The yen is less of a candidate today because Japan is mired in deflation, near depression, and massive government deficits.

Today, the euro is strong and the Chinese yuan is pegged to the dollar. If the Europeans could keep their act together, get their long-term fiscal houses in order, and opt to back the euro with gold, they could displace the dollar as the world's reserve currency.

We think that's a very big if. Remember, Europe is aging faster than we are, and its population is declining. Their generational storm will be worse than ours. But we find it significant that European governments are no longer selling their gold. Indeed, Europe knows the value of gold: if you take a close look at a euro note, it features a circle of stars that slowly turn gold in color.

With a market region as populous as the United States, filled with high incomes and well-educated people, Europe would start to reap the benefits of being a reserve currency as soon as convenient 500 euro notes started to replace the billions in $100 bills circulating in Eastern Europe, the former Soviet Union, the war-torn nations of Africa, and the banana republics of South America.

They'd love to do it too.

The Chinese yuan is an even better candidate if you look ahead twenty years. Their currency is undervalued. They have decades of investment ahead of them. They have the largest trade surplus in the world. They have the largest pool of labor in the world. They could even repatriate generations of immigrants: millions of highly skilled, well-educated Chinese. With or without gold backing, the yuan could become the world's reserve currency. The center of global power could shift from Washington to Beijing, just as it passed from London to Washington less than a century ago.

China could become not only the most populous nation in the world; it could become the most economically powerful. The same development would also mark an increasing global demand for natural resources, particularly oil.

That's why we think every American's savings should have a material dollar-hedging element. In addition to a core holding of I Savings Bonds (for taxable savings) and Treasury Inflation Protected Securities (for qualified accounts) to protect against garden-variety inflation, this element could be a portfolio consisting of:

• Shares in unhedged international bond funds
• Shares in mutual funds that specialize in precious metals

• Shares in energy mutual funds

• Shares in international equity funds, particularly those specializing in China

As much as possible, all of these investments should be low-cost passive index funds.

The Core Fixed-Income Investment: Inflation-Protected Securities

Individuals can buy up to $30,000 of I Savings Bonds a year. Since both the interest and the inflation-based accretion of principal that the bonds earn is tax deferred until the bonds are redeemed, these bonds are great tools for saving or giving. In addition to the advantage of tax-deferred compounding, the bonds have a seldom-considered advantage when they are redeemed: Only the accumulated interest and accrued inflation principal is taxable; the original principal isn't taxed.

This is a minor point until considered from a cash flow point of view. Suppose you put $10,000 into an I Savings Bond when you are 60 and the bonds grow at a compound rate of 7 percent. By age 70, the bonds will be worth $20,000. You could redeem $10,000 worth of bonds, and you'd only need to pay taxes on $5,000. Take $10,000 from your IRA rollover, however, and the full $10,000 will be taxable. If you happen to be in "the zone" for having your Social Security benefits taxed, a portfolio of I Savings Bonds can help you reduce the additional tax burden.

Although they have been available for quite a few years, the financial community has been slow to understand the benefits and uses of Treasury Inflation Protected Securities and I Savings Bonds. We think they are powerful tools for risk-averse investors seeking a simple way to insure their savings against inflation. *Worry-Free Investing: A Safe Approach to Achieving Your Lifetime Financial Goals* (2003) by Zvi Bodie and Michael J. Clowes, is a good primer on the use of these instruments.

Today, only a handful of retail mutual funds specialize in inflation-protected securities.[21] We wish more 401(k) plans offered an inflation-protected fund choice. While Treasury Inflation Protected Securities are subject to the same interest rate upheavals as conventional coupon bonds, we believe these securities are an important asset class. They can be an important part of your financial plans, particularly as you get close to retirement.

Beyond the Core I: International Bond Funds and Foreign Currency Certificates of Deposit

As investors seeking pure, unmanaged asset class investments with minimal expenses, we're a bit frustrated here. While any investor can invest in the broad domestic bond market through funds such as Vanguard Total Bond Fund, there is no equivalent for bonds issued by other nations.

Recently, there were 191 mutual funds that invested in either international bonds or emerging markets obligations. While the actual number of distinct portfolios is much smaller due to the proliferation of fund marketing arrangements—"A" shares, "B" shares, down to "529A" shares—the vast majority of these funds invest in foreign securities but hedge out the currency risk. This eliminates them as candidates since we are looking for funds that accept the risk that exchange rates may shift and affect portfolio returns.

So we're left with a make-do situation, picking through the existing offerings and having to accept higher expenses for management than index investments. There are two large no-load funds with low expense ratios that invest in international bonds without hedging their portfolio. T. Rowe Price International Bond Fund (ticker: RPIBX) is the larger of the funds and clearly shows the benefit of an unhedged fund when the dollar is declining. American Century International Bond (ticker: BEGBX) is a somewhat smaller fund with a lower expense ratio and a better track record. It would be our (reluctant) choice in lieu of a global bond index fund.

Another way to have money invested for return in other currencies is through foreign currency certificates of deposit. These aren't widely available. Fidelity Investments, the nation's largest mutual fund company, offered them for a period but stopped several years ago. You can, however, invest this way through Everbank, which offers CDs in a variety of currencies, including euros and yen. More recently, Everbank introduced savings accounts denominated in yuan. Learn more by visiting its Web site, www.Everbank.com.

Beyond the Core II: Precious Metals Funds

Gold mining companies tend to be relatively small. The largest domestic gold company is Newmont Mining (ticker: NEM), with a recent total market capitalization of $9.2 billion. The second largest is Barrick Gold (ticker: ABX). Its market capitalization is only $6.2 billion. Either company would disappear inside General Electric or Microsoft, each valued at over $250 billion. As a consequence, we suggest buying your gold hedge in a diversified low-cost mutual fund. Again, we'd prefer an index fund because our object is to own gold as an asset class, but the option isn't available. The three largest funds are Fidelity Select Gold (ticker: FSAGX), American Century Global Gold (ticker: BGEIX), and Vanguard Precious Metals (ticker: VGPMX). The Vanguard fund has the lowest expense ratio (0.6 percent a year) and an excellent track record but is closed to new investors. The Fidelity fund, unfortunately, is burdened with an expense ratio of 1.24 percent, twice the ongoing cost of the other two funds. We'd watch for a reopening of the Vanguard fund.

Beyond the Core III: Energy Funds

Unlike gold, the energy sector offers index investments in the form of exchange-traded funds. There are now five such funds: Energy Select Sector SPDR (ticker: XLE), iShares Dow Jones U.S. Energy (ticker: IYE), iShares Goldman Sachs Natural Resources (ticker: IGE), iShares S&P Global Energy Sector (ticker: IXC), and the recently announced Vanguard Energy Index Fund. The indexes reflect the highly concentrated energy industry, with ten holdings accounting for about 70 percent of the assets in each fund.

For a single-purchase broad stake, we suggest the largest, least costly, and best-performing of the mutual funds: Vanguard Energy (ticker: VGENX). T. Rowe Price New Era, which is chartered to invest broadly in commodities, is a good second choice (ticker: PCNEX). Indeed, since this fund has significant gold mining holdings, as well as a broad selection of natural resource stocks, this fund could serve as a kind of uber-fund for inflation and currency hedges.

We suggest that you start with the Vanguard or T. Rowe Price fund. You might also get a "double-play" by investing in Petrochina (ticker: PTR), one of the world's largest oil companies with vast reserves of oil and natural gas. Warren Buffett has already purchased a large position in Petrochina.

This doesn't exhaust possible energy investments. If you are willing to do the homework, it would also be worthwhile to own shares in some of the domestic royalty trusts and some of the larger independent domestic oil and gas producers.

Beyond the Core IV: International Equity Funds, particularly China Funds

Modern portfolio theory tells us to diversify our portfolios by holding international as well as domestic equities. We can accomplish this in a single step by investing in a global index fund based on the broad Morgan Stanley Indexes. Vanguard Total International Stock Fund (ticker: VGTSX) is a sister fund to Vanguard Total Stock Market Fund, which replicates the broadest index of domestic stocks. Divided about 45 percent Europe, 45 percent Pacific, and 10 percent emerging markets, this fund allows broad diversification in a nondomestic asset class at minimal cost.

Investors with larger portfolios (or more interest in investing) would do well to explore the rapidly expanding world of exchange-traded funds where smaller slices of the world's equity markets can be had. We'd start with the iShares MSCI Pacific Ex-Japan Index (ticker: EPP, expense ratio 0.50 percent). This puts us in the growth area of the world and gives exposure to a region rich in natural resources. Indeed, seven of the ten largest holdings in the fund are Australian companies.

Unfortunately, none are in China. Worse, there is no inexpensive way to invest in China. There is no exchange-traded fund (ETF) for

China on a domestic exchange. (Barclays Global, however, has a China ETF that trades on the Hong Kong Exchange and follows the Morgan Stanley Capital International index for China.) Hong Kong, Singapore, and Taiwan, each has ETFs that trade on a domestic exchange but not China.

What to do?

Punt. While we would much rather invest in a broad global index to achieve diversification away from domestic inflation and currency decline, the most populous nation is the world is not included in the passive investing universe. The reluctant alternative is the handful of managed mutual funds that specialize in China. They tend to be small, managed, and expensive. Matthews China (ticker: MCHFX), for instance, has only $50 million in assets under management and an expense ratio of nearly 2 percent. Investec China and Hong Kong has $59 million in assets and an expense ratio just more than 2 percent. The least expensive China-only fund we could find was Fidelity China Region (ticker: FHKCX), the largest of the China funds, which has an expense ratio of 1.31 percent and about $100 million in assets.

Fortunately, there are also closed-end funds that specialize in China. Their assets under management are relatively large. Still better, they have sold at a discount to portfolio value for most of their history, and their expense ratios are no worse than the ratios for the open-end funds. The China Fund (ticker: CHN) has $117 million in assets, sells at a small discount to net asset value, and has an expense ratio of 2.28 percent. The Templeton China World Fund (ticker: TCH) has $168 million in assets, sells at a small discount to net asset value, and has an expense ratio of 1.68 percent. Both funds have sold at discounts approaching 25 percent in the past three years, reflecting the ups and downs of expectations for China. The discounts to net asset value may compensate for the relatively high annual expense ratios. Of the two, the China Fund has provided the better performance, expense ratio notwithstanding.

Given the ephemeral nature of superior management, we'd simply divide the China investment, buying some of Fidelity China Region and some Templeton China World. If China does as many expect, its currency will rise, its stocks will rise, and investors may well pay a premium when late arrivers start to chase performance.

The Alternative Portfolio

Don't get carried away with this! We've always felt a little sorry for the annual gathering of gold bugs in New Orleans. They have held their gold coins for more than two decades, waiting for the day they would be proved right and gold would be the coin of the realm. During those twenty years, they missed the biggest bull market in history in both bonds and stocks. What the hard money, libertarian types regularly forget is the flexibility of our system and the relentless creativity of politicians. Moreover, it's never been a good idea to short America or the dollar, if only because our fiscal sins pale when compared to those of other countries.

So we suggest that you be very measured about this change in your portfolio. Do first things first. So that you will see this in proportion, here are the steps:

1. Shift to low-expense domestic index investments for your primary portfolio. This will liberate you from financial malpractice. It will also allow you to focus on how much you save rather than the magic of investment returns.

2. Substitute inflation-protected investments for traditional bond funds. This will also cut your expenses (eliminate them if you buy I Savings Bonds) and eliminate inflation risk.

3. After that—*and only after that*—build a small alternative portfolio that is parallel to a conventional balanced portfolio, treating international bonds and gold-based investments as fixed income and energy funds and international and China equity funds as your alternative for domestic equities. If you have 20 to 30 percent of your *total* financial assets in your alternative portfolio, you've got a good start and better diversification.

You'll be able to run your conventional portfolio for an average of 20 basis points—less if you're a substantial investor who would benefit from Vanguard's Admiral Funds (minimum investment $250,000) or the low-cost broad ETFs. The low-cost exchange-traded funds can cost as little as 0.09 percent a year. With care, you'll be able to keep the annual cost of your alternative portfolio under an average of 1.00 percent (see table 8.8).

Table 8.8
Building your alternative portfolio

Asset Type	Conventional	Alternative
Equity	Total U.S. market index funds	Total International Equity Index Asian Equity Funds, particularly China; Energy funds
Fixed income	Inflation-protected security funds, I Savings Bonds	Unhedged international bond funds, Large gold funds

What we've laid out so far has been defensive, protecting against inflation and a weak currency. We'd also like to make a positive suggestion. With health care costs and spending certain to rise in the future, health care investments offer a positive opportunity to participate in the inevitable aging of America and the planet.

How do we do it?

Simple. We can invest in one of the exchange-traded index funds that specialize in health care (four at this writing). Unfortunately, these funds have costs in the vicinity of 0.60 percent a year, nearly twice the cost of the Vanguard Healthcare Fund (ticker: VGHCX, expense ratio 0.31 percent). While we prefer index investing, it seems silly to pay a premium to invest in one, particularly since the managed fund has ranked in the top 1 percent of all health care funds over the past 15 years, according to Morningstar.

We also urge moderation. Health care stocks account for nearly 15 percent of all market value in America, so if you own a broad index, you already have 15 percent of your money invested in health care. If your additional health care commitment was 10 percent of your broad equity portfolio, your total commitment to health care would be nearly 23 percent.

The biggest opportunity in health care is personal—tending to your health.

Eat Broccoli

Live hard. Die young. That's the thumbnail prescription for solving the best problem any generation of human beings has ever had to solve—

very long lives. Financing a long retirement won't be a problem if we take up smoking, eat as much as possible (preferably fast food), and avoid exercise of any kind. But why stop there? Let's also ignore those automobile safety belts and drive as fast as possible to the nearest opportunity for some unsafe sex.

Some part of that idea doesn't appeal to you?

Well, it doesn't appeal to us either. But if you take a close look at the cause of our personal and national financial worries, they are rooted in biology and medicine. We're not going broke because we can't afford the price of oil. We're going broke because we "live too long." We spend a great deal of money on health care in the last years of our lives, much of it in the last days and weeks.

In fact, while the entire retirement-investment complex focuses on financing the day-to-day living expenses of long retirements, a closer look at the unfunded liabilities we face shows that 84 percent of the problem is a health care problem. It's fundamentally biomedical, not financial. In 2002, for instance, economists Jagadeesh Gokhale and Kent Smetters estimated the total unfunded liabilities of government would be $46.9 trillion in 2004. Of that, $7.4 trillion was in the Social Security retirement income program, while $38.7 trillion was attributed to soaring costs for Medicare Parts A and B. (Only a virtual trace amount, $753 billion, was attributed to all other government programs.)

Don't get us wrong. Retirement income funding is a major problem. That $7.4 trillion shortfall is the reason we're getting those letters from Social Security warning us about 27 percent benefit cuts in the future.

But the health care problem is *five times larger*.

If a number like $38.7 trillion doesn't mean much to you, think about it this way. If you went around the United States and got each and every citizen to contribute everything they now own—their houses, cars, bank accounts, life insurance cash values, stocks, bonds, and mutual funds, less their mortgages and consumer debt—you'd have the problem covered with about $1 trillion to spare.

Like it or not, the health care problem will be topic number one for the rest of our lives. Nothing is more certain. We think this creates an opportunity for personal action that will save us money and improve our lives. While we're helping ourselves, it may also chop that $38.7 trillion into a smaller number.

We can take responsibility for our personal health. Instead of expecting that a doctor can give us a pill to cure anything and everything—and that someone else will pay for it—we can change our relationship to ourselves, to our doctors, and to the insurance companies that infuriate both doctor and patient.

In an ideal world we would all be like "the Wonderful One Horse Shay"—the Oliver Wendell Holmes poem about a carriage built to last exactly one hundred years. We would be vital and fully functional until suddenly all our parts wore out simultaneously and we died. Instead, most of us get a feeling that our basic warranties have run out sometime after middle age. Then we spend decades fretting over various losses. Some losses are serious, some not. Some people deal with it well, like the 83-year-old friend who smiles when he tells us that he's really not 83 if you average in the age of his many new replacement parts.

Other people don't deal well with aging.

The differences in our lifetime experiences—both our raw physical health and our satisfaction in life—give strong hints of just how much we might accomplish by assuming more responsibility for our personal well-being.

Some confirming evidence comes from longitudinal studies of personal development. One study followed a group of Harvard graduates from their graduation in the early 1940s to the present. Another followed a group of exceptionally bright women through their lifetimes. And another followed a group of inner-city men through their lifetimes. The task of managing all three studies, known as the Harvard Study of Human Development, and then interpreting more than six decades of data, fell to Dr. George E. Vaillant, a Harvard Medical School psychiatrist.[22]

With most of the subjects now well into their 80s, Vaillant divided them into three basic groups: the happy-well, the sad-sick, and the dead. Then he went backward in time. He started to look for signs that might have predicted, at age 50, the destiny of each subject. What he learned was surprising. Having a happy (or unhappy) childhood didn't tell much about your future. Neither did your education level or your income level.

Indeed, most of the "touchy-feely" measures weren't very good as indicators.

So were there any reliable predictors?

Yes. The two most powerful predictors of being among the happy-well were that you didn't smoke and didn't abuse alcohol. It also helped if you weren't overweight, did some exercise, and had a stable marriage. If you smoked or drank heavily, the odds were you were either among the sad-sick or were already dead.

Concern about the sad-sick isn't unique to the United States. As life expectancy has increased around the world, doctors and public health specialists have started to create new measures of expectancy and health that incorporate disability. Called DALE, for Disability-Adjusted Life Expectancy, the World Health Organization has examined the health data in every nation in the world to come up with comparable figures. Starting with life expectancy, they subtract years of ill health after weighting the level and duration of each disability.[23]

And guess what?

The United States is a noncontender in the Life Expectancy Olympics. Our poor showing extends to the DALE contest. In 2000 the World Health Organization found that twenty-four nations had DALEs of at least 70 years. Japan ranked first at 74.5 years, followed by Australia (73.2), France (73.1), Sweden (73.0), Spain (72.8), Italy (72.7), Greece (72.5), Switzerland (72.5), Monaco (72.4), and Andorra (72.3).

Note that the United States, a nation that spends more on health care than any other nation on earth, is not among the top ten. Indeed, we're twenty-fourth on the list. We scored 70 years of healthy life expectancy for babies born in 1999. The United Kingdom, Malta, and Israel scored better. Christopher Murray, director of the WHO's Global Program on Evidence for Health Policy, noted, "The position of the United States is one of the major surprises of the new rating system. Basically, you die earlier and spend more time disabled if you are an American rather than a member of most other advanced countries."

How can this be?

According to the World Health Organization, we lose ground for a number of reasons. One is that some portions of our population are very poor and suffer from the poor health "more characteristic of a poor developing country rather than a rich industrialized one." Another is AIDS. It affects more of our population than other industrialized countries. We also have a high level of violence compared to other industrialized nations. But we also have a high rate of coronary disease (in spite of reductions in recent years), and we are "one of the leading countries for cancers relating to tobacco."

We can get some idea of tobacco's impact by examining figures from Canada, the twelfth-ranked nation on the WHO list with an overall DALE of 72. Canada's two-year advantage over the United States is greater than the 1.6-year lead we have on . . . are you ready for this? Cuba.

A Canadian man age 45 in 1995 had an expectancy of 28.1 years if he was a smoker, 7 years less than the additional 35.5 years of life a male nonsmoker of the same age could expect. The additional years were also healthy years. Similar figures applied to women. A 45-year-old woman who smoked could expect to live another 30.5 years while a 45-year-old nonsmoker could expect another 40.8 years. That's a ten-year difference in life expectancy. Smoking had a similar impact on disability-free life expectancy. Male smokers age 45 could expect to live 18 years "without some form of related disability," 7 years less than the 25 years a nonsmoker could expect. Women nonsmokers of the same age could expect 8 more disability-free years.[24]

Whether it is lung cancer, chronic obstructive pulmonary disease, or circulatory and heart problems, much of the disability and eventual death that many Americans suffer can be traced directly to smoking.

We suffer similar results from our national habit of overeating and underexercising. With obesity at all ages now at epidemic levels, we can look forward to rising levels of diabetes, colorectal cancers, heart problems, joint problems, and more.

A century ago, the best way to increase life expectancy was through public health—better water, sewage systems, lower infant and child mortality. Today, the main levers on health and longevity are directly related to personal choices. Do we smoke? Do we drink too much? Do we eat too much? Do we bother to exercise? The choice is ours.

You can get some idea of the life expectancy gains possible by visiting some of the Web sites that calculate life expectancies.[25] While there is no way you can overcome a family history of early death from cancer or heart disease, gains in life expectancy can be had from exercise, weight loss, diet change. There is even a gain from regular teeth flossing. Like all things in the future, the exact amount of your possible gain from any self-care decision is uncertain. Also, different Web sites use different methods to make their calculations.

Even so, the potential is enormous. Consider this juxtaposition: It has taken well over two centuries for Americans to accumulate their current household wealth, a net value of some $39 trillion. *Decisions for self-care that we make over a much shorter period, the next seventy-five years, can have a dramatic effect on Medicare's $38.7 trillion unfunded liability.* If you avoid becoming part of the statistics that create the liability, your personal health and financial future will be improved. This puts a new twist on the famous line from President John F. Kennedy's first inaugural address: "Ask not what your country can do for you—ask what you can do for your country."[26]

Significantly, there is an increasing body of evidence that personal responsibility and engagement works at multiple levels. Not only can it improve our health and finances at the level of personal habit, it can also improve our health and finances where we engage the health care delivery system.

Contrary to popular thought, remedies for various illnesses are not known, fixed, and unwavering. Medical treatments for the same illness vary wildly from region to region. So do the outcomes and the expenses.

We know this from groundbreaking research by Dr. John E. Wennberg, director of the Center for the Evaluative Clinical Sciences at Dartmouth Medical School. Wennberg produces *The Dartmouth Atlas of Health Care*, a massive exercise in medical data collection and analysis. Here are some examples from the 1999 atlas for the Medicare Program,[27] with all results adjusted for age, sex, and race:

• In Binghamton, New York, only 0.5 of every 1,000 Medicare enrollees had radical prostatectomies. The rate was nine times higher, 4.7, in Baton Rouge, Louisiana. The national average was 1.9 per 1,000.

• In Beaumont, Texas, more than three times as many Medicare enrollees had cardiac catheterization (36 per 1,000) as in Temple, Texas (11.4 per 1,000). The national average was 22.7 per 1,000.

• In Miami, Florida, (109.6 per 1,000) four times as many Medicare enrollees had carotid duplex diagnostic procedures as the Medicare enrollees in Lafayette, Indiana (26.5 per 1,000). The national average was 53.0 per 1,000.

• While 80 percent of patients wish to avoid hospitalization and intensive care during the terminal phase of illness, 20 to 50 percent of all deaths occurred in acute care hospitals. Nationally, 33 percent of all Medicare deaths occurred in hospitals, but there was a 49 percent chance of dying in a hospital in Newark, New Jersey, and only a 17.2 percent chance in Bend, Oregon.

• Since you have to be in a hospital to build a hospital bill, the cost of inpatient care during the last six months of life also varied a great deal. It was $17,797 in Manhattan but only $6,198 in Bend, Oregon, compared to a national average of $9,943.

While the usual medical question is whether a procedure was done right, Wennburg and his research team now ask whether doctors were *doing the right thing.*

Enter George B. Bennett, chairman and CEO of Boston-based Health Dialog, a company premised on the idea of shared medical decision making—what he calls collaborative care. Health Dialog has trained nurses on phone lines ready to walk health plan members through the complexities of any medical decision.

In a recent visit, Bennett explained that fully informed patients routinely made care decisions that reduced costs rather than increased them. For specific examples, he pointed out that women suffering from uterine fibroids would often be offered relief through a hysterectomy. But when the women were informed that many of the symptoms disappear after age 50, some decided not to have surgery. Similarly, many men defer treatment for benign prostate disease when they are fully informed of its side effects and learn that for every man who dies *of* prostate cancer, 150 die *with* it.[28]

Bennett emphasizes that lower costs are a *side effect* of shared decision making, not a goal. This is an important distinction: every audience that has ever seen the movie *As Good As It Gets* hisses when a restrictive HMO is mentioned because HMOs—which have largely failed—

were premised on the idea of containing medical costs by restricting health care choices. The same applies to insurance-based fee-for-service: restricting health care choices attempts to control costs.

When medical decision making is shared, we tend to make more conservative—and less costly—decisions. That's why Bennett says that shared decision making could cut Medicare costs an estimated 30 percent while producing more satisfied patients.

We could, in other words, realize an $11.7 trillion "dividend" by being engaged and informed in our health care decisions. To put this in perspective, the health dividend is more than our collective equity in our homes—about $7.6 trillion at the end of 2002 according to Federal Reserve figures.

Personal responsibility is the great opportunity of this century, physically and financially.

Quit Your Job (or Have Your Spouse Quit His)

Take this job and shove it / I ain't working here no more.
—David Allan Coe

The ever-popular song is visceral and tough, but the sentiments are appropriate. Most of us have felt that way at one time or another. In fact, this is a good time to question the wisdom of work.

The United States, with a population over 285 million and a workforce of some 146.5 million people, recently employed some 137.7 million people in a mind-boggling array of tasks. That's a lot of people at work. It should put some perspective on the 8.8 million who are currently unemployed, between jobs, or otherwise short some paychecks.

Indeed, our national labor force participation rate—the proportion of all eligible people who are actually in the workforce—is near record levels, an impressive 66.4 percent in spite of a soft economy. The record, established in the late 1990s, was 67.1 percent. In some cities and states, the figure is higher. Equally important, many are working far more than forty hours a week. We live in a workaholic age.

You can see just how workaholic we are by comparing the current labor force participation rate with those from earlier times. As recently as 1980, it was 63.8 percent. It was still lower in 1970, 1960, and 1950 when the figures were 60.4 percent, 59.4 percent, and 59.2 percent, respectively. The increase occurred in spite of rising levels of education. In the past fifty years, college educations have supplanted high school educations, and graduate and professional degree study has soared. So a larger percentage of us are working today in spite of more years in school before work life begins and a rising tide of early retirements and downsizing when work life ends.

The single largest contributor to the rising participation rate is the two-earner household. Once rare, it is now the standard. If you are married and under the age of 60 in America, odds are that both husband and wife are employed. The labor force participation rate for women, as we pointed out earlier in this book, has nearly doubled in a half-century, rising from 33.9 percent in 1950 to nearly 60 percent recently.

Which leads us to an interesting question: *Does the two-earner household make economic sense?*

This is not a question of social values. We'll leave that to others. A visit to any bookstore will acquaint you with the growing library of titles suggesting that it doesn't make social sense, psychological sense, family sense, child-rearing sense, or community sense to have two earners in the same household. A few of these books even question whether the two-earner family makes economic sense, pointing to high taxes, work-related costs, child care expenses, and stress-induced spending.[29]

Ironically, virtually all of these voices of social and economic concern *understate* the problem because they consider only the immediate costs. With generational accounting, the lifetime costs become visible. We learn that the lifetime marginal tax rate for second workers can be over 100 percent.

Yes, you read that right: 100 percent. In some households, adding a second worker means a *loss* of lifetime income. Fortunately, the costs are only that draconian in low-income households, representing the loss of welfare and health benefits that households can experience when they go from unemployed to employed at low wages.

How about middle-income households?

Better, but not much. While the highest published marginal tax rate (the rate at which the last dollar of income is taxed) was 38.6 percent

Table 8.9
The lifetime net tax rate for spouses

	Wife's earnings		
Husband's earnings	$20,000	$30,000	$40,000
$20,000	80.6%	66.4%	58.6%
$30,000	43.8	43.5	42.6
$40,000	45.3	46.1	45.6

Source: Jagadeesh Gokhale and Laurence Kotlikoff, "Does It Pay Both Spouses to Work? www.ncpa.org.

on taxable income over $311,950—before the 2003 tax reduction—a second earner who adds $30,000 of income to a primary earner who also earns $30,000 faces a *lifetime* marginal net tax rate of 43.5 percent. This happens because the second earner pays full payroll taxes but gets virtually no increase in Social Security benefits. Expand the earnings combinations considered up to a total of $150,000, and the lifetime marginal rate will often exceed 60 percent (see table 8.9).

Faced with a lifetime tax rate in the vicinity of 50 percent, it gets a lot easier to question whether it's worth getting out of bed in the morning. Subtract work-related expenses, and it gets still harder. When push comes to shove, the second earner has very little to show for his or her work, and the net take-home pay per hour is so low many wonder if their time could be more fruitfully spent at home.

We think so. We can't think of a bigger incentive for do-it-yourself projects than a 50 percent tax rate—unless it's a 60 percent tax rate. The longer we put off making changes that will avert the coming collision between solemn promises and the ability of our children and grandchildren to carry the burden we've created for them, the higher that tax rate will rise. And the worse off our country will be for many years to come.

Epilogue

Our problems are man-made, therefore they may be solved by man. And man can be as big as he wants. No problem of human destiny is beyond human beings.
—President John F. Kennedy

In our every deliberation, we must consider the impact of our decisions on the next seven generations.
—From the great law of the Iroquois confederacy

As we write, federal debt held by the public exceeds $4 trillion. Spread over 280 million Americans, that's more than $14,300 a person. Some people react to this figure with dismay.

We don't.

That $14,300 a person represents all the formal debt our country has accumulated since the First Continental Congress. It includes what we paid France for the Louisiana Purchase, what we paid Russia for Alaska, the money borrowed to finance every hot and cold war we've ever fought, the money borrowed to finance the Works Progress Administration during the Great Depression, and over seventy years of programs to stimulate the creation of jobs and economic growth.

Not all of that borrowed money was well spent, but we're not here to quibble. We know that the true cost of what was purchased far exceeds the amount borrowed. It includes tens of thousands of lives given in wars, years of life volunteered to service, and generation after generation that came, labored, and sacrificed for their children and their children's children.

No generation gave more to our nation than the one now passing—Americans in their late 70s and older who have rightfully been called the

Greatest Generation because they endured the Great Depression and fought World War II. As with every other generation before them, they left us a tremendous legacy.

At a mere $14,300 per head, the formal debt attached to that legacy makes Club America the greatest bargain in history. It's small wonder that untold thousands of illegal immigrants risk their lives each year to live and work in the land of the free, the home of the brave, and the richest country on earth.

But here's the rub. The American dream is becoming prohibitively expensive. *And unless we act soon, the Greatest Generation will be the last to leave its children and grandchildren a better country.*

The problem, as shown throughout this book, is that the government's informal obligations—its promises of old age income and medical care—dwarf its formal commitments. These promises, which are codified in federal law and protected by legions of AARP members, are as real as any U.S. Treasury bond.

The Treasury Papers—the study that former Treasury Secretary Paul O'Neill commissioned and that the Bush the Second administration subsequently expunged from the FY2004 Federal Budget document—record a fiscal gap (the present value difference between our government's projected expenditures and receipts) of $45 trillion—now $51 trillion, thanks to the new Medicare drug benefit. That's more than eleven times the official debt. Equally distributed, it is $159,000 per American man, woman, and child. That's $159,000 each that we can pay off today—or if we want to wait, it's $159,000 we can pay with interest over time.

The longer we delay addressing this massive red hole, the bigger it gets. Indeed, thanks to the truly amazing aging of our country and the miracle of compound interest, the fiscal gap is now growing by more than $1 trillion a year. Worse yet, we seem to have every intention of dumping the entire bill in our children's laps. Nice try, but this bill is far too big for our kids to handle. We need to face that reality and protect them to the greatest extent possible from the economic monster we've created.

Unfortunately, even with the best reforms, our kids are going to get clobbered. And, as a consequence, we'll never measure up to the

Greatest Generation. But unless we get our act in gear, we'll end up being known as the Worst Generation.

As pointed out in chapter 4, we can run, but we can't hide from our government's bills. Economic growth is not going to bail us out. Nor will our parents, our trading partners, our immigration policy, our bosses, our technology, or our retirement behavior. Our only hope lies in immediately and radically reforming the Social Security and Medicare systems along the lines recommended in chapter 6.

Like the proverbial road to hell, our leaders paved the path to national bankruptcy with good-sounding intentions and well-delivered speeches. They wanted to help the old and the sick and the overburdened taxpayers—and who could blame them? They just never wanted to know who would pay for their largesse. Worse, they worked overtime to make sure no one asked that question.

Generational accounting, which is designed to show which generations will pay the government's bills, has been around for more than fifteen years, but both parties have repeatedly suppressed its uncomfortable findings. Instead, both parties have used an economically meaningless but infinitely malleable fiscal measuring rod, the federal budget deficit, to disguise their true actions.

The result is clear. Fiscally and generationally, our government is driving blind.

Sound insane?

Sure sounds that way to us, but to check, we went to Google and typed in "the definition of insanity is" and discovered that *the definition of insanity is doing the same thing, over and over, and expecting a different result*. Some Web sites attribute this definition to Benjamin Franklin, others to Albert Einstein. Whatever the source, the quotation is one of the key mantras recited at Alcoholics Anonymous, Narcotics Anonymous, Sex Addict Anonymous, Overeaters Anonymous, and other groupings of addicts.

Unfortunately, the political junkies running the country are in denial and see no need to attend recovery meetings. Each session of Congress and each election leads to the same thing: talk and more talk about reforming Social Security and Medicare, but either no action or a concerted effort to make matters worse. When things really start looking grim, Congress or the president or both organize a commission to study the issue and then promptly dump its report in the trash when they're told things they don't want to hear.

Truth be told, our politicians care more about their next fix—the next election—than they do about the next generation. And they're not going to clean up their act unless and until they are confronted with a major crisis. Hence, as crazy as it sounds, our only real hope is that the economy will go critical sooner rather than later.

The current administration has certainly been doing its level best to hasten that day. It has cut taxes three times, legislated a huge increase in Medicare benefits, and jacked up discretionary spending. In the process, it has achieved the impossible—given voodoo economics a bad name.

As we write, the bond traders seem to be starting to take notice. Long-term interest rates are nudging up and the dollar is heading down. If these rates hit the double-digit levels that are justified by our country's fiscal condition, the politicians may finally connect the dots and engage in reforms that will diminish the prospect of the boogeyman. We refer, of course, to very high rates of inflation arising from our government's doing what every other irresponsible government has done for two millennia: print money to pay its bills.

We've written this book in the bloodless and realistic prose of economics and money, but there's an underlying passion in our message. Our children are facing a terrible bind. Like those who came to America over the past three centuries, our kids may spend their adult years yearning for another shore, wondering where their America went and where they can go to find it. Some will leave. New Zealand sounds good. Australia is resource rich. And property's cheap in Argentina.

Unless we act now, those who stay will become increasingly frustrated with us, their parents, for doing the absolutely unimaginable—bringing an end to the American dream, which our forefathers risked their lives and fortunes to preserve.

The obligation to set things right lies with all Americans, but it rests particularly with the massive baby boom generation that is scheduled to exact such an awful toll on the next generation. The boomers spent their youth defying the status quo and decrying their lack of power. Now they are the establishment. They run the PTAs, staff the police forces, control the government, and send soldiers to war. Like it or not, the boomers have no one to blame but themselves for preserving the policies now in place.

Boomers are in power, but they are not solely in charge. Each of us—young, middle aged, and old—is responsible for forging the path ahead. And each of us must decide whether to be part of this problem or part of its solution. Now as always, there is no middle ground in matters of right and wrong. Indeed, as President Kennedy reminded us, *"the hottest places in hell are reserved for those who in a period of moral crisis maintain their neutrality."*[1]

And make no mistake. This is not just a moral crisis of the first order. This is *the* moral crisis of our age. We are collectively endangering our children's economic futures without giving them the slightest say in the matter. We are doing this systematically and with malice aforethought. Worst of all, we are pretending not to notice.

Whether or not we can handle that truth, we must now face it. Our country has spent decades piling up astronomical bills for the next generation to pay. Forcing them to do so will destroy their lives and ruin our country. The only solution is to radically, but rationally, reform our social insurance institutions and take other critical steps to prevent our nation's bankruptcy.

Let this book then be a call to duty—the duty to protect the children and nation that we so dearly love.

Notes

Chapter 1

1. John W. Rowe and Robert L. Kahn, *Successful Aging* (New York: Dell), 1999, p. 6. Other sources have smaller projections. The United Nations, which regularly projects population and demographic figures for every nation and area of the world, estimates 473,400 centenarians in the United States by 2050 and 3,218,900 in the world.

2. U.S. Department of Commerce, *Statistical Abstract of the United States*, (Washington, D.C.: U.S. Government Printing Office, 1997), table 46.

3. "Population Distribution by Age, Race, Nativity, and Sex Ratio," www .infoplease.com/ipa/A0110384.html.

4. Population Reference Bureau, "U.S. Fertility Trends: Boom and Bust and Leveling Off," www.prb.org.

5. Old Age, Survivors and Disability Insurance, "Assumptions and Methods Underlying Actuarial Estimates," 2002, www.ssa.gov/OACT/TR/TR02/V _demographic.html.

6. The combined employer/employee tax rate rose from 3 percent in 1950 to 15.3 percent in 2000.

7. Jim Oeppen and James W. Vaupel, "Broken Limits to Life Expectancy," *Science*, May 10, 2002.

8. Kevin Kinsella and Victoria A. Velkoff, "An Aging World: 2001," in *Life Expectancy and Changing Mortality*, p. 31. (Washington, D.C.: U.S. Census Bureau, November, 2001) www.census.gov/prod/2001pubs/p95-01-1.pdf.

9. Thomas T. Perls, "The Oldest Old," *Scientific American*, January 1995, 70–75.

10. Economist, *Pocket World in Figures*, (New York: Wiley, 1999), pp. 70–71.

11. Barbara W. Tuchman, *A Distant Mirror: The Calamitous Fourteenth Century* (New York: Knopf, 1978), p. 97.

12. David Brooks, *BOBOS* in Paradise: The New Upper Class and How They Got There* (New York: Simon & Schuster, 2000), p. 14.

13. Ibid.

14. "Median Age at First Marriage," www.factmonster.com/ipka/A0005061 .html.

15. T. J. Mathews and Stephanie J. Ventura, "Birth and Fertility Rates by Educational Attainment: United States, 1994," *Monthly Vital Statistics Report* 45, no. 10 Supplement (April 1997) www.cdc.gov/nchs/data/mvsr/supp/mv45 _10s.pdf.

16. Cheryl Russell, "Demographics of the U.S.: Trends and Projections," in *Labor Force by Sex and Age, 1950 to 2025* (Ithaca, N.Y.: New Strategist Publications, 2000), p. 237.

17. Howard N. Fullerton, Jr., "Labor Force Participation: 75 Years of Change, 1950–98 and 1998–2025," *Monthly Labor Review* (December 1999): 3.

18. Another recent example of growing unrest is Elizabeth Warren and Amelia Warren Tyagi's, *The Two Income Trap: Why Middle-Class Mothers and Fathers Are Going Broke* (New York: Basic Books, 2003). Discussing the option of having no children, the authors write, "Childlessness may not be a calculated economic strategy, but it has powerful economic consequences. By foregoing childbearing, a woman decreases her chances of going bankrupt by 66 percent. She reduces the likelihood that she will ever deal with a collection call or worry about a repo man, and she increases the chances that she will hold on to her home. And this improved financial security will last a lifetime: By remaining childless, a woman greatly improves her odds of having a comfortable retirement."

19. Robert Byrne, *The 2,548 Best Things Anybody Ever Said* (New York: Fireside Books, 2003), #2022.

20. For countries with the highest divorce rates in the world, see www.aniki .com/divorce.html.

21. For an international comparison of divorce rates, see www.jinjapan.org/ stat/stats/02VIT33.html.

22. Matthew D. Bramlett and William D. Mosher, "Cohabitation, Marriage, Divorce, and Remarriage in the United States," *CDC Vital and Health Statistics* (July 2002): 2.

23. Rose M. Kreider and Jason M. Fields, "Number, Timing, and Duration of Marriages and Divorces: 1996," *Current Population Reports* (February 2002).

24. Laurence J. Kotlikoff and John N. Morris, "How Much Care Do the Aged Receive from Their Children? A Bimodal Picture of Contact and Assistance," in *The Inquires in the Economics of Aging* (Cambridge, Mass.: National Bureau of Economic Research, 1989). ed. David A. Wise.

25. http://www.brainyquote.com/quotes/quotes/p/phyllisdil136115.html.

26. Kenneth W. Wachter, "2030s Seniors: Kin and Step-Kin" (working paper, University of California, Berkeley April 1995), paper www.demog.berkeley.edu/ ~wachter/WorkingPapers/kinpaper.pdf.

27. United Nations Report, "World Population Aging: 1950–2050," 2002.

28. Richard S. Wheeler, *The Buffalo Commons* (New York: Forge, 1998).

29. A more recent report took a much darker view and chopped future population estimates in Africa.

Chapter 2

1. Professor Michael Boskin of Stanford University and professor Joseph Stiglitz of Columbia University are two exceptions.

2. The CBO claims that it is just following the law in formulating its budget projections. There is some truth to this in that Congress requires the CBO to forecast discretionary spending based on what is currently legislated. However, the CBO is free to make and release alternative projections. It could, if it so chose, label the official projection as the "Unrealistic Official Projection" and label the unofficial projection as the "Realistic Unofficial Projection." Furthermore, it could, if it chose to, refrain from publicizing the unrealistic projection on its Web site and elsewhere. Whether it were to use precisely this alternative language or this publication strategy is not critical. What is critical is directing the attention of the public, the press, and, indeed, members of Congress to the most realistic budget forecast.

3. If, for example, we're talking about receiving or paying $50,000 not next year but in three years, the discount factor would be 1.10 raised to the power three or 1.10 times 1.10 times 1.10. Dividing $50,000 by this factor yields $37,565.74. To check that having $37,565.74 today has the same value to you as having $50,000 in three years, note that investing that sum for three years at 10 percent yields $37,565.74 × (1.10) × (1.10) × (1.10) or $50,000.

4. Estimates for gross government liabilities as a ratio of GDP obtained from the OECD Web site at www.oecd.org/dataoecd/5/51/2483816.xls.

5. See President's Council of Economic Advisors, *The Economic Report of the President* (Washington, D.C.: U.S. Government Printing Office, 1982) p. 131.

6. See Paul Begala, *It's Still the Economy Stupid* (New York: Simon & Schuster, 2002) which he dedicates to "Bill and Hillary Clinton, Al and Tipper Gore, and all the people [read staffers] who made the Clinton economic success a reality."

7. Remember, when your earned income rises, your future Social Security retirement benefits also rise.

8. The source of these net marginal tax rates are Jagadeesh Gokhale and Laurence J. Kotlikoff, *Does It Pay to Work* (Washington, D.C.: The American Enterprise Institute, forthcoming).

9. The households considered in table 2.1 feature a husband and wife, both of whom are initially age 18 and live at most to age 95. The couple has two children, one at age 25 and one at age 27. Both spouses earn the same income and

work through age 64. Their initial annual earnings, which grow by 1 percent in real terms each year, are multiples of the minimum wage times 40 hours per week times 52 weeks. Both children attend college between ages 19 and 22. Couples with annual earnings below $105,000 pay one-third of their total initial real annual earnings in college tuition and room and board for each child for each year of education. For couples earning $105,000 or more, college support payments are capped at $35,000 (one-third of $105,000). The couple initially rents a house for 25 percent of its total initial annual earnings. But at age 25, the couple purchases a house for three times initial earnings. This purchase is financed with a 20 percent down payment and an 80 percent mortgage carried at an 8 percent nominal interest. The couple earns a 4 percent real pretax return on assets. Funeral expenses for each spouse are 10 percent of each spouse's initial annual earnings, up to a maximum of $10,000. There are no bequests apart from the value of home equity when the last spouse dies, since the couple never sells its home.

10. See Jagadeesh Gokhale and Laurence J. Kotlikoff, "Is War Between the Generations Inevitable?" National Center for Policy Analysis Policy Report no. 246, November 2001. The lifetime net tax rate reported in this study for future generations is 18 percent rather than 20 percent. But we've increased its size to account for fiscal policy changes that have occurred since the study was written.

11. The CBO projections were generated by John Sturrock, a senior economist at the Congressional Budget Office.

12. The fiscal gap, G, can be expressed as $G = C + D + V - T - A^*$, where A^* is the present value of the net taxes of future generations assuming they pay the same lifetime net tax rates as current generations.

13. "Balance Sheet of Household and Nonprofit Organizations," available at: http://www.federalreserve.gov/releases/Z1/.

14. Jagadeesh Gokhale and Kent Smetters, "Fiscal and Generational Imbalances: New Budget Measures for New Budget Priorities," Federal Reserve Bank of Cleveland, Policy Discussion Paper, March 2002.

15. Even though the infinite horizon liability is three times the seventy-five-year liability, the immediate and permanent payroll tax hike required to pay off the infinite horizon liability is not three times larger than the tax hike needed to pay off the seventy-five-year liability. The reason is that the tax base used to determine the requisite infinite horizon tax hike is the present value of taxable payroll over the infinite horizon rather than just the next seventy-five years.

Chapter 3

1. See Laurence J. Kotlikoff, *Generational Policy*, (Cambridge, Mass.: MIT Press, 2004.)

2. Note that when the government changes its labeling, it does so with respect to the new young generation around at the time. It doesn't change the labels of

the payments or receipts it makes to or receives from the initial set of elderly (those elderly alive at the time of the change in labeling).

3. For example, the discounted present value of paying taxes of $1,000 when young net of the discounted present value of receiving a transfer of $1,000 when old is $90.90. But so is the discounted present value of paying no taxes when young but $100 in taxes when old.

4. Scott Burns, "IOUs: A Tale of Strife," *Dallas Morning News*, August 23, 2003, examines the reality of the Social Security Trust Fund through the story of a married couple's finances: http://www.dallasnews.com/business/ scottburns/columns/2003/stories/082403dnbusburns.95124.html.

Chapter 4

1. In rural Santa Fe County, in a state that has only one area code, Qwest was still burying fiberoptic cable in the spring of 2002.

2. Joelle Tessler, " 'Off-the-Scale' Fiber Glut Rocks Telecom Industry," *Mercury News*, April 13, 2002.

3. Jagadeesh Gokhale and Kent Smetters, "Fiscal and Generational Balances: New Budget Matters for New Budget Priorities," Federal Reserve Bank of Cleveland, Policy Discussion Paper, March 2002.

4. This abstracts from the important issue of whether the private sector can manage publicly owed assets better than can the government.

5. Even American corporations, which are no longer regarded as bastions of accounting integrity, distinguish between ongoing revenue and asset sales.

6. See Laurence J. Kotlikoff, Kent Smetters, and Jan Walliser, "Finding a Way Out of America's Demographic Dilemma," National Bureau of Economic Research Working Paper, no. 8258, 2001.

7. Samuel P. Huntington, *The Clash of Civilizations and the Remaking of World Order* (New York: Touchstone Books, 1997), pp. 86–88.

8. Robert B. Avery and Michael S. Rendall, "Estimating the Size and Distribution of Baby Boomers' Prospective Inheritances," in *1993 Proceedings of the Social Statistics Section* (Alexandria, VA: American Statistical Association 1993) pp. 11–19.

9. See Jagadeesh Gokhale, Laurence J. Kotlikoff, and John Sabelhaus, "Understanding the Postwar Decline in U.S. Saving," *Brookings Papers on Economic Activity* 1 (1993): 315–390.

10. See John Ameriks, Robert Veres, and Mark J. Warshawsky, "Making Retirement Income Last a Lifetime," *Journal of Financial Planning* (December 2001):60–76.

11. Gokhale, Kotlikoff, and Sabelhaus, "Understanding the Postwar Decline," 361.

12. Ibid., p. 340.

13. Laurence J. Kotlikoff and John Morris, "Why Don't the Elderly Live with Their Children? A New Look," in David A. Wise, ed., *Issue in the Economics of Aging* (Chicago: University of Chicago Press, 1990), pp. 149–172.

14. Many of these studies are either presented or discussed in Laurence J. Kotlikoff, *Essays on Saving, Bequests, Altruism, and Life-Cycle Planning* (Cambridge, Mass.: MIT Press, 2001).

15. See Gokhale, Kotlikoff, and Sabelhaus, "Understanding the Postwar Decline in U.S. Saving."

16. Congressional Budget Office, "Utilization of Tax Incentives for Retirement Saving" (August 2003).

17. See Laurence J. Kotlikoff and David A. Wise, *The Wage Carrot and the Pension Stick* (Kalamazoo, Mich.: W. E. UpJohn Institute for Employment Research, 1989).

18. Statement of Steven A. Kandarian, executive director of the Pension Benefit Guarantee Cooperation before the Government Affairs Committee Subcommittee on Financial Management, the Budget, and International Security, U.S. Senate, September 15, 2003.

19. Olivia S. Mitchell and Stephen P. Utkus, "The Role of Company Stock in Defined Contribution Plans," NBER Working Paper, no. 9250, October 2002.

20. Ibid.

21. Ibid.

22. Scott Burns, "The 401(k) Lottery, by Industry," *Dallas Morning News*, January 27, 2002, and "Examining Your Gift Horse," *Dallas Morning News*, April 17, 2001.

23. See table 7 in James Poterba and David A. Wise, "Individual Financial Decisions in Retirement Savings Plans and the Provision of Resources for Retirement," NBER Working Paper, no. 5762, September 1996.

24. Employee Benefit Research Institute, "Retiree Health Benefits: Public Perception vs. National Reality," September 2002, http://www.ebri.org/hcs/2002/hcs-ret.pdf.

25. Patrick J. Purcell, "Older Workers: Employment and Retirement Trends," *Monthly Labor Review* (October 2000).

26. See table 1 in John Attarian, *Immigration: The Wrong Answer for Social Security* (Raleigh, N.C.: American Immigration Control Press, 2003).

27. Alan J. Auerbach and Philip Oreopoulos, "Analyzing the Fiscal Impact of Immigration," *American Economic Review* 89, no. 2 (May 1999): 176–180.

Chapter 5

1. This chapter draws on an article that appeared in fall 2003 issue of the *National Interest* entitled "Going Critical" that Kotlikoff coauthored with Niall Ferguson.

2. Scott Burns, "The Emperor's Clothes," *Dallas Morning News*, January 17, 1999   http://www.dallasnews.com/business/scottburns/columns/archives/1999/990117SU.htm.

3. Concern about immediate Brazilian default has subsided of late as investors realized that newly elected President Lula is not loo loo, but the perceived probability of default over the next few years remains high.

4. See Glyn Davies, *A History of Money* (Cardiff: University of Wales Press, Cardiff, 1994).

5. We refer here to the government's nominal debt, not its inflation-indexed debt.

6. Under Secretary of the Treasury Peter R. Fisher put it another way. Speaking to the Columbus, Ohio, Council on World Affairs on November 14, 2002, he said, "To say that doing this would 'make it easier' to meet our future liabilities is misleading. It's like telling a man that it would easier for him to jump across the Mississippi River if he took a running start." http://www.ustreas.gov/press/releases/po3622.htm.

7. To be fair to those programs, other labeling conventions wouldn't necessarily single them out.

Chapter 6

1. See John F. Cogan and Olivia S. Mitchell, "Perspectives from the President's Commission on Social Security Reform," *Journal of Economic Perspectives* 17, no. 2 (spring 2003): 149–172.

2. Compared with other Republican plans, the President's Commission plan (Model 2) is less sanguine about the return on the stock market. Consequently, the commission assumed that workers would contribute roughly 40 percent of their Social Security payroll taxes to the new accounts. But since this costs the system a lot of money, the commission also assumed that workers would not only have their Social Security benefits reduced via switching from wage indexing to price indexing, but they'd also have their Social Security benefits reduced by a special retirement tax calculated as their contributions to the new accounts accumulated at a real 2 percent return. The commission's plan also calls for significant additional general revenue finance of the Social Security System. So the plan screws workers in three ways—by price-indexing benefits, establishing the retirement tax, and imposing additional general revenue finance. Some plan!

3. This abstracts from benefit reduction that occurs because of early receipt of dependent and widow benefits.

4. See Jagadeesh Gokhale and Laurence J. Kotlikoff, "Social Security's Treatment of Postwar Americans. How Bad Can it Get?" in *The Distributional Effects of Social Security Reform*, ed. Martin S. Feldstein and Jeffrey Lieberman, 207–262. (Chicago: University of Chicago Press, 2002).

5. The size of the untruncated Social Security long-term liability would be even larger were the trustees to adopt more realistic assumptions about how quickly

the baby boomers will die. Most top academic demographers appear to believe that the trustees are substantially understating future increases in longevity. See, for example, Ronald Lee and Hisashi Yamagata, "Sustainable Social Security: What Would It Cost?" *National Tax Journal* 56, no. 1 (2003): 27–43.

6. Aficionados of the current Social Security system will object that we're being too generous in defining accrued benefits because young workers will be treated as lifetime poor workers due to the progessivity of the Social Security benefit schedule. We understand their concern, but think it's important to pay current workers every penny of their accrued benefits. This way current workers will be assured that the reform is giving them every penny they earned under the old (current) Social Security system.

7. That is, for purposes of computing survivor and disability benefits, the Social Security administration would not enter zeros into workers' earnings records after the reform.

8. If a low-cost global index fund sounds far-fetched to you, we suggest that you check the rapid development of exchange-traded funds. Although only a few years old, they now number over 100 and provide instant passive access to equity markets around the world. More recently, Barclays Global introduced first fixed-income exchange-traded funds. And today, if you visit the Dow-Jones Web site, you'll find risk-graded global index portfolios. We think it won't be long before those indices—or a close relative—will be offered as one-stop shopping global portfolios. If this were expensive, it wouldn't work. Exxon Mobil, however, has index fund choices in its 401(k) plan that cost 3 to 7 basis points. That's .03 to .07 percent a year. If Exxon Mobil can get such low costs with a $5 billion plan, imagine what the new Social Security Administration can do with its billions. The Federal Employee Retirement System has a similar plan with very low costs.

9. These annuities would be "priced" (their levels would be determined by) the prevailing life expectancy for the cohort whose account balances are being annuitized. To accommodate unexpected increases in cohort longevity, a portion of each PSS participant's account balances would be held in reserve rather than annuitized.

10. See table 2 in Jagadeesh Gokhale and Kent Smetters, *Fiscal and Generational Imbalances* (Washington, D.C.: American Enterprise Institute Press, 2003).

11. We use the word *seem* again because what is and isn't called Medicare receipts in calculating Medicare's liability is arbitrary. Medicare has two parts, A and B, corresponding to the HI, or Hospital Insurance, program and SMI of the Supplemental Medical Insurance program. The HI program has a $21.1 trillion unfunded liability, and the SMI program has a $16.5 trillion unfunded liability. This is based on ascribing only 2.9 percentage points of the total 15.3 percentage point FICA tax to Medicare and ascribing none of the general revenues used to pay for Medicare Part B to that program. Were the government to use different conventions in designating its tax revenues, Medicare could look in much better and, indeed perfect, fiscal shape.

12. This figure is based on CMS data at http://cms.hhs.gov/publications/trusteesreport/2002/tabivb1.asp.

13. See table 5 in Gokhale and Smetters, *Fiscal and Generational Imbalances*.

14. See "Private Plans Again Seen as Aid to Medicare," *New York Times*, July 5, 2003, p. 1.

15. George F. Will, "Bush's Bad News for the Right," *Boston Globe*, July 24, 2003, p. A11.

16. See Peter Ferrera, John C. Goodman, Gerald Musgrave, and Richard Rahn, "Solving the Problem of Medicare," National Center for Policy Analysis Policy Report, no. 109, January 1984, and Andrew Rettenmaier and Thomas R. Saving, "Saving Medicare," National Center for Policy Analysis Policy Report, no. 222, January 1999.

Chapter 7

1. Text from August 2003 letter. Much the same was said the previous year: "Changes will be needed to meet the demands of the times. We're living longer and healthier lives, 79 million 'Baby Boomers' are approaching retirement, and in about 30 years, there will be nearly twice as many older Americans as there are today.

"Social Security now takes in more in taxes than it pays out in benefits. The excess funds are credited to Social Security's trust funds, which are expected to grow to over \$4 trillion before we need to use them to pay benefits. In 2018, we'll begin paying more in benefits than we collect in taxes. By 2041, the trust funds will be exhausted and the payroll taxes collected will be enough to pay only 73 percent of benefits owed.

"We'll need to resolve long-range financial issues to make sure Social Security will provide a foundation of protection for future generations as it has done in the past."

2. The 1994 Social Security and Flying Saucers Survey, http://www.thirdmil.org/publications/surveys/surv7.html.

3. Alicia Munnell, *The Declining Role of Social Security*, http://www.bc.edu/centers/crr/jtf_6.shtml.

4. Historical Tables, Budget of the United States Government, Fiscal Year 2004, http://w3.access.gpo.gov/usbudget/fy2004/maindown.html.

5. George F. Gilder, *Sexual Suicide* (New York: Quadrangle Books, 1973).

6. Congressional Budget Office, Long Range Fiscal Policy Brief, "A 125-Year Picture of the Federal Government's Share of the Economy, 1950 to 2075," revised July 3, 2002, http://www.cbo.gov/showdoc.cfm?index=3521&sequence=0. See table, following page.

7. Ibid., p. 3.

They've seen the future: And spending will double by 2075

Fiscal year	Social Security (1)	Medicare (2)	Medicaid (3)	Total (1 + 2 + 3)	All other except interest	Interest expense	Total
1950	0.3%	NA	NA	0.3%	13.5%	1.8%	15.6%
1970	2.9	0.7	0.3	3.9	12.8	1.4	19.3
1990	4.3	1.9	0.7	6.9	11.7	3.2	21.8
2010	4.4	2.7	1.8	8.8	7.6	0.8	17.2
2030	6.2	4.9	2.8	13.9	7.1	-0.2	20.8
2050	6.0	6.7	3.9	16.7	7.1	3.1	26.9
2070	6.2	8.9	4.9	20.0	7.1	9.4	36.5
2075	6.2	9.6	5.3	21.1	7.1	11.5	39.7

Note: This CBO study assumes that government revenues remain fixed at 19 percent of GDP in the future and spending over that amount is financed. As a result, interest expense starts to rise rapidly after 2040. The alternative is to virtually double revenue collections. Note that expenditures on other government functions remain fixed at 7.1 percent, which is below their current level.

8. U. S. Senate and House of Representatives, Joint Economic Committee, October 24, 2002, www.house.gov/jec/press/2002/10-24-02.htm.

9. Ben S. Bernanke, "Deflation: Making Sure 'It' Doesn't Happen Here," National Economists Club, November 21, 2002, www.federalreserve.gov/boarddocs/speeches/2002/20021121/default.htm.

10. Ibbotson Associates, *Stocks, Bonds, Bills, and Inflation, 2003 Yearbook* (New York: John Wiley & Sons, 2003).

Chapter 8

1. Peter Lynch, "Fear of Crashing," *Worth* (September 1995).

2. Scott Burns, "Dangerous Advice from Peter Lynch," *Dallas Morning News*, October 1, 1995, www.scottburns.com.

3. www.financialengines.com.

4. www.troweprice.com.

5. Laurence J. Kotlikoff is one of the developers of this software.

6. To be fair, TIAA-CREF's Web site also features a slightly less primitive life insurance calculator.

7. Scott Burns, "The Lessons of Really Long Term Investing," *Dallas Morning News*, November 3, 2003.

8. A firm like Sanford Bernstein, which deals with high-net-worth individuals, is a good example—it walks clients through the consumption/giving/estate trade-offs.

9. A variety of on-line portfolio survival calculators can be found at www.retireearlyhomepage.com.

10. Vanguard, for instance, recently introduced six "target retirement" funds that use combinations of six different index funds. This is in addition to its "Balanced Index" fund, which has done better than 76 percent of its competing managed balanced funds. Fidelity has its "Four-in-One" fund that uses four index funds.

11. "How America Saves," a report on Vanguard defined contribution plans, cites Social Security Administration figures for 2002 indicating that 20 percent of older Americans get 100 percent of their income from Social Security, another 11 percent get 90 to 99 percent of their income from Social Security, and 33 percent get 50 to 89 percent of their income from Social Security.

12. www.ssa.gov.

13. Scott Burns, "Score Yourself for Wealth, the Sequel," *Dallas Morning News*, September 7, 2003.

14. Scott Burns, "The Investment Equivalent of Working at Wal-Mart," *Dallas Morning News*, March 9, 2003.

15. Scott Burns, *Home, Inc.: The Hidden Wealth and Power of the American Household* (New York: Doubleday, 1972).

16. Scott Burns, "Home Ownership and Taxes," *Dallas Morning News,* April 22, 24, 27, 2003.

17. http://www.cardweb.com/.

18. This assumes a 5 percent interest rate on a loan of $25,000 for five years, giving a monthly payment of $471.78.

19. Currency in circulation at www.fms.treas.gov/bulletin/b13uscc.doc.

20. Gold at Fort Knox: www.usmint.gov/about_the_mint/fun_facts/index.cfm? flash=yes&action=fun_facts13.

21. Currently, only five mutual funds specialize in inflation-protected securities: American Century Inflation Protected Bond Fund (ticker: ACITX), Fidelity Inflation Protected Securities Fund (ticker: FINPX), Vanguard Inflation Protected Securities Fund (ticker: VIPSX), PIMCO Real Return (ticker: PRTNX), and TIAA-CREF Institutional Inflation Linked Bond Fund (ticker: TCILX)

PIMCO Real Return is available in a good many 401(k) plans. If you buy the fund in an IRA or other independent account, we suggest using the Vanguard fund—it has the lowest expense ratio. Daily updated information on these and other funds is available on the Morningstar Web site, www.Morningstar.com.

22. George E. Vaillant, *Aging Well* (Boston: Little, Brown, 2002).

23. www.who.int/inf-pr-2000/en/pr2000-life.html.

24. "Impact of Smoking on Life Expectancy and Disability," *Daily/Statistics Canada,* June 22, 2001.

25. There are many life expectancy calculators on the Web. One of the easiest to use is on MSN Moneycentral, http://moneycentral.msn.com/investor/calcs/ n_expect/main.asp. Another is the "Living to 100" Web site, www. livingto100.com/. Still another takes the opposite tack and calculates our "real age," adjusting of chronological age up and down for various factors: www.realage.com.

26. Leonard Roy Frank, *Quotationary* (New York: Random House, 2001), p. 153.

27. "The Quality of Medical Care in the United States: A Report on the Medicare Program," in *The Dartmouth Atlas of Health Care 1999* (Chicago: AHA Press, 1999), Web site: www.dartmouthatlas.org.

28. Scott Burns, "The $35.5 Trillion Medicare Elephant," *Dallas Morning News,* August 10, 2003.

29. The best recent book is Ann Crittenden's The Price of Motherhood: Why the Most Important Job in the World Is the Least Valued (New York: Holt, 2001).

Epilogue

1. Kennedy was quoting Dante.

Index